Regulating the Security Industry

It is widely acknowledged that the size of the security industry has increased in virtually every country around the world, often eclipsing conventional police forces in personnel numbers and expenditures. Security providers differ from law enforcement officers in many ways, yet the nature of their crime reduction activities brings them into frequent contact with citizens, drawing to the forefront issues of training, professionalism and accountability. Unlike police officers, whose training and licensing standards are well established, regulations for security providers are often minimalist or entirely absent.

This volume brings together research on regulatory regimes and strategies from around the globe, covering both the large private security sector and the expanding area of public sector 'non-police' protective security. It examines the nature and extent of licensing and monitoring, and the minimum standards imposed on the industry by governments across the world.

The chapters in this book were originally published in various issues of the *International Journal of Comparative and Applied Criminal Justice*.

Mahesh K. Nalla is Professor in the School of Criminal Justice at Michigan State University, USA.

Tim Prenzler is Professor in the School of Law at the University of the Sunshine Coast, Australia.

T0346608

Regulating the Security Industry

Global Perspectives

Edited by
Mahesh K. Nalla and Tim Prenzler

LONDON AND NEW YORK

First published 2018
by Routledge
2 Park Square, Milton Park, Abingdon, Oxon, OX14 4RN, UK

and by Routledge
52 Vanderbilt Avenue, New York, NY 10017

First issued in paperback 2020

Routledge is an imprint of the Taylor & Francis Group, an informa business

Chapter 5 © 2018 Taylor & Francis
All other chapters © 2018 School of Criminal Justice, Michigan State University

British Library Cataloguing in Publication Data
A catalogue record for this book is available from the British Library

ISBN 13: 978-0-367-58869-4 (pbk)
ISBN 13: 978-1-138-54170-2 (hbk)

Typeset in Minion Pro
by RefineCatch Limited, Bungay, Suffolk

Publisher's Note
The publisher accepts responsibility for any inconsistencies that may have
arisen during the conversion of this book from journal articles to book chapters,
namely the possible inclusion of journal terminology.

Disclaimer
Every effort has been made to contact copyright holders for their permission to
reprint material in this book. The publishers would be grateful to hear from any
copyright holder who is not here acknowledged and will undertake to rectify
any errors or omissions in future editions of this book.

Contents

Citation Information

The following chapters were originally published in the *International Journal of Comparative and Applied Criminal Justice.* When citing this material, please use the original page numbering for each article, as follows:

Preface

Chapter 1

Chapter 2

Chapter 3

Chapter 4

Chapter 6

Chapter 7

Critiquing the regulation of private security in the United Kingdom: views from inside the sector
Rob Mawby and Martin Gill
International Journal of Comparative and Applied Criminal Justice, volume 41, issue 4 (November 2017), pp. 259–272

Chapter 8

Common past - different paths: Exploring state regulation of private security industry in Eastern Europe and post-Soviet republics
Mahesh K. Nalla and Anna Gurinskaya
International Journal of Comparative and Applied Criminal Justice, volume 41, issue 4 (November 2017), pp. 305–321

Chapter 9

Private security services regulations in the United States today
Robert McCrie
International Journal of Comparative and Applied Criminal Justice, volume 41, issue 4 (November 2017), pp. 287–304

The following chapter was originally published in *Policing and Society*. When citing this material, please use the original page numbering, as follows:

Chapter 5

The Taming of the Japanese Private Security Industry
Naoko Yoshida
Policing and Society, volume 9 (1999), pp. 241–261

For any permission-related enquiries please visit:
http://www.tandfonline.com/page/help/permissions

Notes on Contributors

Julie Berg is Associate Professor in the Public Law Department, and Director of the Institute for Safety Governance and Criminology, at the University of Cape Town, South Africa.

Mark Button is Director of the Centre for Counter Fraud Studies at the Institute of Criminal Justice Studies, University of Portsmouth, UK.

Martin Gill works for Perpetuity Research and Consultancy International, Tunbridge Wells, Kent, UK.

Anna Gurinskaya is Associate Professor in the Faculty of Liberal Arts and Sciences at St. Petersburg State University, and the Faculty of Law, at the Russian State Pedagogical University of Herzen, St. Petersburg, Russia.

Simon Howell is a Senior Researcher in the Institute for Safety Governance and Criminology at the University of Cape Town, South Africa.

Dae Woon Kim is a Lecturer in the Department of Police Administration at Yeungnam University, Republic of Korea.

Rob Mawby is a Visiting Professor of Criminology and Criminal Justice at Harper Adams University, UK.

Robert McCrie is Professor of Security Management at John Jay College of Criminal Justice, The City University of New York, USA.

Mahesh K. Nalla is Professor in the School of Criminal Justice at Michigan State University, USA.

Kris Pillay is Director of the School of Criminal Justice at the University of South Africa, Pretoria, South Africa.

Tim Prenzler is Professor in the School of Law at the University of the Sunshine Coast, Australia.

Rick Sarre is Professor of Law and Criminal Justice at the University of South Australia, Adelaide, Australia.

Peter Stiernstedt is a PhD candidate in Social Sciences at the University of Portsmouth, UK, studying the perception of corruption.

Ronald van Steden is Associate Professor in Public Administration and Political Science at the Vrije Universiteit Amsterdam, The Netherlands.

Naoko Yoshida is a Lecturer in Law, at the University of Kyoto-Sangyo, Japan.

Preface

Tim Prenzler

It is now a truism of criminology that the global security industry has been growing at a faster rate than regular police services and is now much larger in many locations in terms of personnel and expenditures. It is less widely recognised that the industry has played a key role in the large reductions in crime seen around the world since the 1990s, and that the industry plays a vital role in the primary prevention of offending and protection of potential victims of crime (Farrell, Tilley, & Tseloni, 2014; van Dijk, 2008, 2012). There are a number of possible reasons why these achievements receive so little attention. One is that the sector is practice focused. Claims about success in stopping crime tend to be confined to advertising – sometimes exaggerated – with little consideration given by industry members to scientific evidence about the effects of their work. Additionally, the growth of the industry – leading to its near-ubiquitous presence in all aspects of people's lives – is widely seen as a major contributor to a surveillance-based and highly segmented society in which the wealthy and political elites exploit security services to protect their privileges and lifestyle at the expense of the poor and marginalised. Furthermore, the industry often attracts attention, especially from the media, over security failings and scandals – including fraud, violations of privacy, harassment, and assaults.

The main take-home message from the increasing body of research demonstrating the value of security is that we need more security – but more security that is better managed and that serves a wider public interest. There are two keys to significantly enlarging the social benefits of security. One is for governments, NGOs, and private companies with a social conscience, to target more security to those who need it but cannot afford it. Better security in the public sector should extend to public housing, schools, hospitals, and parks, with subsidies for security in private sector areas such as public transport and rental accommodation. The second key involves the optimal regulation of the industry. Security providers cannot be effective in crime prevention if they are inadequately trained, out-of-date with technical developments, incompetent, unhelpful, negligent, corrupt, or committing crimes against their clients.

There is now a fairly well-developed scientific literature on security industry regulation, dating back to the 1970s, which has established a set of basic requirements around the concepts of "comprehensive" and "smart" regulation (Button & Stiernstedt, 2016; Prenzler & Sarre, 2014). The model involves a licencing regime for all providers, with a primary role for independent control through a specialised government agency, but with close consultation with both security managers and practitioners. It involves dynamic training, character checks, monitoring, and complaints investigations and discipline. The model has a strong universal dimension, based on the common nature of security work and ethical risks. At the same time, it can accommodate variations in local needs and government capacity through a hierarchy, starting with minimalist elements – such as disqualifying offences and mandated basic training for operatives – through to more advanced elements – such as a research-driven quality improvement process and mandatory training for security managers.

To what extent, then, is the security industry effectively managed in the public interest in different countries? To what extent has the ideal model outlined above been implemented? And what are the obstacles to adequate adoption of the model? Answering these questions is the aim of this special issue of the *International Journal of Comparative and Applied Criminal Justice*. The idea for an international review of current practice in the field germinated over two years ago, with a particular interest in global coverage – something that had never been achieved before. The idea led to approaches to, and commitments from, all the authors. However, as anyone knows who has tried to conduct research in the area, this is not an easy field in which to obtain adequate and current data – even in relatively open and wealthy countries. Consequently, the research and finalisation of papers was a protracted process, but one which I feel, as special issue editor, was well worth the effort.

The first paper charts the growth of security industry regulation in the European Union (EU), where some of the most advanced regulatory systems are now in operation. EU governance and the single market appear to have contributed to higher standards, and the EU has some of the best data on regulation via the Confederation of European Security Services. Despite this situation, the authors identify considerable inconsistencies in regulation amongst the member states, so that ensuring consistency in best practice is now a primary challenge. The UK currently remains an EU member, and the following paper provides a more in-depth assessment of current regulatory issues in this relative newcomer to industry-specific government regulation. The study employed surveys of security company managers and also security clients. The results identified broad support for the system to-date – in terms of improved standards and reduced criminality – but with a consensus in favour of better coverage of all security providers, especially in regard to training; more proactive monitoring and enforcement of standards; and improved consultation with stakeholders by the regulator. The paper usefully highlights private providers' commitment to better regulation as something benefitting both legitimate businesses and "the public good".

The next paper addresses the topic of industry regulation in Africa. The paper provides a continent-wide overview, with particular attention to the challenges of hybrid forms of public and private security; low pay, long hours and high turnover amongst operatives; collusion and corruption in contracting; and the limited resources of many governments. Moving north-west, the next paper in the special issue assesses the situation in that world powerhouse of capitalism: the United States. The paper identifies a common reluctance by member states to interfere in the market, although the terrorist attacks of 11 November 2001 stimulated a greater concern for public safety via marshalling and regulation of the industry. At the same time, regulation remains highly uneven, with some states having next to nothing in terms of direct government control through licencing.

The next paper examines changes affecting security regulation in countries which have transitioned from soviet-dominated socialism towards capitalism and/or democracy. Again, we see enormous diversity in government control of the industry, with specific problems in some locations in regard to government ownership of security businesses and also a problem with the infiltration of fledgling businesses by organised crime groups. With the multiple challenges entailed in these seismic shifts in government and society, it is not surprising that many of these new states have engaged in only very minimal control of private security.

The final paper, from Australia, is focused on the core issue of training. Australia has, in the past, been described as a "social laboratory" of progressive ideas. Unfortunately – despite the long-term stability of its democratic institutions, leanings towards big government, and high standard of living – national efforts to establish consistent standards across the states and territories are shown to have signally failed. The paper concludes by articulating the lessons for effective training, particularly in terms of specifying standards in areas such as hours of instruction and modes of assessment.

Together, these papers make for a unique collection of cutting-edge empirically grounded reviews of contemporary security industry regulation globally. Despite the diversity of regions, methods, and specific areas of focus, the collection makes for some strong common findings. First, the papers demonstrate large advances in many jurisdictions towards more comprehensive and more effective regulatory systems, consistent with the comprehensive/smart model advocated by security scholars. Secondly, they point out inconsistencies, limitations, and pitfalls when the model is not properly designed or implemented at the jurisdictional level. Thirdly, the papers chart a way forward towards best practice – in part through greater recognition of the benefits of good regulation. In the majority of cases, the contributions provide updates and refinements of previous studies, mainly from established democracies. Of particular note is the ground-breaking work on emerging democracies in Africa and post-socialist states. I am particularly grateful to these authors for their hard work and commitment to the project.

I am of course grateful to all the contributors. It is easy to say "yes" to a request for a paper when the due date seems to be well in the future. It is another thing again to provide a quality paper on time, then respond politely to the special editor's request for changes, and then respond again to recommended changes from the reviewers. Fortunately, all the authors were extremely cooperative through the elongated process of bringing the issue to final fruition. I am also grateful to the anonymous referees, whose assessments and helpful suggestions have contributed further to the quality of the special issue.

References

Button, M., & Stiernstedt, P. (2016). Comparing private security regulation in the European Union. *Policing and Society*, 1–17. Pre-print online. doi:10.1080/10439463.2016.1161624

Farrell, G., Tilley, N., & Tseloni, A. (2014). Why the crime drop? *Crime and Justice: A Review of Research, 43*(1), 421–490. doi:10.1086/678081

Prenzler, T., & Sarre, R. (2014). Regulation. In M. Gill (Ed.), *Handbook of security* (pp. 857–878). Houndmills: Palgrave-Macmillan.

van Dijk, J. (2008). *The world of crime*. Thousand Oaks, CA: SAGE.

van Dijk, J. (2012, June). *Closing the doors: Stockholm prizewinners lecture 2012*. Paper presented at the Stockholm Criminology Symposium, Stockholm.

Introduction

Mahesh K. Nalla and Tim Prenzler

Over the past 60 years, since the 1960s, the global security industry has grown to a point where it is pervasive in all aspects of people's lives: in operating a telephone or a motor vehicle, getting on board a plane, accessing one's workplace, making purchases by plastic card, logging on to the internet, or reporting crimes at transport hubs or shopping malls. In terms of personnel, numbers vary significantly between countries. Police are often used as a yardstick, and data indicate ratios of approximately one-to-one in many locations, but as high as two or three security officers to every one police officer in some locations (CoESS, 2011; Nalla & Crichlow, 2014; chapter 1 of the present book). While much of the research on the industry is focused on the private sector and frontline guarding services, the industry is highly diverse – including a large public sector component, and also numerous specialist agencies in areas such as copyright compliance or covert anti-fraud surveillance (Prenzler, 2014).

Most studies attribute the growth of the industry to a major shift from reliance on police for crime prevention and law enforcement to self-protection in response to the rapidly rising rates of crime from the 1970s to the 1990s – a process referred to as "responsive securitization" (van Dijk, 2012, p. 10). On the occasion of winning the Stockholm Prize for Criminology in 2012, Jan van Dijk observed that:

> Investments in self-protection have since the 1970s been a mass phenomenon, impacting on almost all aspects of society. A prime example is the huge increases in private security guards and alarm centres ... Measures to prevent crime have become ubiquitous in all corners of modern society. Harnessing new technology, security provisions have been built into homes, cars, stores and parking lots, public transport and public/social housing, schools and hospitals, offices and other work places, entertainment venues and sports stadiums, airports and seaports, and to warehouses and transportation terminals.
>
> (2012, p. 11)

Other influences on growth include increased litigation for security lapses, improved security technology, and expanded workplace health and safety legislation (see chapter 1 of the present book). There is a growing body of research demonstrating the potential large benefits of the industry in terms of reduced victimization and increased feelings of safety. In fact, an increasing number of studies are attributing much of the large reduction in crime internationally since the 1990s to securitization (de Waard, 2017; Farrell, Tilley, & Tseloni, 2014). In addition, a number of studies have shown the benefits of close partnerships between police, other governments authorities, and private security providers in combatting crime (Prenzler & Sarre, 2016).

Security is all around us, entailed in almost everything we do, and often highly visible in the form of uniformed guards, entry-exit screening points and security hardware. When a lock fails, a password doesn't work or a car alarm works when we don't want it to – then security is inconvenient, frustrating and deeply annoying. Unfortunately, there has also been a much darker side to the industry in the form of insider crime, fraud, harassment, assaults, breaches of privacy, corruption and negligence (Prenzler & Sarre, 2014). The growth of the industry has also provoked a wider social justice critique regarding the role of security in protecting privilege and power, while also sounding the alarm over the ever increasing surveillance of ordinary citizens in the name of protection from terrorism and crime. These recurring problems, evident wherever the industry has been studied, has given rise to the gradual, often reluctant, enlargement of government regulation intended to curtail abuses and ensure minimum standards for both security clients and members of the public (Nalla & Crichlow, 2014; Prenzler & Sarre, 2014). Industry regulation primarily involves licensing through a specialist agency via mandated training, the application of disqualifying offences, and independent complaints resolution – applied primarily to the guarding and investigation sectors. This approach can take highly diverse forms, across a spectrum between rigorous and very lax enforcement. A large number of additional measures are possible beyond the basic framework, including comprehensive licensing of all security activities; secure weapons storage; drug and alcohol testing; mental health tests; insurance requirements; specialist training programs; and the use of inspections, intelligence and surveillance. In theory, optimal regulation will not only protect against misconduct but facilitate better security from a wider public interest perspective: better security in public places and improved security in rental accommodation, welfare housing and in public institutions such as schools and hospitals.

The mix of developments described above leads to a number of fundamental questions about regulation. How has regulation been applied in different countries or different jurisdictions? How effective has regulation been in curbing misconduct, raising standards and enhancing confidence in the industry? What factors have led to the adoption of different regulatory strategies, and what factors have limited their adoption? The purpose of the present book is to provide answers to these questions by bringing together recent cutting-edge research from around the world. The editors have selected a set of nine papers – most very recent as well as a few slightly older ones – that provide a useful coverage of the field in terms of depth and breadth, and history and geography, with a focus on lessons for improved practice.

Chapter 1, by Ronald van Steden and Rick Sarre, sets the context for the book. The authors take on the challenging task of assessing the strength of private security guard employment and comparing global trends, in essence to capture the "breadth and depth" of the core element of the industry. Building on earlier contributions from de Waard (1999), van Steden and Sarre expand the scope of their coverage by examining employment trends in Africa, the Americas, Australasia and Europe, to the extent that data were available. In addition to assessing the size of the sector, they offer comparative data on employment of public police officers to identify discrepancies in the employment ratios of public and private police. Among the factors that drive increases in the numbers of security guards are spatial changes and the growth of private spaces where much public life occurs, fear of crime and an increasing demand for safety and security, the expansion of global markets for guard services, and the forces of globalization that allow for growth of transnational security conglomerates.

Chapter 2 by Kris Pillay provides an in-depth examination of the development of security industry regulation in South Africa, where there has been enormous growth in the private sector component. The author draws contrasts between the "pre-Apartheid dispensation" and "post-Apartheid expansion". Pillay offers a comprehensive description of the various state legislations relating to a variety of security services that include guards, investigators and locksmiths, both in terms of regulation and minimum standards for recruitment and employment. Clearly, the origins and development of private police in South Africa are distinct compared to the developments in other former African colonies.

The next chapter addresses the under-researched field of security industry regulation in Africa. Julie Berg and Simon Howell provide a unique overview of developments across the continent, with a particular focus on hybrid security services involving combinations of private and public providers. Particular challenges for regulators include low pay and long hours for many operatives, high turnover amongst employees, issues of corruption and collusion across the sectors, and the limited capacity of many governments to adequately resource regulatory agencies.

In Chapter 4, Tim Prenzler, Rick Sarre and Dae Woon Kim make a detailed case study of policy developments and practice in the area of mandated security training. The Australian security industry has been beset by recurring scandals around competency and conduct. Efforts to clean up the industry through enhanced training were undermined by inconsistency across state jurisdictions, so that operatives with substandard qualifications have been able to work in jurisdictions with higher standards. The chapter charts the evolution of this problem – one that faces all federal systems where security licensing is the responsibility of states or provinces – and recent attempts to develop uniform national standards.

The next chapter also focuses on developments and issues in one country, in this case Japan. Naoko Yoshida's case study provides an overview of this country with historically low crime rates, where citizens still have a high regard for and confidence in their public police relative to the discernable level of acceptance of private security guards. Yet, data suggests that there are more private security guards relative to public police officers. Yoshida, however, notes that the state police have become a supervisor of private security services, thus showing confidence in this secondary line of crime control functionaries, clearly suggesting a junior partner role played by private security, and has actually initiated many private policing programs. Unlike in the West, which experienced an expansion of mass private properties that generated an increase in demand for private security, Japan had experienced a sharp increase in 24-hour retail units owned and operated by large corporations resulting in a similar demand for security guards. Yoshida outlines the various facets of the legal framework that governs the guarding sector (e.g., minimum standards and training) as well as regulatory powers of the police in its role as overseer of the industry.

Chapter 6 then moves the book back to the issue of attempted coordination across a set of jurisdictions. Regulation of the industry in the European Union should be of particular interest in that some of the most advanced forms of government control are evident there. Mark Button and Peter Stiernstedt begin by examining historical phases of security industry expansion in the EU. A key finding regarding current standards is that, despite the EU's support for a common framework, there has been reluctance to intervene with member states. This means there is still considerable fragmentation in practice, and this has adverse implications for the idea of a common market. In light of this, the authors argue that the time is right for a more directed approach to ensure consistently high standards across the Union.

The United Kingdom was a surprising latecomer to the field of security industry regulation, despite its membership of the EU, with specific legislation only enacted in 2001. Chapter 7, by Rob Mawby and Martin Gill, reports on the results of valuable stakeholder research on the effects of UK regulation, through surveys of clients of security companies and security company managers. The results support findings made elsewhere: that stakeholders support the basic elements of the standard licensing model in improving competencies and reducing misconduct, but they also see the need for more comprehensive and proactive regulation. The latter includes greater consultation by the regulator, licensing of persons engaged in all types of security tasks, more depth in training, and closer monitoring and enforcement of license conditions. The chapter is particularly valuable in showing how regulation is good for both the clients of security firms and the wider public.

Chapter 8, by Mahesh Nalla and Anna Gurinskaya, analyzes the state of industry regulation in the post-Cold War period amongst nations which have made the transition away from soviet-governed socialism towards market-oriented and/or democracies. The spread of private security has been an important part of this enormous upheaval, accompanying the growth of freedom for ordinary people and large increases in private wealth. What we see from this pioneering study is extensive diversity in state regulation – as seen in other cross-jurisdictional studies – although with a generally minimalist profile consistent with the limited resources at the disposal of many post-communist governments. Some of the problems identified in Africa are also apparent here, including conflicts of interest related to state owned security enterprises. For regulators, there is also the particular challenge posed by the involvement of organized crime groups in the ownership or control of security businesses.

The final chapter, by Robert McCrie, examines the state of play in that bastion of democracy and capitalism, the United States of America. Here we see a strong culturally-based reluctance to interfere in market mechanisms, with diverse but generally very light forms of regulation. This is despite the strong counter-terrorism agenda in the post-9/11 period, and attempts to enlarge and blend private and public sector security providers into the homeland security mandate. McCrie concludes that regulatory mechanisms in the US lag well behind best practice and that a much more responsible approach needs to be taken by governments to protecting clients and members of the public from irresponsible security providers.

As editors, we are excited to be able to bring these studies together in this one volume. As noted, the papers have been carefully selected to provide the best available global coverage of the issues. Our interest is in evidence-based assessments and honest critique, acknowledging achievements where they have occurred and identifying the need for improvements where the evidence is clear. Our primary focus is on lessons for practical, fair and efficient ways to optimize the contributions of the security industry. The size and scale of the ongoing crime problem, despite reductions in many locations in recent decades, makes this an urgent task. The world needs better security. Private security can respond well to this need, as history demonstrates the role it played in social regulation and order maintenance (Johnston, 1992), providing tailor-made solutions to crime challenges faced by individuals and corporations with the resources to engage in self-protection. This will help free up police resources to more directly serve public needs, regardless of capacity to pay. This should be augmented with government-provided protective security services, delivered either directly or through partnerships with the private sector. But to effectively protect ordinary people from crime, as well as businesses and government assets, the security industry needs to be subject to democratic control through an appropriate mix of basic and advanced regulatory mechanisms.

References

CoESS (2011). *Private security services in Europe: CoESS facts and figures 2011*. Wemmel: Confederation of European Security Services.

De Waard, J. (2017). *What Works?: A systematic overview of recently published meta evaluations/synthesis studies within the knowledge domains*. The Hague: Ministry of Security and Justice, Law Enforcement Department, Unit for General Crime Policy.

Farrell, G., Tilley, N., & Tseloni, A. (2014). Why the crime drop? *Crime and Justice: A Review of Research*, 43(1), 421–490.

Johnston, L. (1992). *The Rebirth of Private Policing*. London: Routledge.

Nalla, M. K., & Crichlow, V. (2014). Have the standards for private security guards become more stringent in the post 9-11 era? An Assessment of security guard regulations in the US from 1982 to 2010. *Security Journal*, 30(2), 523–637.

Prenzler, T., & Sarre, R. (2016). Public-private crime prevention partnerships. In T. Prenzler (Ed.), *Policing and security in practice: Challenges and achievements* (pp. 149–167). Houndmills: Palgrave-Macmillan.

Prenzler, T. (2014). The security industry: Dimensions and issues. In T. Prenzler (Ed.), *Professional practice in crime prevention and security management* (pp. 129–147). Brisbane: Australian Academic Press.

Prenzler, T., & Sarre, R. (2014). Regulation. In M. Gill (Ed.), *Handbook of security* (pp. 857–878). Houndmills: Palgrave-Macmillan.

Van Dijk, J. (2012, June). Closing the doors: Stockholm prizewinners lecture 2012. Paper presented at the *Stockholm Criminology Symposium*, Stockholm.

The Growth of Privatized Policing: Some Cross-national Data and Comparisons

RONALD VAN STEDEN[1]

RICK SARRE[2]

The policing services offered by private security companies have been embraced enthusiastically by public and private entities the world over. It is argued in this paper that the
impact of the "privatization" trend is, however, underestimated and understudied. In order
to understand the importance of the phenomenon, and to measure its impact, it is important
for researchers to undertake international comparisons of both the reach of private security
and the extent to which its industries shape and complement the policing task. In pursuit of
that end, this paper is designed to provide a snapshot description of the coverage of private
security industries worldwide (where current information is available), along with an
analysis of their impact.

INTRODUCTION

Over the last two decades, a significant restructuring of policing, especially
in North America and the European Union (EU), has led to private industries
now occupying a major position in "police extended families" (Law Commission of Canada, 2002; Johnston, 2003; Crawford and Lister, 2004). Indeed,
the commercial market for private policing generally and private security more
specifically expands inexorably. As Clifford Shearing and colleagues signaled
a quarter-century ago: "[p]rivate security has developed so rapidly and unob-
trusively, that its presence represents nothing less than a quiet revolution in
policing" (1980, p. 1). The trend continues. Those who were pioneers in
developing and building private security industries are witnessing a lucrative
return on their investments. One recent estimate suggests that world demand
for private contractual security service will grow 7.7 per cent annually until at
least 2008 (Freedonia, 2005).

All of this is not particularly surprising, given that the publicly funded
agencies of order maintenance that evolved and grew during the nineteenth-
century development of modern policing never really eradicated the private
forms of policing that had preceded them (Johnston, 1992). The upshot of this
resurgence is a modern mix of public and private options and roles. According
to Lucia Zedner,

> the publicly employed officers of state police have been generally regarded as
> synonymous with the criminal justice state. It now appears increasingly possible

> that this model of the police may come to be seen as an historical blip in a more enduring schema of policing as an array of activities undertaken by multiple private and public agencies, and individual and communal endeavours. In the longer term, that archetypical modern state venture—the criminal justice system—may itself be regarded as historical anomaly (2006, p. 81).

Uniformed security guards are, by far, the most observable exponents of private security occupations. Their presence has considerably intensified alongside the police and police-like bodies (e.g. city wardens) safeguarding urban areas (Crawford et al., 2005). It is especially in mass private-property environments such as shopping malls, airport terminals, holiday resorts, industrial complexes and office parks that private guarding is on the rise (Sarre, 2005). Private personnel have thus become an integral part of overall policing strategies, or, as some would prefer to say, "governance of security" (Johnston and Shearing, 2003, p. 9).

In order to facilitate these developments, private security industries are now actively promoting an image of a sector that is able to distance itself from an unsavory reputation (O'Connor et al., 2004). Moreover, they are now offering a kaleidoscope of professional services and a greater variety of products than ever before, including manned guarding (both "in-house" and "contract"), alarm monitoring, security equipment production and installation, transportation of cash, investigation of white-collar crime and provision of advice on risk management (George and Button, 2000; Button, 2002).

Given the "silent rise" of private security, it is remarkable that the body of knowledge on the extent and powers of private security, although steadily evolving, is still rather limited. There is, to date, very little knowledge about the size and nature of the security industry worldwide. Clifford Shearing observes that

> [w]hile private security is certainly no longer a subject that languishes on a forgotten scholarly back burner, it remains surprisingly under researched. Despite its obvious importance to the governance of security, scholars continue to focus far more attention on the police than they do the various other agents and agencies that provide for security (Shearing, 2003, p. xvii).

Researchers, but also politicians and policy-makers, often take the presence of private players simply for granted as "minor" players in the policing landscape. Their prominence is, however, overlooked at one's peril. It is essential that researchers devote greater attention to the blossoming of private security companies in order to determine what they can and cannot offer society in terms of upholding social order.

In order to pursue that goal, this article will address five main issues. First, we underline that the mushrooming of commercial guarding agencies poses a challenge to the sovereignty of nation states. Policing is scattered away from 'blue colored' forces, thus challenging the traditional centralized methods of regulating society. Second, attention is paid to the barriers encountered when one attempts to measure the size of private security industries around the globe, although some useful, albeit cautious, estimates can still be made. Third, a modest international comparison of private security companies and firms is presented. Fourth, after describing trends in private security, we use an analytical lens through which to identify and explain why private security will continue to dominate the policing "market" into the foreseeable future, and finally, the article concludes with a research agenda, which stresses the need for good data and well-informed debate.

Why Private Security is a Challenge for Societies

The provision of policing is rapidly being redesigned across the globe. Its private forms disperse in a number of ways. "Commercialized" or "paid" security is the most pervasive and challenging one. David Bayley and Clifford Shearing state that the augmentation of specialized security companies, along with other non-state bodies and agents, into the field of policing implies

> a watershed in the evolutions of their systems of crime control and law enforcement. Future generations will look back on our era as a time when one system of policing ended and another took its place (1996, p. 588).

Their premise assumes that the "governance of security" is no longer, if it ever was, the sole monopoly of the constitutional state. Today the growth of "mass private property" such as shopping malls and airport terminals, in company with a growing complexity and social heterogeneity within urban societies, erodes the "steering" role of governments and their police forces. Policing is being restructured along the lines of markets, residential communities and cultural communities, a tendency which overthrows the "Hobbesian-Weberian framework where the public sphere is the sphere of the governors and the private sphere is the sphere of the governed" (Shearing, 2006, p. 31). Crime control has, in other words, become everybody's business. Nowadays, security guards, community volunteers and other private policing providers regularly patrol the vast majority of spaces where people spend their daily lives.

Trevor Jones and Tim Newburn (2002, 2006) have warned that one must not generalize too widely in making these observations lest one lose sight of the different historical paths that "local political cultures" follow (2006, p. 9.). But despite disagreements about how to interpret what is evolving, scholars widely recognize the process of "pluralization" (more specifically, "privatization") of policing and the unique challenge this phenomenon poses to modern order maintenance.

Determining the Breadth and Depth of the Private Security "Industry"

On an empirical level, private security is difficult to define. Indeed, Elizabeth Joh refers to it as a "paradoxical" term (2004). Although the law draws a clear distinction between 'public' and 'private,' both sectors are increasingly difficult to tell apart. Today, the police and the private security industries perform many of the same tasks and have many of the same sorts of responsibilities. As Philip Stenning outlines,

> it is now almost impossible to identify any function or responsibility of the public police which is not, somewhere and under some circumstances, assumed and performed by private police in democratic societies (2000, p. 328).

Additionally, and to make things more complicated, the private security "industry" is not some clearly defined homogenous group, but rather a multitude of sectors, large and small, all related to the provision of security and investigation services, crime prevention, systems planning, technical consulting and security design (George and Button, 2000, p. 15). Often these industries are very different from each other in structure, authority, purpose and method, and when one adds the sheer variety of private security occupations, trying to determine the size of the industry becomes an almost impossible task (Jones and Newburn, 1995, pp. 223-224).

Moreover, the quality of accessible data varies considerably from source to source. Indeed, "[w]hat has mostly been available are fragments of information, mixed with speculation and dramatic claims, especially when the media get involved" (Sarre and Prenzler, 2005, pp. 7-8). For example, registration systems do not always differentiate between full-time personnel and the sizeable group of part-time personnel. This lack of clarity about the number of staff employed probably leads to an over-estimation of the actual work forces of security industries. On the other hand, however, "in-house" staff are sometimes not counted, so it could also be argued that the numbers of private security are, in reality, *under*-estimated. Furthermore, most private firms do not like to advertise their earnings and personnel numbers. Because competition is fierce amongst companies, they are, quite understandably, not eager to disclose confidential and sensitive information about market share and revenues. Finally, private security tasks are now being undertaken by a variety of businesses. For example, accountancy firms have been known to set up forensic services for clients, and sometimes offer private detective work. Private security companies not uncommonly undertake related activities such as limousine hiring or facility management alongside their general policing activities. The private security industry thus flows into a range of markets, making counting a precarious undertaking.

Cross-national Comparisons

Despite the fact that any attempt to measure the scope of the industry should be hedged with caveats, there is consensus among observers about the mounting pervasiveness of private companies and personnel in many countries, referred to (collectively) below as "private security services" or

"PSSs." The following snapshots from a variety of countries and regions have been drawn from the growing list of reports and reviews devoted to the subject of privatized provision of policing. Information on legislative authority and regulatory conditions is also included in the discussion below, where such information is available and of interest.

We begin with a comparative picture based upon information available from Northern and Southern America, Asia, Australia, the Middle East and Africa. Thereafter, the available data from the 27 EU member states is presented, followed by information gleaned from agencies in countries proximate to the EU. The information contained in each of the three tables is drawn from a number of sources.

Americas	Private security force
USA	+1,500,000
Canada	82,000
Mexico	+153,885
Brazil	400,000
Asia	
Japan	459,305
South Korea	115,845
Pacific	
Australia	+90,000
Middle East	
Saudi Arabia	16,000
Africa	
Nigeria	+100,000
Kenya	48,800
Sierra Leone	+3,000
South Africa	+250,000

Table 1: Private security services in selected international countries. Sources: Van Steden and Huberts (2005), Manning (2006), Law Commission of Canada (2002), Reames (2005), Wood and Cardia (2006), Yoshida and Leishman (2006), Sarre and Prenzler (2005), Abrahamsen and Williams (2005, a,b,c), Button et al (2006), Shearing and Berg (2006) and De Jong (2002).

The Americas

Security industries are so diverse in North America that their data, while not difficult to find, are difficult to compare. Early estimates indicate that 429,000 private staff, compared to 694,000 public law enforcement personnel, were employed in the **United States** in 1972 (Kakalik and Wildhorn, 1977, p.

18). According to the so-called Hallcrest report, this number had grown to almost 1 million private employees by 1990 (Cunningham et al., 1990, p. 196-197). One-and-a-half decades later the USA boasts some 60,000 security companies, and private industries employ approximately 1.5 to 2 million guards (Manning, 2006, p. 110). One estimate puts the number of security workers in **Canada** at around 82,000 compared to just over 59,000 police (Law Commission of Canada, 2002, p. 9-10). In **Mexico**, approximately 10,000 private security firms operate within the country. Yet fewer than half of these firms have employees who possess an official permit. In December 2000, there were 153,885 registered employees, but their actual number is probably significantly higher (Reames, 2005, p. 1192). In South America, the data are very difficult to find. Only **Brazil** provides some information for our purposes. A case study suggests that 1,200 private security companies with a total workforce of 400,000 were available for hire in 1998 (Wood and Cardia, 2006, p. 154). Indeed, the federal police contract with private guards to protect persons, property and assets, especially in metropolitan areas such as Sco Paulo. Since 1983, the Brazilian security industry has been covered by specialist legislation.

Asia

According to some reports, the security industry in **Japan** has grown from 775 companies employing 41,146 guards in 1972 to 8,669 companies employing 377,140 (full-time and part-time) guards in 1996. The security industry significantly outnumbers the Japanese police force, comprising, on 1996 figures, over 225,000 officers (Yoshida, 1999). The latest data from Japan indicate that this number has continued to grow since then, to 459,305 security guards and approximately 240,000 police officers in 2003 (Yoshida and Leishman, 2006). Government authorities hold powers to sanction security firms that violate the rules, by the imposition of strict penalties, imprisonment or the suspension and even termination of business. Even in the centralized market economy that is **China**, approximately 250,000 security service companies had been brought into existence by 1999 as free market competitors to the internal security system (Guo, 1999). In the **Republic of South Korea**, the rate of change has been rapid. From 1978 to 2005, the number of security personnel rose to well over 115,000 (compared with 93,271 police officers), a growth rate of 2,320 per cent (Button et al., 2006).

Australia

It is difficult to obtain an accurate picture of the size of the private policing and security markets in **Australia**. In 1998-99, the Australian Bureau of Statistics (ABS, 2000) recorded 1,714 businesses in security services industries, employing over 31,700 persons (Prenzler, 2005). This list included those firms that identified themselves as such, typically private detectives and inquiry agents, but did not include government security agencies, locksmith services, alarm wholesaling, and security equipment installation. Licensed security agents, on figures supplied by state licensing agencies in 2003, numbered approximately 140,000, but this figure includes individuals who hold multiple licenses. One should compare the number (approximately 48,000 on 2003 figures) of sworn police officers in Australia. Census data show that between 1996 and 2001 the Australian population increased by 6.0 per cent, police numbers increased by 6.5 per cent and security providers by a staggering 31.1 per cent (Prenzler and Sarre, 2006).

The Middle East

It is difficult to obtain accurate data about private security in the Middle East. Countries are mostly governed by strict Islamic regimes which exercise strong control over information on "sensitive" topics such as crime and safety. Nonetheless, De Jong (2002, p. 36) has conducted explorative research on the situation in **Saudi Arabia** and reports that four large security (guarding) companies employ approximately 3,500 staff throughout the country. They are part of a larger industry covering some 40 companies and 16,000 staff. Special legislation dates back to 1992 when the Ministry of the Interior issued *Rules of Private Civil Security*. Strikingly, this law obliges owners of, for instance, banks, jewellery shops and residential compounds to hire commercial guards, boosting the industry's growth throughout the 1990s. There is, however, no evidence that the industry has expanded since then.

Sub-Saharan Africa

Data on **Nigeria**, **Kenya** and **Sierra Leone** have been gathered recently by Abrahamsen and Williams (2005 a,b,c).[3] In Nigeria, private security is the second largest income earner for the nation after oil and gas. Numbers in the security guard sector may be as high as 100,000. Virtually any business, embassy, non-governmental organization (NGO) and residential compound will have contracts with (armed) private security personnel. Given the huge socio-economic inequalities that exist throughout Kenya, private security is a major industry, generating as many as 48,800 jobs. Regardless of the risks they run, security guards are not permitted to carry firearms. Because of a brutal civil war which raged across Sierra Leone from 1991 to 2002, security remains a top political priority, hastening a rapid expansion of commercial guarding services. Although numbers may be much higher, there may be as many as 30 security companies operating, employing approximately 3,000 persons.

South Africa

The security sector in **South Africa** may be expanding by as much as 30 per cent per year. 1999 figures indicate that, apart from 60,000 "in-house" personnel, the industry employs 350,000 guards. When only counting the number of "in-house" and "contract" security guards, the police/private security ratio would be 1:3.1, or it could be as high as 1:4 (Minnaar and Ngoveni, 2004, p. 45). However, Shearing and Berg (2006) are more moderate in their estimates. They assume the size of registered security officers was 250,000 in 2004, representing a doubling since 1997. Since the fall of the apartheid regime a number of multinational firms have become established in South Africa. These massive corporate players absorbed a vast number of local security businesses, whose numbers dropped from 5,185 in 2001 to 4,271 in 2003.

The European Union

Previous comparative research has indicated the significant contribution of security companies to internal security within the EU (Ottens et al., 1999; Van Outrive, 1999; Van Steden and Huberts, 2005; De Waard, 1999), although the information has been somewhat fragmented. Given the absence of firm and comparable data, Jaap de Waard, a Dutch civil servant working for the Ministry of Justice, published a comprehensive international study of private security, covering 27 countries including all the countries of the EU at the time plus 12 others. His study was based upon reports from the European Commission Directorate-General for Employment, Industrial Relations and Social Affairs in 1996. De Waard estimated that there were 592,050 security personnel in Europe in a population of 369 million. That meant that there were 160 security personnel per 100,000 people, compared to 375 police per 100,000. He further estimated that 75 per cent of security personnel worked for contract firms, with the remainder "in-house." De Waard found very large variations in personnel numbers between countries. Great Britain and Germany had the most security personnel, with 275 and 217 respectively per 100,000. Finland and Greece had the lowest proportions with 69 and 19 respectively. Overall, these 1999 data suggest that, in indicative terms only, police outnumbered security personnel in the EU by a very rough estimate of 2:1.

On 1 May 2004, 10 new member states successfully joined the existing 15 member states, and then on 1 January 2007 Bulgaria and Romania were added to the EU bringing the total number to 27. These events had considerable implications for the number of police officers and commercial security personnel previously counted by De Waard. His estimates are now well and truly in need of revision. The statistical snapshot presented below in Table 2 provides a timely update of the best available employment figures in the public and private policing sectors in the EU. The data are gleaned mainly from a report published by Morré (2004) and draw on figures collected by the Confederation of European Security Services (CoESS), the European umbrella association for private security industries.[4] Other data are drawn from SEESAC (2005).

Table 2 summarizes the latest estimates of private security industries in the 27 EU member states.

Country	Total Police	Total Private Security	Private Security/ Population Ratio	Private Security/ Police Ratio
Austria	30,000	6,790	1/1,208	0.23
Belgium	39,000	18,320	1/562	0.47
Bulgaria	28,000	130,000	1/58	4.6
Cyprus	3,000	1,500	1/517	0.50
Czech Republic	47,400	28,100	1/363	0.59
Denmark	14,000	5,250	1/1,010	0.38
Estonia	3,600	4,900	1/286	1.36
Finland	7,500	6,000	1/867	0.80
France	145,000	117,000	1/516	0.81
Germany	250,000	170,000	1/485	0.68
Greece	49,900	25,000	1/428	0.50
Hungary	40,000	80,000	1/125	2.00
Ireland	12,000	20,000	1/195	1.67
Italy	280,000*	55,000	1/1,056	0.20
Latvia	10,600	5,000	1/460	0.47
Lithuania	20,000	10,000	1/360	0.50
Luxembourg	1,573	2,200	1/210	1.40
Malta	1,800	700	1/572	0.39
The Netherlands	49,000	30,000	1/543	0.61
Poland	103,309	200,000	1/193	1.94
Portugal	46,000	28,000	1/375	0.61
Romania	45,830	37,291	1/597	0.81
Slovakia	21,500	20,840	1/259	0.97
Slovenia	7,500	4,500	1/444	0.60
Spain	193,450	89,450	1/450	0.46
Sweden	18,000	10,000	1/530	0.56
United Kingdom	141,398	150,000	1/401	1.06
Total	**1,609,360**	**1,255,841**	**1/395**	**0.78**

Table 2: Police forces and private security services in 27 EU-Member States. Sources: Morré, 2004 and SEESAC, 2005. Complements and updates data from van Steden and Sarre, 2006.

* This number is based on De Waard's (1999) estimate of the Italian police force numbers, because of missing data in the CoESS report.

Western Europe

Germany, the **United Kingdom** and **France** are indisputably the leaders in Western Europe in providing PSSs. As seen in Table 2, in sheer numbers, Germany takes the first position with approximately 170,000 personnel, although informed estimates place the number of employees in the United Kingdom much higher than the 150,000 reported by the sources available to Morré. For example, Button (2002, p. 99) arrives at a figure of 217,000 private security staff, whereas Jones and Newburn (1995, p. 229) counted over 300,000 people engaged in private "policing" occupations. Even with the lower number, police officers are outnumbered by private security in the UK by a ratio of 1 to 1.06. In France, the ratio is 1 to 0.81, and Germany is slightly lower again at 1 to 0.68.

Germany has implemented trade regulation laws that apply to security enterprises, but legal standards are also embedded in other acts. Training and education are provided by the Chamber of Commerce and Industry and by professional organizations. Operational staff undertake mandatory instruction (theory) of 40 hours. Managerial staff must attend 80 hours of theory. Specialized private security personnel (for example, guards at military installations) are allowed to carry guns.

In France, commercial security institutions hold a strong position. CoESS probably underestimates the French public policing system (145,000), for previous studies show a police strength of at least 227,000 officers (De Waard, 1999, p. 155; Ottens et al., 1999, p. 81). Ocqueteau (2006) maintains that private security does not challenge the sovereign role of police and the gendarmerie. Rather, the industry complements the state's security resources. Nevertheless, he concludes that commercial security is an irreversible phenomenon, which will continue to grow in the future.

Legislation for the private security sector in the United Kingdom did not exist until relatively recently. Private guards, investigators and door supervisors relied upon voluntary self-regulation (Button, 2002). In 2001, however, the parliament passed the *Private Security Industry Act*. It was the first attempt to regulate contract and "in-house" security guards, the CIT sector, private investigators, wheel clampers, security consultants, and bodyguards. Its main contributions were the introduction of a licensing system and the creation of a Security Industry Authority (SIA) to monitor the quality and legitimacy of security industry services.

The **Republic of Ireland** has a huge private security presence (approximately 20,000 strong) and its ratio of police to private security indicates that the former are well outnumbered by the latter (1 to 1.67). The number of private personnel per head of population (1 per 195) is one of the highest in Europe. Yet Ireland was one of the later countries to set out detailed legal standards for the industry. The parliament finally passed its *Private Security Services Act* in 2004.

In the **Grand Duchy of Luxembourg** there are more private security personnel (the overwhelming majority in full-time roles) than police officers (a ratio of 1 police officer to 1.4 security officers). Possible explanations for this are the fairly large banking sector and the fact that some central EU institutions are based in Luxembourg. With regard to the private security/population ratio, **Austria** has a rate that is the lowest in Europe at 1 private officer per 1,208 population. Nevertheless, there are 200 companies (on 2003 figures) active in Austria, employing 6,790 people. The annual turnover of €200 million (2001) is steadily increasing by 2 per cent to 3 per cent per year. While there is no specific law for the Austrian security market, there are a few commercial laws with relevance to specialized (guarding) companies.

Belgium and **The Netherlands** have moderately-sized private security industries, with a similar ratio of population to private security. The ratio of police to private security personnel (1 to 0.47 and 1 to 0.57, respectively) is similar, too. Both countries have laws that regulate the industry beyond manned guarding, and include private detectives, alarm monitoring systems, the cash-in-transit (CIT) sector and "in-house" security workers in their purview. The key points of Belgian and Dutch laws are similar too, and include strict regulation of uniforms, training, and criminal background checks. Contrary to the situation in The Netherlands, however, some Belgian guards are permitted to carry firearms. The Dutch division of Group 4 Securicor has been granted permission to provide custodial services to detention centers, which puts the company in a unique business position (Van Steden and Huberts, 2006).

Central and Eastern Europe

The collapse of socialist bureaucracies and the consequent sale of state assets have presumably contributed to the spectacular growth of private security industries in former Soviet bloc or Warsaw Pact countries (Brodeur et al., 2003, p. 6). Moreover, Central and Eastern EU member countries have reportedly suffered from waves of criminal activities within their own borders, thus providing an incentive for those who can afford it to seek supplementary policing (Caparini and Marenin, 2005).

Hence, in Central and Eastern Europe, private security companies have been mushrooming in an array of locations since the fall of the Berlin Wall in 1989. Countries like the **Czech Republic, Latvia, Lithuania**, and **Slovenia** are now witnessing strong growth in private security markets. Other Central and Eastern European EU members have also seen a significant rise in the number of private security and protection agencies in a growing market. In **Slovakia, Estonia, Hungary**, and **Poland** private security personnel now match or exceed their corresponding police numbers. In the cases of Poland and Hungary they are double the police numbers. According to CoESS, the yearly financial turnover is massive, for example, €40 million in Estonia (2001 figures) and €933 million in Poland.

The monitoring of private security in these regions is best described as a "work in progress." Two of the Baltic states, Estonia and Latvia, regulate manned guarding services and related areas by their respective security acts. Lithuania has implemented a law on individuals and property safety. The same trends are observed in most of the newly admitted EU member states. Except for the Czech Republic, all governments have instigated specific legal guidelines addressing private security. Requirements such as criminal background checks, identifications cards and special permission to carry handguns are standard and, in some cases, mandatory (for example, Czech guards). The Czech Republic and Slovenia offer university training for both public policing and private policing. Police practitioners and students seeking a career in an assortment of (governmental) security agencies are taught at the Police Academy in Prague and the College of Police and Security Studies in Ljubljana.

In **Romania**, along with **Bulgaria**, the privatization of security has expanded significantly over the last decade. These countries host the most developed and professional security industries in the region. Given that up-to-date numbers on police for these two nations are available from SEESAC (2005, p. 109), it is possible to make a rough estimate of the ratio of police to private security. In Romania the ratio (0.81) is around the average for the EU, assuming, that is, that one can rely upon the data. This may be problematic, as many guards work without permission and are paid "under the table" (Gounev, 2006, p 117). The Bulgarian ratio (28,000 police to 130,000 private security) is 4.6, or the highest for the EU, again assuming the data are accurate. A 2005 business survey indicated that 54,000 of these are contract guards paid by PSSs, while the other 70,000 to 80,000 are in-house guards. According to SEESAC, issues such as the absence of democratic oversight, ineffective implementation of legislation and rivalry between police forces and security companies are of major concern to observers (SEESAC, 2005).[5]

Southern Europe

There is a relatively low private security/police ratio in Southern European countries. In **Greece**, for example, a security market barely existed until 1997 (Rigakos and Papanicolaou, 2003, 298). At present, however, there may be as many as 25,000 to 30,000 private security personnel, which is about half the number of police officers (Papanicolaou, 2006, p. 86). Legislation was introduced in 1997 to mandate a number of requirements covering security licensing, uniforms, training and dogs. The license-holder's criminal record must be checked and he or she is obliged to have joined the Greek army.

Police in **Italy** employ 280,000 officers, five times the estimated number of people employed by private security agencies. Likewise, **Cyprus**, **Malta**, **Portugal**, and **Spain** make more use of police officers than security guards. Nevertheless, with the exception of Cyprus, these governments have provided comprehensive governing frameworks to achieve some form of regulation.

Even taking into account the problems of accurately measuring private security personnel numbers, we can safely assume that there are over one million people employed in private security industries in the EU following its expansion in 2004. Given De Waard's figure of almost 600,000 employees based upon 1996 figures, this amounts to an increase of perhaps 500,000 employees across EU member states in less than a decade. The police/private security ratio, too, has moved up to 1 to 0.71 overall in 2004 compared to the EU average of 1 to 0.43 in 1999 (De Waard, 1999, p. 156). Although these findings are very tentative, and must be treated with caution, it is impossible not to conclude that there has been a significant growth in private security in the EU. One can assume that there are a number of factors for this rise, not only "natural growth" by virtue of the addition of new member states, but also the belief that PSSs are an appropriate means by which to deal with perceptions of growing lawlessness generally, as well as the move to market economies following the collapse of the Soviet Union.

Scandinavia

Reliable estimates of private security personnel are available in the three Scandinavian countries that are members of the EU: **Denmark**, **Finland**, and **Sweden**. In each country, the private security industry is, in absolute and relative terms, small. A plausible explanation for this might be the traditionally low crime rates officially reported in Scandinavian countries. Furthermore, as De Waard (1999, p. 167) notes, the Danish police, historically, do not enter into so-called commercial public-private partnerships. The government is thus reluctant to cooperate with security services. Nevertheless, the latest figures indicate that there may be over 5,000 private security personnel in Denmark (for a ratio of 1 to 0.38, police to private security) and double that number in Sweden, for a not dissimilar ratio of 1 to 0.56.

Finland has a higher level of private security in comparison with its police force, although, per head of population, it has fewer security personnel (1 per 867) than Sweden (with 1 per 530). Finland's *Act on Private Security Services* (along with supplementary decrees) governs several "guarding" and "protection" sectors. We find the same kind of regulatory systems in Denmark. Sweden's regulatory regime covers most private security areas except alarm stations, in-house security and cash-in-transit (CIT). In Sweden and Finland, but not in Denmark, firearms carriage is permitted with special authorization. All Scandinavian EU countries require basic training for private security employees.

Southeastern Europe, Russia, Ukraine, and Georgia

The renaissance of private security in the EU is not exceptional to the region. The following information, as set out in Table 3, offers a useful insight into PSSs in the regions and nations proximate to the EU, and allows some preliminary comparisons to be made.

Eastern Europe (non-EU), Russia and Ukraine	Private security force
Albania	4,100
Bosnia and Herzegovina	12,000
Croatia	115,000
Kosovo	2,580
Macedonia	3,000
Moldova	+3,000
Montenegro	+1,900
Serbia	130,000
Russia	+850,000
Ukraine	+33,000

Table 3: Private security services in selected non-EU countries or entities. Sources: Van Steden and Huberts (2005), SEESAC (2005), Volkov (2002), Hiscock (2006).

The growth of private security companies in Southeastern Europe is probably a direct result of perceptions of a growing "market of violence" in the region (Eppler, 2002). Hence, private security companies have emerged in the former Yugoslavian countries, such as **Serbia**, **Croatia**, and **Bosnia-Herzogovina**. However, in these countries (if not **Albania**), concerns have been raised relating to the (mis)use of weapons, including automatic weapons, by private security (SEESAC, 2005). Moreover, they have been linked with armed ethnic minorities in **Kosovo**.

The collapse of the Soviet Union and a "hidden" private security legacy prior to the break-up both contributed to the spectacular growth of the private security industry in **Russia** (Favarel-Garrigues and Le Huérou, 2004). The protection market is, by and large, divided between detective agencies, PSSs and private protection companies (PPCs). In 1999, statistics indicated that almost 200,000 licensed employees (that is, those who are entitled to carry a firearm) are working for security services and protection companies, but their total number probably exceeds 850,000 (Volkov, 2002, p. 137). Not unlike the position in Southeastern Europe, regulatory structures for the private security industry are weak in Russia. Despite a 1992 federal law on private detective and protective activity which gave legal status to the commercial provision of security, business relations are still highly informal. This informality has had a negative impact on the transparency and accountability of the industry.

Ukraine, according to 2006 figures, has 33,000 people licensed to undertake protection work in over 3,000 enterprises, a number that is expanding rapidly. PSSs in the Ukraine, according to Hiscock, have been known to engage in illegitimate cooperation with the state (Hiscock, 2006, p. 136). There is little known about the employment scale of the private security market in Georgia, although estimates suggest that there may be as many as 250 to 300 PSSs (Hiscock, 2006, p. 141). There are very few rules that regulate PSSs and their staff.

Transnational Developments

Allied to the explosive growth of private security is the ascendancy of transnational security conglomerates mentioned above. Giant multi-nationals such as the Securitas Group, Group 4 Securicor, Tyco International, Secom, The Brink's Company, Sohgo Security Services, Chubb, Corrections Corporation of America and Prosegur have allowed a "globalization" of commercialized security provision to develop (Johnston, 2000, 2006; Walker, 2003; Wood and Kempa, 2005). Group 4 Securicor employs an astonishing 405,000 staff, working in over 100 countries and generating a yearly turnover of €6.1 billion.[6]

Moreover, a diversity of commercial security activities is penetrating into national and sub-national institutions such as fire departments, ambulance services, car assistance services, custodial services and even military operations (Group 4 Securicor, 2004; Singer, 2003). One can thus safely predict that transnational contract security will increasingly expand their functions in securing local (urban) and national domains across every continent.

Factors Driving Private Security: Discussion, Analysis, and a Research Agenda

How can we explain such a remarkable renaissance and durability of non-state forms of order maintenance? It is hard to answer this question unequivocally as pluralization and privatization affect policing "in different ways and at different speeds depending on the nature of the social, political and cultural circumstances in which they are taking place" (Jones and Newburn, 2006, p. 5). Nevertheless, the policing, sociological and criminological literature offer valuable analytical tools for explaining the growth of private security internationally. The first explanation is that the quest for guards and additional private supervisors can be situated within the context of *spatial changes* (Shearing and Stenning, 1981). Particularly in urban areas, the hegemony of consumerism stimulates the emergence of "quasi-public" spaces, such as shopping malls, sports stadiums and leisure facilities (Wakefield, 2003). Because of risks related to deviant behaviour disturbing the ambience of such sites, a "mixed economy" of security staff is routinely active here. These are predominantly security guards, but other agents such as crowd controllers and stewards are often present.

The *fear of crime* explanation is a useful one too. Crime rates have risen sharply over recent decades. Garland (2001) even portrays Western societies as "high crime cultures." The terrorist acts of (and since) September 11, 2001, have posed new dangers to national security and have enhanced citizens' "search for security" (Law Commission of Canada, 2002), which has become a "normal" fact of life. Moreover, governments have attempted to "responsibilize" civil society for its own risk management (Garland, 2001). For example, the Dutch police openly assert that

> security is not a matter exclusively for the police. The police need partners and are therefore looking for ways of establishing worthwhile collaboration ... by which many police forces aim to establish closer ties with local people. (Ministry of the Interior and Kingdom Relations, 2004, p. 8)

Closely related to this point, Button argues a lack of government performance and the financial weakness of states has contributed to the shift in emphasis (Button, 2002). Police are simply not capable of reassuring everybody. As governments try to reduce their spending by restricting the funding of public services such as the police, society is left with a "security vacuum," which is filled by private agents and agencies. In circumstances where private security is unregulated or under-regulated (George and Button, 2000), entrepreneurs may start businesses without being hindered by legal red-tape, with sometimes adverse public-image consequences (Livingstone and Hart, 2003).

Finally, in the context of a *liquid modernity* (Bauman, 2000) where extraordinary dynamism and agility find their counterparts in (ontological) feelings of uncertainty and insecurity, people are collectively yearning for *safe freedom* (Boutellier, 2004). The vitality of contemporary western life goes hand in hand with an obsessive desire for protection. This paradoxical situation creates the optimal circumstances for private security systems to proliferate.

As the security industry has grown worldwide, so has debate over the "quality of life impact" of this development (Prenzler, 2004, p. 283). According to some commentators, private security has the potential to disregard democratic rights, particularly the equality, privacy, and personal freedoms that citizens should be able to enjoy (Sarre and Prenzler, 2005, p. 202), given "that they must *sell* security" (Rigakos, 2002, p. 13; italics in the original). Their overarching interest, thus, is to "pursue their client's objectives" (Joh, 2004, p. 61) and make profitable business deals (South, 1988). Private security personnel generally work under an assumption that victims, especially their fee-paying institutional victims, should be given priority over all other concerns within civil society (Shearing and Stenning, 1983, p. 9). Thus there are many issues around private security, its purposes and accountabilities that remain unresolved.

In an attempt to address these questions, observers must continue to turn their gaze to four key research agendas (Sarre, 2005). Researchers should, first of all, map out generic patterns of privatized policing internationally and highlight the differences and similarities between countries. Only through this exercise can patterns and trends be observed and analyzed.

Researchers should also continue to explore and compare preferred forms (and forums) of accountability for private security and other auxiliary police options and come up with "what works best" in given situations. In doing so, they are better equipped to advise policy-makers to develop "law and justice" criteria to judge the quality of private accountability systems in various national and international settings. The research task must also include a discussion of the competing principles that public police and private security espouse, and the precise relationships both sectors should develop with each other, for despite decades of the development of private/public partnership models, the relationships between police and their private security counterparts remain guarded and tentative.

Finally, researchers should continue to examine the principles, interests, powers, mentalities, technologies and working methods of private security businesses (both national and transnational) in order to determine the effects of private policing on civil liberties, privacy, access to information, human rights and personnel safety.

CONCLUSION

Commercial security providers, at the very least, in terms of numbers of personnel and annual expenditures, now dominate the policing landscapes in many nations of the world (Sarre and Prenzler, 2005, p. 9). The current shifts towards private options in policing are likely to continue apace. Commercial integration and the freedom to move goods, capital and services are becoming progressively more common in a number of regions of the world, and there is little reason to suspect that there will not be a similar integration of security services.

The appropriate call is for governments to serve as central anchor points to facilitate and direct private policing activities and to fund research into them. Governments cannot shirk their responsibility to coordinate security (facilitated by public and private funding) to ensure that not only are their citizens enjoying a satisfactory level of protection at an appropriate cost, but that they are being protected by a blend of public and private policing that does not compromise fundamental accountabilities, rights and freedoms.

NOTES

1. Contact information: Ronald van Steden, Ph.D. student, Vrije Universiteit, Amsterdam, Netherlands. E-mail: R.van.Steden@fsw.vu.nl

2. Contact information: Rick Sarre, Professor of Law and Criminal Justice, School of Commerce, University of South Australia, and Visiting Professor, Law Department, Umeå Universitet, Sweden. GPO Box 2471, Adelaide, South Australia 5001. Tel: ISD 61 8 8302-0889, Fax: ISD 61 8 8302-0992. E-mail: rick.sarre@unisa.edu.au

3. For the on-line publications see **http://users.aber.ac.uk/rbh/privatesecurity/ publications.html**.

4. See **www.coess.org** for the full report.

5. For more information on the security situation in former Yugoslavia and elsewhere in the Balkans, see the Balkan site within **www.seesac.org**, the official website of the South Eastern and Eastern Europe Clearinghouse for the Control of Small Arms and Light Weapons.

6. For more information see **www.G4S.com**.

REFERENCES

Abrahamsen, R., & Williams, M. C. (2005a). *The Globalization of Private Security. Country Report: Nigeria*. University of Wales: Aberystwyth.

Abrahamsen, R., & Williams, M. C. (2005b). *The Globalization of Private Security. Country Report: Kenya*. University of Wales: Aberystwyth.

Abrahamsen, R., & Williams, M. C. (2005c). *The Globalization of Private Security. Country Report: Sierra Leone*. University of Wales: Aberystwyth.

ABS (2000). *Security Services Australia. Catalogue 8557.0*. Canberra: Australian Bureau of Statistics.

Bauman, Z. (2000). *Liquid Modernity*. Cambridge: Polity Press.

Bayley, D., Shearing, C. (1996). The Future of Policing. *Law and Society Review, 30*(3), 585-606.

Boutellier, J. C. J. (2004). *The Safety Utopia: Contemporary discontent and desire as to crime and punishment*. Dordrecht: Kluwer.

Brodeur, J-P., Gill, P., & Töllborg, D. (2003). Introduction. In J-P. Brodeur, P. Gill, and D. Töllborg (Eds.), *Democracy, Law and Security: Internal security services in contemporary Europe*. Aldershot UK: Ashgate.

Button, M. (2002). *Private Policing*. Cullompton: Willan.

Button, M., Park, H., & Lee, J. (2006). The Private Security Industry in South Korea: A familiar tale of growth, gaps and the need for better regulation. *Security Journal, 19*, 167-179.

Caparini, M., & Marenin, O. (2005). Crime, Insecurity and Police Reform in Post-Socialist CEE [Central and Eastern Europe]. *The Journal of Power Institutions in Post-Soviet Societies* (Special Issue 2: Reflections on Policing in Post-Communist Europe: **www.pipss.org**).

Crawford, A., & Lister, S. (2004). *The Extended Policing Family: Visible patrols in residential areas*. York, UK: Joseph Rowntree Foundation.

Crawford, A., Lister, S., Blackburn, S., & Burnett, J. (2005). *Plural Policing: The mixed economy of visible patrols in England and Wales*. Bristol: Policy Press.

Cunningham, W. C., Strauchs, J. J., & Van Meter, C. W. (1990). *The Hallcrest Report II: Private security trends 1970-2000*. Boston: Butterworth-Heinemann.

De Jong, M. (2002). Peace of Mind? Perceptions of Contractual Security Guarding at Commercial Banks in Saudi Arabia. *Security Journal, 15*(1), 33-47.

De Waard, J. (1999). The Private Security Industry in International Perspective. *European Journal on Criminal Policy and Research, 7*(2), 143-174.

Eppler, E. (2002). *Von Gewaltmonopol zum Gewaltmarkt? [From a Monopoly on Violence to a Market of Violence?]*. Frankfurt am Main: Suhrkamp.

Favarel-Garrigues, G., & Le Huirou, A. (2004). State Policing and the Multilateralization of Policing in Post-Soviet Russia. *Policing and Society, 14*(1), 13-30.

Freedonia (2005). *World Security Services to 2008, Study #1917*. http://www.freedoniagroup.com/

Garland, D. (2001). *The Culture of Control: Crime and social order in contemporary society*. Oxford: Oxford University Press.

George, B., & Button, M. (2000). *Private Security*. Leicester: Perpetuity Press.

Gounev, P. (2006). Bulgaria's Private Security Industry. In A. Bryden, & M. Caparini (Eds.), *Private Actors and Security Governance*. Zürich: Lit. 109-128.

Group 4 Securicor. (2004). *Group 4 Securicor International Magazine*, October, 2004.

Guo, T. (1999). Private Security in China: A note of recent developments. *Security Journal, 12*(4), 43-46.

Hiscock, D. (2006). The Commercialization of Post-Soviet Private Security. In A. Bryden, & M. Caparini (Eds.), *Private Actors and Security Governance*. Zürich: Lit, 129-148.

Joh, E. (2004). The Paradox of Private Policing. *The Journal of Criminal Law & Criminology, 95*(1), 49-131.

Johnston, L. (1992). *The Rebirth of Private Policing*. London: Routledge.

Johnston, L. (2000). Transnational Private Policing: The impact of global commercial security. In J. W. E. Sheptycki (Ed.), *Issues in Transnational Policing*. London: Routledge, 21-42.

Johnston, L. (2003). From "Pluralization" to the "Police Extended Family": Discourses on the governance of community policing in Britain. *International Journal of the Sociology of Law, 31*(3), 185-204.

Johnston, L. (2006). Transnational Security Governance. In J. Wood, % B. Dupont (Eds.), *Democracy, Society and the Governance of Security*. Cambridge: Cambridge University Press, 33-51.

Johnston, L., & Shearing, C. D. (2003). *Governing Security: Explorations in policing and justice*. London: Routledge.

Jones, T., & Newburn, T. (1995). How Big is the Private Security Sector? *Policing and Society, 5*, 221-232.

Jones, T., & Newburn, T. (2002). 'The Transformation of Policing? Understanding Current Trends in Policing Systems. *British Journal of Criminology, 42*(1), 129-146.

Jones, T., & Newburn, T. (2006). *Plural Policing: A comparative perspective*. London: Routledge.

Kakalik, J. S., & Wildhorn, S. (1977). *The Private Police: Security and danger*. New York: Crane Russak.

Law Commission of Canada (2002). En Quête de Sécurité: Le rôle des forces Policières et des agences privées'; [In Search of Security: The role of public police and private agencies]. Ottawa (discussion paper).

Livingstone, K., & Hart, J. (2003). The Wrong Arm of the Law? Public Images of Private Security. *Policing and Society, 13*(2), 159-170.

Manning, P. (2006). The United States of America. In T. Jones, & T. Newburn (Eds.), *Plural Policing: A comparative perspective*. London: Routledge, 98-125.

Ministry of the Interior and Kingdom Relations (2004). *Policing in the Netherlands*. Government Report, The Hague, Netherlands: Ministry of the Interior and Kingdom Relations.

Minnaar, A., & Ngoveni, P. (2004). The Relationship Between the South African Police Service and the Private Security Industry: Any role for outsourcing in the prevention of crime?. *Acta Criminologica, 17*(1), 42-65.

Morré, L. (2004). *Panoramic Overview of Private Security Industry in the 25 Member States of the European Union*. Brussels: CoESS/Uni-Europa.

O'Connor, D., Lippert, R., Greenfield, K., & Boyle, P. (2004). After the "Quiet Revolution": The self-regulation of Ontario contract security agencies. *Policing and Society, 14*(2), 138-157.

Ocqueteau, F. (2006). France. In T. Jones, & T. Newburn (Eds.), *Plural Policing: A comparative perspective*. London: Routledge, 55-76.

Ottens, R. W., Olschok, H., & Landrock, S. (1999). *Recht und Organisation Privater Sicherheitsdienste in Europa [Legislation on, and Organization of, Private Security Services in Europe]*. Stuttgart: Boorberg.

Papanicolaou, G. (2006). Greece. In T. Jones, & T. Newburn (Eds.), *Plural Policing: A comparative perspective*. London: Routledge, 77-97.

Prenzler, T. (2004). The Privatisation of Policing. In R. Sarre, & J.Tomaino (Eds.), *Key Issues in Criminal Justice*. Unley: Australian Humanities Press, 267-296.

Prenzler, T. (2005). Mapping the Australian Security Industry. *Security Journal, 18*(4), 51-64.

Prenzler, T., & Sarre, R. (2006). Australia. In T. Jones, & T. Newburn (Eds.), *Plural Policing: A comparative perspective*. London: Routledge, 169-189.

Reames, B. (2005). Mexico. In L. E. Sullivan, & M. R. Haberfeld (Eds.), *Encyclopedia of Law Enforcement (Volume 3)*. Thousand Oaks: Sage, 1186-1193.

Rigakos, G. S. (2002). *The New Parapolice*. Toronto: University of Toronto Press.

Rigakos, G. S., & Papanicolaou, G. (2003). The Political Economy of Greek Policing: Between neo-liberalism and the sovereign state. *Policing and Society, 13*(3), 271-304.

Sarre, R. (2005). Researching Private Policing: Challenges and agendas for researchers. *Security Journal, 18*(3), 57-70.

Sarre, R., & Prenzler, T. (2005). *The Law of Private Security in Australia*. Pyrmont, New South Wales: Thomson LBC.

SEESAC (2005). *SALW and Private Security Companies in South Eastern Europe: A cause or effect of insecurity?* Belgrade: South Eastern Europe Clearinghouse for the Control of Small Arms and Light Weapons (SEESAC). http://www.seesac.org/

Shearing, C. D. (2003). Preface. In A. Wakefield. (2003). *Selling Security: The private policing of public space*. Cullompton: Willan.

Shearing, C. D. (2006). Reflections on the refusal to acknowledge private governments. In J. Wood, & B. Dupont (Eds.), *Democracy, Society and the Governance of Security*. Cambridge: Cambridge University Press, 11-32.

Shearing, C. D., & Berg, J. (2006). South Africa. In T. Jones, & T. Newburn (Eds.), *Plural Policing: A comparative perspective*. London: Routledge, 190-221.

Shearing, C.D., & Stenning, P. C. (1981), Modern Private Security. In M. Tonry, & N. Morris (Eds.), *Crime and Justice (volume 3)*. Chicago: The University of Chicago Press, 193-245.

Shearing, C. D., & Stenning, P. C. (1983). *Private Security and Private Justice: The challenge of the 80s*. Montreal: The Institute for Research and Public Policy.

Shearing, C. D., Farnell, M. B., & Stenning, P. C. (1980). *Contract Security in Ontario*. Toronto: Centre of Criminology, University of Toronto.

Singer, P.W. (2003). *Corporate Warriors: The rise of the privatized military industry*. Ithaca: Cornell University Press.

South, N. (1988). *Policing for Profit: The private security sector*. London: Sage.

Stenning, P. (2000). Powers and Accountability of Private Police. *European Journal on Criminal Policy and Research, 8*(3), 325-352.

Van Outrive, L. (1999). Morphologie des Agents et Agences Privés dans Six Pays. In J. Shapland, & L. Van Outrive (Eds.), *Police et Securité: Controle social et interaction public/privé; [Policing and Security: social control and the public-private divide]*. Montreal: L'Harmattan, 179-194.

Van Steden, R., & Huberts, L. (2005). Private Security Growth in Western Countries. In L. E. Sullivan, & M. R. Haberfeld (Eds.), *Encyclopedia of Law Enforcement (Volume 3)*. Thousand Oaks: Sage, 1261-1268.

Van Steden, R., & Huberts, L. (2006). The Netherlands. In T. Jones, & T. Newburn (Eds.), *Plural Policing: A comparative perspective*. London: Routledge, 12-33.

Van Steden, R., & Sarre, R. (2006). The Growth of Private Security: Trends in the European Union. *Security Journal*, forthcoming.

Volkov, V. (2002). *Violent Entrepreneurs: The use of force in the making of Russian capitalism*. Ithaca, New York: Cornell.

Wakefield, A. (2003). *Selling Security: The private policing of public space*. Cullompton: Willan.

Walker, N. (2003). The Pattern of Transnational Policing. In T. Newburn (Ed.), *Handbook of Policing*. Cullompton: Willan, 111-135.

Wood, J., & Cardia, N. (2006). Brazil. In T. Jones, & T. Newburn (Eds.), *Plural Policing: A comparative perspective*. London: Routledge, 139-168.

Wood, J., & Kempa, M. (2005). Understanding Global Trends in Policing: Explanatory and normative dimensions. In J. Sheptycki, & A. Wardak (Eds.), *Transnational and Comparative Criminology*. London: Glasshouse, 287-316.

Yoshida, N. (1999). The Taming of the Japanese Private Security Industry. *Policing & Society, 9*, 241-261.

Yoshida, N., & Leishman, F. (2006). Japan. In T. Jones, & T. Newburn (Eds.), *Plural Policing: A comparative perspective*. London: Routledge, 222-238.

Zedner, L. (2006). Policing Before and After the Police: the Historical Antecedents of Contemporary Crime Control. *British Journal of Criminology, 46*(1), 78-96.

The Proliferation of Private Security Agencies in South Africa and its Concomitant Effect on Crime Prevention and Crime Reduction

KRIS PILLAY

Private security industry is a growing phenomenon in South Africa, similar to the rest of the emerging global markets. This paper outlines the nature of the security industry in South Africa and examines various issues relating to regulation and licensing of this industry as well as its role in crime prevention.

INTRODUCTION

The South African private security industry is of considerable strategic and economic importance. The security industry's strategic role in ensuring safety and security is highlighted by the vast human and material resources it deploys to protect and safeguard people and property in South Africa.

Across the globe, crime remains the single largest threat, and South Africa is by no means an exception. Crime is a threat that not only endangers profitability but may also cause the collapse of an economic system. Following worldwide trends, South Africa has also experienced rapid growth in its private security industry. According to Hollemans (2005), a private security researcher, "The business of private security is growing and has gone through a silent revolution. All over the world, the industry has boomed and it has taken over functions that were previously performed by the police" (p. 2). As in many countries, the growth of the private security sector challenges outdated ideas on the roles of public and private policing. Private policing is said to be reemerging mainly because of its flexibility and responsiveness to consumer demand and because of an apparent loss of faith in some policing standards and an increase in private property ownership.

Growth of the Private Security Industry in South Africa

The rapid growth and expansion of the private security industry in South Africa cannot be ignored or go unnoticed. Minnaar (2004) argues that "internationally the last twenty years has witnessed the growing role and influence of private security in many aspects of social control. This phenomenal growth has been attributed on the one hand to demands by the public for increased personal safety and protection, by business for increased security, the growth not only in the mass property market but also in the size and number of shopping complexes, private security villages and enclosed or gated neighbourhoods'' (p. 42). In human resources terms, the security industry has grown at an average rate of 11% per year over the past 3 years. The strategic importance of the security industry to the country from a safety and security perspective is self-evident. Considerable trust is placed by clients in an industry which has more resources available than the public police service.

On June 1, 2004, there were approximately 132,000 people employed by the South African Police Service. Of these, approximately 98,000 were uniformed police officers performing policing functions. In the recent research conducted by Irish-Qhobosheane (2005), private security officers outnumber police officers by 4 to 1. South Africans seem to be relying more and more on private security, evidenced by the growth of an army of armed and unarmed security guards that seems to be filling in the gaps left by the overstretched police force.

Generally, the private security industry is made up of individuals and companies providing a service to clients or employers and is charged with protecting and safeguarding persons and property. The basic feature of the private security industry in South Africa is that its activities, structures, and performance are based on free enterprise business principles (SOIB Policy Document, 2000, p. 38)

Pre-1994 Apartheid Dispensation

Historical Context of the Private Sector Security Industry in South Africa

In a literature review conducted by Mistry and Minnaar (1999) on the private security industry in South Africa, the following salient points emerged:

- In the period preceding the 1994 democratic elections, the surveyed literature indicated that the growth of the private security industry was linked to the repressive political culture which existed during the 1970s and 1980s in South Africa.

- The apartheid police force was used primarily to uphold the law and enforce discriminatory and racist laws.

- As the opposition to apartheid grew in intensity, the more affluent residents and the corporate world began to take the issue of private security more seriously.

Former Deputy Minister for Safety and Security Joe Mathews asserted the following at a meeting of the Security Officers Interim Board on April 18, 2000:

"We come from a historical situation where security was basically aimed at preventing the emancipation of Black people. That is how people perceived security. That is how they looked at it. And a lot of people believed that the security industry was merely another arm of the security apparatus of the [previous] government. Now we have to remove those perceptions" (SOIB Policy Document, 2000, p. 25).

According to Shaw (1995), the interests of the state and the private security industry coincided on the issue of protecting property belonging to Whites. Consequently, many White residents and the commercial world, who became increasingly afraid for their own safety and security as well as the impact on their livelihood, turned to private security companies for their own protection. Another factor that gave rise to the increasing growth of the private security industry in South Africa was that during the 1980s, the South African Police shifted its emphasis from ordinary policing to controlling political resistance. This left room for an increase in security company activity. The apartheid state actively encouraged the private security sector to fill the gap left by the police as they became over stretched. Consequently, a close relationship formed between the private and public policing sectors and created considerable functional overlap.

According to Schonteich (1999), private policing is reemerging because of its flexibility, responsiveness to consumer demand, and a loss of faith in the standards of certain public policing services.

Post-Apartheid Private Security Expansion

In democratic post-apartheid South Africa, the private security industry contributes substantially to the economic growth of the country because it:

- gives employment to hundreds of thousands of people,

- presents lucrative opportunities for entrepreneurs and investors to be involved in marketing a service for which there is a significant demand; and

- provides for the protection of assets and economic resources worth hundreds of billions of rands (R14b).

According to the Seth Mogapi, Director of the Private Security Industry Regulatory Authority, "even though the number of registered security businesses has dropped to 6,167 in 2001 to its current 4,385, the Authority was expecting a growth in the private security sector, already one of the fastest growing employee industries in South Africa to escalate in 2005" (Smit, 2005, p. 10). Some of the reasons attributed for this phenomenal growth are crime, the perception of crime, the demand for more sophisticated and personalized security, and declining resources available to the South African Police Service.

Regulating the Private Security Industry in South Africa

As far as the existing regulatory framework is concerned, the need for a review and transformation of the private security industry became more apparent for the following reasons:

- Political circumstances in South Africa are now fundamentally different from those that prevailed when the present legislation was adopted.

- Proper effort must be given to the general transformation initiatives of the government since 1994.

- The existing legislation pre-dates the Constitution of 1996 and may not be entirely consistent with all of its values and principles.

- There is a need to ensure that new legislation is consistent with other laws that apply to facets of the security industry.

- There is a general need to effect technical improvements to current legislation and to devise a more sophisticated and modern regulatory framework.

Change in the security industry also has been necessitated by the following factors:

- The need to deal effectively with certain malpractices, abuses, and corruption in the industry and to lower the possibility of harm to public interest.

- The need to address certain unacceptable attempts by members of the industry to avoid the impact of the current regulatory framework.

- The need to ensure access by emerging entrepreneurs to an industry that is perceived by some as displaying some monopolistic tendencies and allowing entrenched positions to previously disadvantaged positions.

- Socioeconomic developments and the substantial growth of the industry.

Who and What is Being Regulated?

The original legislation creating the first Security Officer's Board (the Security Officer's Act 92 of 1987) came into operation on April 3, 1989. The purpose of this legislation was to provide for the establishment of the Security Officer's Board to deal with and to exercise control over the occupation of security officer. As the various amendments to the Security Officer's Act 92 of 1987 indicate, the legislature has been actively engaged in attempts to improve the Act since the early 1990s with new substantive and other formal changes and to address problems that have emerged, as a result of certain shortcomings, including:

- It became apparent that there was a need to put in place effective mechanisms to deal with certain misconduct, abuses and dishonesty in the industry and to reduce the risk of harming public interest,

- At the time there was a need to tackle certain objectionable attempts by members of the industry to avoid the impact of the regulatory framework that was in existence at the time,

- It also emerged that the phenomenal growth of the industry prompted the government to introduce a more acceptable regulatory framework that would serve the wider interest of the public and consumers of various security services.

The mid-1990s saw phenomenal growth in the size of the security industry. This further posed challenges with respect to proper regulation. Moreover, the economic role of private security in providing business opportunities and creating employment has added impetus to the need for proper regulation.

Towards the end of 1994, initiatives to reform the security industry and its regulation were launched. This culminated in the promulgation of the Security Officers Amendment Act 104 of 1997, which provided for the establishment of the Security Officers Interim Board.

In the originally promulgated Security Officers Act, the objects of the Board set out in section 2 were stated to be the exercise of control over, and the maintenance, promotion, and protection of the profession of the security officer. In the Security Officers Amendment Act 104 of 1997, the legislature added two further objects, namely, to ensure that the industry acts in the public interest and for the periodic submission of reports to the Minister on the regulation of the industry. The appointment of an Interim Board, with a mandate to advise on changes in the relevant legislation, is a clear indication that the government is of the opinion that the current legal framework is in need of review and change.

With this background, on January 25, 2002, the South African government enacted the Private Security Industry Regulation Act No. 56 of 2001. The main purpose of this new Act was "To provide for the regulation of the private security industry; for that purpose to establish a regulatory authority; and to provide for matters connected therewith" (Government Gazette, 2001, p. 2).

Chapter 2, Section 3 of Act 56 of 2001 outlines the following Objectives, namely:

> The primary objects of the Authority are to regulate the private security industry and to exercise effective control over the practice of the occupation of security service provider in the public and national interest and the interest of the private security industry itself, and for that purpose, subject to this Act.

The following are subjected to regulatory norm and control:

- Persons (e.g., employers, employees, managers, directors in the "security industry," as well as for certain purposes, consumers of those services);

- Business entities (e.g., companies, close corporations, partnerships, sole proprietorships, and business trusts);

- Activities and practices (e.g., the rendering of certain types of security services and the manner in which this is done);

- Occupations (e.g., security guard, electronic security monitoring officer, private investigator, security consultant, and security manager/supervisor);

- Sectors (e.g., "contract security," "in-house" security, "guarding sector," the "unarmed" sector, and "cash in transit");

- Relationships (e.g., employer/employee, and principal/contractor); and

- Objects or equipment used in providing a security service (security equipment as defined, for example, armoured vehicles, armed reaction vehicles, electronic alarms, electronic alarms, satellite tracking devices, security dogs, fire-arms, etc.).

It is imperative to define "security service" and "security officer" in accordance with current statutory definitions. The current scope of regulation is mainly provided for by two provisions in the Security Officers Act 92 of 1987, which determines what a "security service" and who a "security officer" are.

Section 1(1) of the Act contains the definition of security service, which is currently used for determining the scope of regulation. This definition reads as follows:

"[A] service rendered to by a person to another person for reward by:

- making himself or a person in his employ available for the protection or safeguarding of people or property in accordance with an arrangement concluded with such a person; or

- advising such other person in connection with the protection or safeguarding of people or property in any manner whatsoever, but does not include such a service rendered by an employee on behalf of his employer."

What is Regulation?

Given the above, the Security Officers Interim Board, on which various stakeholder categories in the security industry in South Africa are represented, had the statutory function of advising the Minister of Safety and Security on any future regulatory framework in respect to the security industry. It was therefore an appropriate moment to introduce a new statutory framework that would regulate the South African private security industry.

It may be useful to get an understanding of what regulation means in the context of the private security industry.

The Security Officers Interim Board Policy Paper on the future regulation of the occupation of the security officers and other related matters states the following:

> Regulation generally means that the important aspects of the nature and activities of the security industry, including who is admitted to the industry and the standard of conduct expected of members of the industry, are controlled and shaped through enforcement strategies and actions in accordance with values, principles and standards contained in the applicable regulation (SOIB Policy Document, 2000, p. 12).

In essence, regulation implies that the members of the industry are not allowed to determine or govern all aspects of their professional or occupational activities in terms of self-imposed standards and principles and that the application of general laws is not sufficient.

Therefore, special legal principles are made applicable and an enforcement mechanism is created to monitor and enforce compliance.

Ibbotson (1998) aptly summarizes the objects of regulation in South Africa as follows:

> "Regulation is simply to ensure that security officers — in any security discipline — who interact with the public are trustworthy and competent" (p. 10).

In their policy paper (2000) the Security Officers Interim Board, subscribes to the following:

> "Regulation is intended to ensure a legitimate, trustworthy and competent private security industry which is optimally capable of contributing to the achievement and maintenance of sufficient levels of safety and security in our country" (SOIB Policy Document, 2000, p. 82).

As a point of departure it may be useful to briefly elaborate on some aspects of the industry that are subject to regulation.

Protection and Safeguarding of Property or Persons in General

This topic covers a wide range of activities in the "guarding sector" of the industry such as patrolling, protecting, guarding, watching, or performing access and exit control. Also included are services such as "close personal protection" or "VIP protection" (bodyguarding services).

Reactive Security

This refers to the security service usually described as "armed response" or "alarm response." An alarm signal or other warning is reacted to by the dispatch of armed security personnel to investigate or to take such other necessary steps. Those who monitor alarms and similar equipment (in a control room or elsewhere) or dispatch any security personnel or supervise them are included in the regulation.

Armed Escourt of Valuables (the Provision of a "Secured Transport," "Cash-in-Transit," or "Assets-in-Transit" Service)

This form of security service is already covered by the general description providing for the protection or safeguarding of property. This implies that the fact that cash or other vehicles are being transported or moved while being protected or safeguarded does not render their guarding or protection anything less or else than a security service.

Providing a Service Aimed at Ensuring Order and Safety on the Premises Used for Sporting, Recreational, Entertainment, or Similar Services

This includes the occupational activities of bouncers, crowd controllers, and those providing control at entertainment venues or during so-called "special events." These operators perform important functions in the field of safety and security.

Manufacturing, Importing, Distributing or Advertising of Monitoring Devices as Contemplated in Section 1 of the Interception and Monitoring Prohibition Act, 1992 (Act No. 107 of 1992)

It is common knowledge that the use of electronic security equipment plays a pivotal role in most security systems. The equipment referred to includes equipment or systems concerning the following: vehicle security, intruder detection, fire detection, closed circuit television (CCTV), electronic surveillance, metal detection, X-ray inspection, bomb detection, telephone security, electronic access control, and aspects of telephone security. It is suggested that the activities of those who advise on the use and installation of security equipment at premises, or persons who monitor any signals from such equipment, be subject to regulation. The trustworthiness and competence of these persons should be promoted by subjecting them to an enforceable code of conduct.

Performing the Functions of a Private Investigator

The occupational activities of private investigators or private intelligence agents do not currently fall under the existing Security Officers Act, as amended, and needs to be brought expressly under the provisions of the new legislation and the future regulatory authority.

Some of their activities/services include the following:

- Criminal, financial, forensic, personal, and asset investigations

- The surveillance of persons or the monitoring of some of their activities

- The gathering of business intelligence

- Risk assessment

- Tracing of persons or property

- Counter-intelligence activities

It is self-evident that the above activities pose a significant threat to the rights of individuals, the public interest, and even the interests of the State (internally as well as in its foreign relations). It is therefore necessary to bring the persons involved in such activities within the regulatory framework and make them subject to an enforceable code of conduct.

Provision of Security Training or Instruction

The current definition of a security service does not expressly include the activities of someone who provides training or instruction in relation to a security service. In terms of the proposed new legislation, security training means any training, instruction, or qualification required in terms of any law before a person may be registered as a security service provider or allowed to render a particular security service. Training providers have been included because of various serious malpractices in the security training industry that have highlighted the need for comprehensive and improved regulatory control. Such control will be promoted by requiring registration and compliance with the code of conduct for security officers.

Performing the Services of a Locksmith

A locksmith means a person who, for the benefit of another person:

(a) opens, closes or engages locks, including locking mechanisms operated by means of an electrical, electronic, magnetic or other processes, by means other than keys, objects or procedures normally used;

(b) repairs, replaces, rebuilds or adjusts locks or other locking mechanisms or their components;

(c) manufactures parts designed for use in locks or such other locking mechanisms; or

(d) cuts or reproduces keys or objects used to open, close or engage locks or such other locking mechanisms, but not a person who manufactures such locks, other locking mechanisms, keys or objects, only by repetitive methods. (Government Gazette, 2001, p. 7)

The Role of Private Security Industry in Crime Prevention

It was recently reported that the rapid growth and the increased need for private security services happened without any real development of policy, and some commentators have argued that there has not been any debate on what role private security should play in society.

Minnaar (2004) contends that internationally, the last 20 years has witnessed the growing role and influence of private security in many aspects of social control. This phenomenal growth has been attributed on the one hand to demands by the public for increased personal safety and protection, by business for increased security, and the growth not only in the mass property market but also in the size and number of shopping complexes, private security villages, and enclosed or gated neighborhoods. All of these factors were subtly encouraged by public perceptions of the efficacy of the public police to provide safety, law, and order, coupled with the declining trust and faith in the police to prevent crime.

Irish-Qhobosheane (2005) stated the following: "Thus far, we have talked about how the sector should be regulated, but we have not been making policy or defining the role of the industry. Where does public policing end and private security start? The separation between these roles has become very blurred" (p. 9).

The boundaries between public and private policing are becoming increasingly blurred. The establishment of a strong armed response component within the private security industry has moved the industry one step closer to performing some of the roles traditionally performed by the police. There also is a growing number of businesses and neighborhoods that are employing private security companies to patrol their streets and suburbs. In a number of places around the country, security companies are part of the local community police forums.

South Africa suffers from a kind of siege mentality, where people barricade themselves in their houses. Some of these measures seem a bit drastic, but the fear of crime is not hype. This situation becomes exacerbated because of the fear of existing property crime, which is rooted in economic differences.

> This [protection] can lead to a breakdown in social bonding. It increases de-personalisation and the anonymity of the individual. The sense of responsibility towards other people and the community diminishes, which in turn leads to a breakdown in social control. The fact that we feel the need to hire armed response and move into gated communities and boomed areas is a manifestation of loss of faith in the police. People do not trust the police to effectively protect their area; they buy themselves some safety (Hollemans, 2005, p. 2).

Residents who live in these gated townhouse complexes seem to believe there is safety in numbers. Complexes are guarded full-time and many have guards posted at the front gates.

According to Hollemans (2005), "this is not peculiar to South Africa, but [is] the pattern around the world. Informal settlements and gated communities are the fastest-growing forms of urban development across the world today" (p. 3).

Minnaar (2004) points out that in South Africa, there have also been ongoing efforts by the authorities to increase the regulation of the industry, but this has been met with considerable resistance or reluctance from the private industry. One of the problems has been in defining the parameters of powers that can be delegated to private security officers in any crime prevention policing operations.

Minnaar (2004) further argues that, "the debate has been complicated by the fact that in the last few years the provision of policing and crime prevention by the private sector has and is already occurring even in the absence of any official co-operative and regulatory framework" (p. 15).

The role that the private security industry plays in crime prevention, crime reduction, and crime control in South Africa will continue to supplement the traditional role of the South African Police Service in protecting the citizens of the country.

Duties shared by a partnership between the police and the private security industry include the following:

- responding jointly to crimes in progress

- investigating crimes

- sharing crime intelligence

- joint involvement in crime intelligence gathering (i.e., by means of joint surveillance teams or CCTV operations)

- sharing of expert knowledge (e.g. on the latest technology [private sector] or training methods [police]

- accessing and supplying official crime information

- joint planning and policing of special events

- assistance with training from both sides (e.g., for computer forensics by private sector companies or collecting and correct control of evidence at a crime scene by the police)

- crime prevention advice (i.e., sharing of risk analysis and audits information)

CONCLUSION

Some of the crucial issues that need to be resolved by the state and the private security industry include:

- defining the role of the police versus that of the private security industry;

- developing guidelines and mechanisms to enable the police and the private security industry to work together;

- creating mechanisms to enable the state and the industry to deal effectively with elements in the industry that are involved in illegal activities and practices; and

- protecting the public where they interface with the private security industry.

The first two points should be addressed through clear policy guidelines, the third through the criminal justice system, and the last should be dealt with through the introduction of effective regulation.

REFERENCES

Anon. (2002). Security industry in novel partnership with SAPS. *Security Focus, 20*(10), 5.

Blecher, S. (1996). *Safety in security: A focus on the role of the private security industry and the potential for violence*. Durban, South Africa: Network of Independent Monitors.

Government Gazatte. (2001). Republic of South Africa, Volume 439. Cape Town Private Security Industry Regulation Act, No. 56 of 2001, p. 2.

Hollemans, E. (2005). Private Security: A disturbing peace of mind. *Mail and Guardian*. Online: http://www.mg.co.za/articlePage.aspx?articleid=237054 &area=/insight/insight national   Accessed July 15, 2005.

Ibbotson, J. (1998). How the private security industry should be regulated. *Security Focus, 16*(9), 8.

Irish, J. (1999). Policing for profit: The future of South Africa's private security industry. ISS Monograph 39. Available online at http://www.iss.co.za/Pubs/monographs/No39/contents.html

Irish-Qhobosheane, J., Earl-Taylor, M., & Bremner, L. (2005). Cited in newspaper article "Private security: A disturbing peace of mind" by Ellen Hollemans. Mail & Guardian online, Johannesburg, South Africa. Retrieved May 5, 2005, from http://www.mg.co.za/articlePage.aspx?articleid=237054&area=/insight/insight_national

Johnston, L. (1992). *The rebirth of private policing*. London: Routledge.

Lee, C. M. (2004). Accounting for rapid growth of private policing in South Korea. *Journal of Criminal Justice, 32*(2), 113-122.

Minnaar, A. (1996). The South African private security industry and the police. (Information document prepared for National Policy & Strategy, SAPS.) Pretoria, South Africa: SAPS Research Centre.

Minnaar, A. (1997). Partnership policing between the South African Police Service and the South African private security industry. (Information document prepared for National Policy & Strategy, Division of Management Services, SAPS.) Pretoria, South Africa: SAPS Research Centre.

Minnaar, A. (2004). Private-public partnerships: private security, crime prevention and policing in South Africa. Inaugural Professorial Lecture. [Also available in *Acta Criminologica, 2005, 18*(1), 85-114.]

Minnaar, A., & Ngoveni, K.P. (2003). The relationship between the South African Police Service and the private security industry with specific reference to the outsourcing of certain operational functions in the police: Post-April 1994. Paper presented to the International Conference on Policing and Security: In Search of Security. Montreal, Quebec, Canada. 19-22 February.

Mistry, D., & Minnaar, A. (1999). Literature review on the private security industry. Technikon, South Africa. [IHRCJS research report submitted to the National Secretariat for Safety and Security.]

Nalla, M. K., & Heraux, C. G. (2003). Assessing goals and functions of private police. *Journal of Criminal Justice, 31*(3), 237-247.

Private Security Industry Regulation Act 56 of 2001. Pretoria, South Africa: Government Printer. Available in Government Gazette, 439, No. 23051, Cape Town, South Africa, January 25, 2002, online at http://www.info.gov.za/gazette/acts/2001/a56-01.pdf

Schonteich, M. (1999). Unshackling the crime fighters: Increasing private sector involvement in South Africa's criminal justice system. [ISS Monograph]. Johannesburg: South African Institute of Race Relations.

Security Officer's Interim Board. (2000). *Policy Paper on the principles regarding the future regulation of the occupation of security officer and related matters*. Published May 31, 2000. Pretoria, South Africa: Security Officer's Interim Board.

Shaw, M. (1995). Partners in crime? Crime, political transition and changing forms of policing control. [Research report No. 39, Centre for Policy Studies, Johannesburg.]

Shaw, M. (1995). Privatising crime control? South Africa's private security industry. [Unpublished research paper.] Midrand: Institute for Defence Policy.

Smit, I. (2005). The guarding industry: Facing the challenges that lie ahead. *Security Focus, 22*(1), 22-24.

The private security complex and its regulation in Africa: select examples from the continent

Julie Berg and Simon Howell

ABSTRACT

This article aims to provide an overview of the primary trends and developments of the domestic private security industry in select countries in Africa, while also further reflecting on a selection of operational challenges and obstacles inherent to the industry and its regulation. In particular, field research was conducted in Uganda to explore the nature of the state ownership of private security companies so as to further highlight the regulatory difficulties. Our findings raise a number of questions pertaining to the theorising of private security regulation answers of which, we conclude, may find utility in drawing on the concept of "hybridity" as an alternative heuristic tool to engage with the realities of state regulation in the Global South.

Introduction

There has been much debate within international scholarly circles on the nature of domestic private security regulation from a Global North perspective. For instance, a number of scholars have been instrumental in mapping out the nature of private security regulation in various geographical regions (see, for instance, Button, 2007; Button & Stiernstedt, 2016; de Waard, 1999), conceptualising regulatory trends from a political economy perspective (White, 2010, 2012) as well as within the context of plural policing developments (see Stenning, 2009). The current state of Global North debates on private security regulation is perhaps best described by Loader and White (2015) where they identify two prevailing ways in which private security regulation is, in their view, conceptualised in the literature. One way in which private security regulation is conceptualised is that the industry needs to be "cleansed" through focussing on "deviant sellers" (Loader & White, 2015, p. 1). The other way is that the industry needs to be "communalised" through focussing on the "empowerment of buyers" (Loader & White, 2015, p. 1). According to the authors, both models fail to account for the role that morality plays in the market and so too only focus on either the buyer (the cleansing model) or only on the seller (the communalising model). They therefore offer a third model to mitigate the weaknesses of both conceptualisations, that of "civilising" the market through considering the role of morality and through developing a deeper role for public regulation, while also considering both the role of the buyer and the seller. They acknowledge that certain conditions need to be present for their model to gain traction, including, in their words, "(relatively) efficient, effective, and legitimate public regulators." In other words, their model relies on some form of state regulator.

Of course, the nature of this role has been questioned within criminological debates. It has long been recognised that statutory regulation of private security does not "constitute a sufficient response to the problem" (Johnston, 1999, p. 12). And that in fact private security is regulated in many other ways besides state or public regulation (Stenning, 2000). Johnston (1999, p. 192) also points out that exclusive regulation of private security by the state is in itself a problem, given that the state as "a unified, authoritative, exclusively public body, with an in-built capacity to exercise sovereign control – is becoming a fiction." This is particularly true for what constitutes "statehood" in many parts of Africa. Similarly, White (2010, p. 14), in providing a historical trajectory of the regulation of private security in the UK, found that what he calls the "reform period" in British history was "shaped by self-interested state actors driven more by a desire to protect their professional domains from the competition of private security companies than by altruistic sensibilities." In other words, the state of debates in Global North circles on the one hand normatively favours a public regulatory body to regulate the private security industry, while on the other hand, there is acknowledgement of the difficulties in relying purely on this form of regulation.

In comparison to Global North engagements, debates on domestic private security regulation in Africa have been very limited. Given the difficulty in extracting information on the size and shape of the industry itself, much of the literature consists of a mapping exercise where the existing normative frameworks are described and critiqued (see, for instance, Abrahamsen & Williams, 2009; Gumedze, 2015). South Africa is somewhat of an exception, given the advanced state of its regulatory system (see Berg & Nouveau, 2011, which calls for a more innovative approach to regulation in South Africa). In other words, the literature which does focus on domestic private security in Africa tends to focus on the lack of regulatory systems in place and the need to develop them – the underlying premise is that the state fulfil this role and that the private and public sectors are discrete entities although they operate in fluid networks or "assemblages" where there is a considerable blurring of power relations (Abrahamsen and Williams, 2011).

In light of these debates and considering the relative dearth of information on this issue, the article aims to provide an overview of some key trends and developments within the domestic private security industry in select African countries, while also reflecting on some of the operational challenges faced by the private security sector and its regulation. Although we acknowledge the inevitable blurring of "high" and "low" security activities, this article will not focus on private military and security companies on the African continent per se (Brodeur, 1983). Much has been written on the nature of private military involvement and the political implications of outsourcing conflict in spaces of weak or contested statehood (see, for instance, Musah, 2002). However, this article will focus on what could be considered "low" forms of security provision or domestic private security. In this way, we aim to contribute to debates on the public regulation of domestic private security by reflecting on the role of the state in fulfilling this function. Both as an example and as means of demonstrating the complexity of these challenges, we draw on the findings of field research conducted by a commissioned researcher in Uganda on the ownership patterns of private security companies, drawing on both the literature and numerous semi-structured interviews with key individuals. These findings raise theoretical and pragmatic questions around the issue of private security regulation, particularly with respect to both the role of the state and the efficacy of traditional regulatory frameworks. In this way, the aim of the article is to contribute to theoretical debates on regulation and their applicability by focussing on select African empirical examples. This is, furthermore, to acknowledge that there is often a dissonance between many of the conceptual frameworks used to understand private security on the continent, their operational realities, and the regulation thereof.

Theoretically framing the private security complex

Very few countries in Africa have an accurate or reliable account of the number of companies and security officials in operation. Even South Africa, with its extensive system of regulation and data-capturing mechanisms facilitated by a formal oversight body, has difficulty in keeping track of the approximately two million security officials on its database, of which only approximately 400,000 are accounted for (Gichanga, 2015). In piecing together a picture of the nature of private security on the continent, a useful analytical descriptor of it is that of a "complex." On the one hand, this acknowledges the sheer number of individual companies, corporations, and collectives that have been formed, consolidated, or expanded in the last decade at the local, regional, and transnational levels (see, for example, Diphoorn, 2015; Goodley, 2011; Palmer, 2015). On the other hand, the term also points to the extent of the networks of relationships that have been formed, both between private security companies themselves and between African states, foreign actors, and indeed the international community itself.

In consideration of the above, a useful conceptual tool with which to frame engagements with the realities of private security ownership may be that of "hybridity." The term is usually employed by scholars concerned with peacebuilding and conflict studies and/or with forms of governance in places of limited statehood. Hybridity scholars therefore reject a state-centric approach to engaging with the complexity of governance arrangements in global and local settings (Albrecht & Moe, 2015; Hönke, 2013; Luckham & Kirk, 2012; Millar, 2014). More recent scholarly engagements on hybridity reject also the tendency to present the "state" and "non-state" as binaries, instead urging that the nature of political order should be an empirical question (Albrecht & Moe, 2015). This is also similar to the interpretations of other disciplines in light of the complexity of regulatory arrangements, especially in situations of weak or limited statehood where authority may come from various sources. What makes the hybridity literature appropriate is that scholars reject the binary of "state" and "non-state" because of the possibility of a complete *integration* of the two, not just a grafting or a co-operation, but a merging (Luckham & Kirk, 2012).

Governance scholars within legal discourse and in conflict studies use the concept "hybrid" to mean the ways in which the non-state may borrow or enrol the authority of state entities to fulfil their mandates and the two become blurred (see Black, 2008; Scott, 2000). This also ties into the notion of the "simultaneity of authority," which sees a merging of the state and non-state and where an individual "draws on, articulates, and practises several registers of authority simultaneously" (Albrecht & Moe, 2015). Hybridity understood in this way is a more useful way to explain the merging of state and non-state authorities and formal and informal regulation. As mentioned, Global North debates may normatively favour the state as the public regulator or acknowledge the difficulties in this but not necessarily offer an alternative conceptual framing to understand the nature of relations between the state and the private security industry where there is a merged relationship. What we will show later in this article is that the state as regulator may simultaneously be the primary owner and/or client of private security. To reiterate what many others have found therefore, the concepts "state" and "non-state" and "private" and "public" are not necessarily useful as heuristic devices, and this extends to the issue of regulation, which needs to be conceptualised within an alternative framing. We, therefore, suggest that through employing the concept of "hybridity," we may begin to account for the realities of privatised security, and the many structural differences, between the developing and developed contexts. The remainder of this article will therefore explore trends, developments, and challenges on the African continent with respect to the private security industry and its regulation; highlight an exemplar of the blurring between the private sector and the state through an example from Uganda; and conclude on the way forward with respect to adopting the concept of "hybridity" as an alternative conceptual framing.

Trends and challenges on the African continent

Africa, and the relationships between its member states, people, and industries are themselves intricately enmeshed; such heterogeneity is not only reflected but further magnified when looking

Table 1. Country ranking by private security industry size

Country ranking	Size of private security per 100,000 of the population
1. Hungary	1050
2. Guatemala	944
3. Panama	928
4. Honduras	870
5. South Africa	806

to private security companies, not only because security remains a critical concern in multiple places but because classical distinctions between the state and non-state, between private and commercial interests, between "high" and "low" security, and indeed between what is pre-emptive and preventative are often unclear, as mentioned (Bowling & Sheptycki, 2012; Brodeur, 1983; Kushner, 2015; Williams, 2016). Yet in acknowledging and taking seriously this complexity, it is *not* possible to provide a definitive "map" or complete analytical "outline" of the myriad of ways in which private security exist, operate, and interact in Africa. This being said, it remains possible to reflect on at least some of the central thematic features of this complex and, when narrowed down slightly, possible to give a fair account of the private security industry as it exists in/at the levels of individual countries and regions. Speaking to this, in this section, we provide a brief overview of what are (arguably) the primary thematic trends and challenges that help shape the private security complex on the continent. In providing illustrations to this thematic, we draw secondly on a number of examples from diverse range of African countries to show how this diversity creates both congruencies and disparities.

Beginning with their basic structural features, private security companies in Africa occupy many roles, perform a number of functions, and in totality have an inordinately varied clientele – varying in diversity from the protection of private property to the protection of individuals, from the safeguarding of embassies to the escorting of ships and vessels at sea, and, often in seeming contradictory ways, from facilitating aid projects to coalescing around resource-rich sites and helping to expedite the path of natural resources from source to consumer (Ferguson, 2005; Spearin, 2001). Organisations can also vary greatly in size, the smallest of which are individually run and operated micro-companies, while the largest of which are multinational conglomerates such as G4S which reportedly operates in 24 African countries employing approximately 120,400 people (G4S, 2017).

The demand and need for private security services is in many African countries itself a resource to be mined (Brooks, 2000). In reviewing what is known about private security on the continent, domestic private security is a burgeoning industry. In some countries it is, and has been, growing at an exponential rate for decades. For instance, using data available at the time of writing, South Africa hosts the largest (known) numbers of private security companies and employees on the continent – both per capita and in terms of raw numbers. In 2015/2016, there were over 8692 security companies and approximately 488,666 registered and active private security employees in South Africa compared to 151,834 police officers in the South African Police Service (excluding civilians) and members of the armed forces (Private Security Industry Regulatory Authority, 2016; South African Police Service, 2016). In other words, compared to the state security apparatus, private security outnumbers the public police by 3 to 1. Whereas the public police total 276 personnel per 100,000 of the population of South Africa, the private security industry boasts 889 per 100,000 of the population. Even on the global stage, the country has a particularly large sector as Table 1 shows, drawn from the Small Arms Survey (2011) which reviewed the state of private security in 70 countries.

Knowing this, what is known about other African countries is, as mentioned, limited. Summing up what information exists, in Kenya, "[i]t is estimated that there are currently between 2000 and 4000 such companies operating ... which employ approximately 300,000 guards" (Noor & Wagacha, 2015). In Liberia, estimates from 2012 indicate that there were 87 companies with around 7000 employees outnumbering the approximately 6000 armed forced and police forces combined (Von Boemcken, 2012). In Botswana, there were reportedly 2377 registered private security companies according to an industry association, while in Namibia in 2010, there were 216 companies with an estimate of 20,000 employees (Molomo & Maundeni, 2015; Nakutta, Duminy, & Simamuna, 2015). In Ghana, in 2014, there were reportedly 176 licensed security companies, according to the Ministry of Interior, but reportedly 1053 companies according to Ghana's Association of Private Security Organizations (Owusu, Owusu, Oteng-Ababio, Wrigley-Asante, & Agyapong, 2016). In Senegal, it was estimated that there were 150 security companies and between 25,000 and 35,000 employees in 2008 (O'Brien, 2008). In Sierra Leone, estimates posit that there were from 30 to 50 security companies in 2009 and approximately 3000–5000 employees (Abrahamsen & Williams, 2009).

Regardless of the size of the industry, whether in South Africa, Namibia, Liberia, and Swaziland, private security is one of the fastest growing industries (Grant, 1989; Nakutta et al., 2015; Simelane, 2008; Von Boemcken, 2012). In Liberia, for instance, the private security industry reportedly doubled its revenues between 2004 and 2011, while in South Africa, private security has gone from an industry worth 600 million Rand (USD44 million) in 1986 to current estimates of it being worth 60 billion Rand (USD4 billion) (Grant, 1989; Von Boemcken, 2012). With new markets and new opportunities, such as maritime protection services required by offshore oil drilling, private security growth is aided by some of the largest industries in the world. The Economist (2015) recently stated, for instance, that "between 2007 and 2009, while an insurgency seethed in the fuel-rich region, Shell splurged $383 million, 40% of its global security budget, in Nigeria."

However, as is expanded on below, the provision of such definitional accounts presuppose that there is a clear distinction between the private security industry and other companies, the state, and the communities in which they operate. Such estimates are rarely contextualised in relation to population size or economic growth. Moreover, while private security companies are invariably profit driven, the multiplicity of functions they offer, their embeddedness in the architecture of statehood, informal networks of protection, and indeed the often ill-defined (or poorly enforced) regulatory frameworks and labour practices make neat categorisation of their activities an ongoing challenge. Ironically, the documentation of such indices may not only reflect boundaries, but serve to reproduce them. In direct reference to Africa, such challenges have been noted, both in terms of conceptual and empirical definition (Bearpark & Schulz, 2007).

The lack of verifiable empirical data is itself indicative of the definitional concerns touched on above. The private security complex has become so interwoven into the security/regulation architecture of Africa, and indeed, private security companies and their employees are so embedded in the day-to-day, that in becoming ubiquitous they have become hidden in plain sight. Moreover, their various services and "products" are so widely used – although, it should be said, this use is economically linked – that their employment has become de facto for many organisations, governments, and indeed citizens. This, as has been widely noted, raises a whole raft of regulatory, ethical, and safety concerns (see, for instance, Shearing, 2016). With this in mind, it is important to review some of the regulatory frameworks that are in place to govern the industry on the continent and, moreover, to underscore some of the challenges faced in regulating the complex.

The private security complex *in situ*

There have been a number of different responses by African states to both the challenges and opportunities presented by the strengthening of the private security complex more broadly. Beginning with the largest of these, South Africa has the most sophisticated regulatory framework in place on the continent to regulate domestic private security. Many other African countries see it as an exemplar of what normative provisions should be in place. This stems, however, from the convoluted history of engagement between the private security industry and the state in South Africa – both during and after Apartheid. The earliest legislation stems from the 1980s as a means by which the Apartheid government could harness the private capacities of the industry (that is, the Security Officers Act of 1987 and the subsequent creation of a Security Officers' Board). Therefore, much of the focus on this initial regulation was on professionalising the industry to administer core functions, while the state security agencies could focus on maintaining the apartheid infrastructure. In other words, the industry was both actively and passively recruited to fill the gaps left by the state – the 1980s legislation reflects this.

Revised legislation from the 2000s stems from a wary post-apartheid, democratic government cognisant of the industry's past and its specialist abilities. It is argued that the 1987 legislation was created to protect the interests of the industry, whereas the later legislation (including the amendments of the 1990s) was created to protect the interests of the public, hence explaining why the later legislation takes on a more punitive stance with respect to the treatment of the industry by the new, democratic government (Ibbotson, 1994). The underlying principles of the apartheid and post-apartheid legislation thus reflect the changing regulatory tactics employed by the two state systems. The newer legislation was ultimately designed to tighten the loopholes and fill the gaps of the 1980s legislation as well as to legitimise and professionalise the industry in order that it contributes to the good of society.

The current legislation regulating private security in South Africa is extensive and has already been discussed by scholars in detail (see Berg, 2003; Minnaar, 2007). Therefore, in brief, the primary documents (some of which have since been amended or revised) include the Private Security Industry Regulation Act of 2001, Appeal Regulations of 2002, Improper Conduct Enquiries Regulations of 2003, Code of Conduct for Security Service Providers of 2003, and others. Presently, the Private Security Industry Regulation Act of 2001 provides for the establishment of a regulatory body called Private Security Industry Regulatory Authority (PSIRA) as well as a Council (consisting of a maximum of five persons) which "governs and controls" PSIRA.

A large degree of power has been conferred to PSIRA inspectors to undertake the task of ensuring that companies and officers in the private security industry are registered and comply with the law – a reflection perhaps of the state's desire to regulate the industry in light of its past practices and exponential growth.

South Africa's story is a fairly unique one in terms of the history of the development of private security and the regulatory framework enacted. For instance, in Swaziland, there exists no specific legislation aimed at the private security industry and any regulation in place is constituted through labour law and corporate regulation (Simelane & Maziya, 2015). In effect, this means that "[a]nybody can start a private security company in Swaziland" (Simelane, 2008, p. 605). Although Botswana has a Private Security Bill of 2007, it has yet to be approved and enacted (Molomo & Maundeni, 2015). In the meantime, the industry remains unregulated by the state.

Moving further afield, Namibia has a Security Enterprises and Security Officers Act of 1998, as well as the Security Enterprises and Security Officer Regulation Board, the accompanying regulations, at the time of writing, had yet to be enacted (Nakutta et al., 2015). In Nigeria, there exists the Private Guard Companies Decree of 1986 and the Private Guard Companies Act of 1990, yet there is no regulatory body per se, instead the paramilitary agency, the Nigeria Security and Civil Defence Corps (NSCDC) is responsible for registering private security companies as well as attending to its other tasks focussed on national security (Olawale, 2016; Omotoso & Ader, 2016). In Liberia, regulation is by means of licencing (renewed annually), which is controlled by the Division of Public Safety, Ministry of Justice, headed by the Assistant Minister of Justice, Administration and Public Safety (Ashkenazi & von Boemcken, 2011). In Ghana, private security companies are similarly regulated by the Ministry of Interior and the Ghana Police Service and, as with South Africa, has had a long history of attempts to regulate the industry – dating back to the 1970s through the Ghana Police Service Act (Abudu, Nuhu, & Nkuah, 2013; Owusu et al., 2016). Later, amendments to this Act in the 1990s provide for registration and the provision and renewal of licences as well as regulations on uniforms and firearms (Owusu et al., 2016). Similar to Ghana, private security companies are regulated by the police in Uganda, primarily in accordance with Sections 72 and 73 of the amended Police Act Cap 30, and the Police (Control of Private Security Organisations) Regulations (Nakueira, 2015). While the former is more general, the latter is more specifically focussed on the laws governing the operations of the private security industry, having been developed in 2007 to replace the earlier versions made valid in 1997 and 2004. Under Section 1(w) of the Police Act Cap 303, a private security company is defined as a registered company under the Companies Act, of which only those private security organisations that have registered under this Act are allowed to provide security services (Nakueira, 2015). In terms of regulation and oversight, the Inspector General of Police is primarily responsible for ensuring that all private security companies comply with these regulations and is also responsible for their continued operation and the supervision thereof (Nakueira, 2015). This is similar to the way in which the registration of private security companies takes place in Tanzania (Shadrack, 2011).

The above provides only a snapshot of some of the regulatory trends in a few countries, but what is common to most, if not all, countries on the continent is the challenges faced in terms of the regulatory frameworks in place and their functionality. What follows is a brief overview of some of these challenges.

Political and private challenges

On reviewing the literature on domestic private security in Africa, one of the most pervasive regulatory challenges is the problematic nature of the private security industry itself (see, for instance, Abudu et al., 2013; Ashkenazi & von Boemcken, 2011; Mkutu & Sabala, 2007; O'Brien, 2008; Omotoso & Ader, 2016; Owusu et al., 2016; Simelane, 2008; Von Boemcken, 2012 on which the following section is based). Many countries have the mammoth task of professionalising an industry which is largely unknown, a nebulous entity characterised by poorly paid security guards, with limited or no benefits, low skills, and lack of training often undertaking dangerous jobs in contentious spaces. There is often a blurring of informal and formal activities skirting the line between what is legal and illegal. Although difficult to expose, the industry is often accused of criminal practices, having links to organised crime and/or committing human rights abuses in the course of their duties. There are concerns in many African countries about the involvement of foreign nationals in the ownership of private security companies, particularly given the history of private military companies on the continent and the influx of ex-combatants into the industry. Some countries have opted for a ban on foreign ownership (such as Nigeria, Liberia, and Senegal), while some are still considering the economic and political effects thereof (such as South Africa) (Ashkenazi & von Boemcken, 2011; O'Brien, 2008).

The increasing size and diversity of the industry has left governments feeling uncomfortable with the incursions into what was considered the traditional role of the state – hence for instance, stricter regulations on uniforms, insignia, and weapons, to prevent companies from emulating the state and encroaching on state authority. The industry is also beset by inequalities – particularly gender inequalities – with long hours, limited benefits, and dangerous conditions being cited as the primary reasons for the industry remaining a male-dominated one. Many of these challenges are contingent on a market which is a highly competitive one, where low costs trump quality service and security guards are a readily available commodity for short-term contracts. Collusion and corruption during tendering processes only add to this problem.

There are also challenges faced by the regulatory agencies themselves. Given the diversity of activities undertaken by the industry, its in-house component, and the blurring of high and low forms of security, one of the greatest challenges is in defining the industry. A definition too broad or too narrow may result in an industry too unwieldy to regulate or not regulated sufficiently. As mentioned, whereas some countries have developed regulatory provisions in place, others simply have no direct state regulation of the industry. Those countries which do have laws in place usually experience problems of a lack of/or low resources, lack of capacity and staffing, and a general lack of political will to properly fund regulatory efforts. For instance, even for a fairly well-resourced country, like South Africa, PSIRA struggles with capacity issues with respect to the number of inspectors allocated to inspect private security businesses.

One of the primary challenges faced is the difficulty in controlling those who enter the industry – vetting entry and screening applicants is a considerable task given the high turnover rates of guards entering and exiting the industry on short-term contracts. Although firearms may be outlawed in some countries (such as for instance Nigeria, Liberia, Swaziland, and Botswana), those countries which do allow private guards to be armed face the added difficulty of ensuring that firearms are legally acquired and used by competent personnel (Ashkenazi & von Boemcken, 2011). This is particularly problematic if regulatory frameworks and agencies are not equipped to manage unregistered, unlicensed, or fly-by-night companies. What adds to this problem is when state security agencies (police or military units) are mandated with the task of regulating the industry over and above their core functions. In reference to Nigeria, but pertinent to many countries across the continent, Abrahamsen and Williams (2009, p. 10) observe that it is "often difficult to determine where public force ends and private security begins."

What then are the implications of a state security agency serving as the primary regulator of the private security industry? Similarly, what are the implications for state regulation when the state is the primary client, such as is the case in Swaziland? (Simelane, 2016). Furthermore, consider the involvement of the state in the ownership of private security companies. In Liberia, for instance, private security companies are often owned by government officials. According to Ashkenazi and von Boemcken (2011), the Minister of Defence owns "the largest Liberian-managed firm" and smaller companies are often owned by police officials. So too, in Senegal, according to O'Brien (2008), most private security companies are owned by ex-military or police personnel with some companies being owned by those still in office. Personal connections to the state play an important role in some countries; for instance, in Senegal, "[p]ersonal ties are important, as companies that have the strongest ties to the state security system or to the state bureaucracy are more likely to win licenses" (O'Brien, 2008, p. 658).

Similarly in Nigeria, if one has political connections to the minister or the president, then starting a private security company is a far less onerous and bureaucratic affair (Olawale, 2016). In Tanzania, it has been observed by Shadrack (2011, p. 54) that private security companies are largely owned and/or run "by current serving members and ex-members of the armed forces with political influence thus, in one way or another, blocking any move towards effective regulation." Likewise in the Democratic Republic of Congo, undertaking successful business ventures is contingent on personal and political ties, as outlined by Hönke (2013, p. 74):

> In Southern Katanga, as in many other African countries, working with the state depends entirely on having personal contacts within it. … good relations with key people in central government are essential for successfully running a large business in the DRC.

This brings to the fore another regulatory challenge which questions the normative stance that the state should be the primary regulator of the industry. This extends far beyond logistical questions around registering and licencing security guards or ensuring compliance with uniform codes – this speaks to the heart of how private security can and should be regulated in contexts where the default regulatory agent, the state, may be compromised.

The case of Uganda

In order to explore this issue further, preliminary field research was conducted in Uganda in the latter part of 2015 to explore the nature of relations between the state and private security companies. The country is of specific interest as a representative example of some of the many challenges faced by both the security industry and indeed the state in finding effective mechanisms of regulation. The research presented here was specifically commissioned and is based on both a review of the literature and semi-structured interviews conducted by a field worker (Nakueira, 2015) over the course of some three months in 2016 with numerous key participants in the security and regulatory spheres. Where necessary or requested, the interviews have been anonymised.

In Uganda, as noted above, the private security complex is not a "clearly defined homogenous group" (United Nations Office on Drugs and Crime, 2014). This is a product of ill-defined and highly malleable regulatory framework and because the distinction between "the public" and "the private" and "formal" and "informal" is not easy to make. The findings reveal, for instance, that

> ... the public is very much aware that the state has infiltrated every sector with spies. These spies are said to include "boda-boda" (taxi-motorcyclists), street vendors, waiters as well as people who are deemed to be mentally ill and wandering the streets. This state-run private security network is reported to include regular people working in various public and private agencies to spy on the public for the state. (Nakueira, 2015)

In this sense "private security" is much more than the formal system of registered security guards and by no means a distinct entity from the state.

Considering the political context of Uganda, in which numerous forms of corruption remain problematic, difficulties in the effective implementation of regulation are enmeshed in deeper concerns with corruption and accountability. As the research (Nakueira, 2015) further discovered that:

> An interview with the Registrar of private security organisations revealed that in reality the number of registered companies was 151. He however explained that because he had not yet inspected the premises of 20 of the newly registered companies, the list he gave me reflected only 131.

Uganda, unfortunately, remains notorious for the high prevalence levels of corruption, with the public procurement sector having suffered losses amounting to an estimated USD258.6 million per year (Nakueira, 2015).

In essence, the research in Uganda found that most owners or directors of private security companies are members of parliament or close relatives (mostly children) of prominent politicians (including the president's office) and or ex-military or National Resistance Movement (NRM) affiliates. They also all belong to the same ethnic groups. This is summed up by Nakueira (2015) as follows:

> The presence of a strong state influence in the private security industry can be reasonably understood to emanate from the state's inauguration into power. Control of the private security industry in Uganda is intimately connected with ex-military or current political affiliates of the ruling party. For example ... many of the directors or owners of the private security organisations in Uganda are children of (as well as ex-members of) the former rebel group the National Resistance Army that is now in power. Therefore, the private security industry's ties to the state can be properly be described as consisting of ethnic, family and close friends to the state.

Much of these findings are confirmed by others, where it has been found that political, ethnic, or kinship connections with state officials (as mentioned, going right up to the president's office and family) are necessary for private security companies to arm their guards. The implication of this is that only those with connections are able to provide armed guards, which are in greater demand than unarmed guards. In essence, what has been found by the research is as follows:

> On the face of it, the private security industry looks like a mundane security machine going about its operations in a country where the state police is barely visible. However, a more nuanced analysis suggests that the private security industry in Uganda is run by an army of Museveni loyalists, NRM apologists and business opportunists who benefit from the lucrative deals and the "stable" security status quo. (Nakueira, 2015)

It goes without saying that effective, formal regulation of the industry is severely hampered by informal connections. Politically connected private security companies in Uganda are essentially an extension of state security, and when considering that the state is a "politically contested regime," it becomes all the more apparent than that private security is a useful back-up to protect prevailing state interests should they be threatened (Nakueira, 2015). This has profound implications with respect to the nature of state regulation.

The impacts on state regulation were further articulated in some of the interviews conducted in Uganda; for instance, when asked whether the state's involvement in the private security industry was problematic, the Director of a Procurement Agency commented as follows:

> Definitely yes, because the ownership of most security firms is linked to high profile government persons the regulation is affected, the Ministry of Internal Affairs does the vetting and issuing of licences to operate the security firm, this in itself is a challenge especially to entry in the market sector. Also when the security firm staff are involved in any form of criminal offence during work the cases are not properly handled by the police. (Nakueira, 2015)

This is further emphasised by the comment made below by a former auditor of a private security company with state connections in Uganda:

> Politicisation as witnessed in other sectors especially the public sector has had the effect of undermining institutions (especially regulatory) and in the process making them ineffective and redundant in most cases. While the private security sector is still loosely regulated, politicisation of the sector presents the risk of making this worse. Case in point was the ban on [the] use of automatic rifles by security firms that the government laid down years ago but failed to implement it for [a state-owned private security company]. Which in turn caused other firms to drag their feet on implementation .... (Nakueira, 2015)

In this sense, the state "regulates" the private security industry in a manner wholly different from the normative idea of the state as formal, independent regulator set-up to protect the interests of the public or the public good. In other words, in a formal sense, private security is "loosely regulated" through the law and through the regulatory obligations of the Inspector General of Police. In practice, formal regulation is ineffectual and informal systems of regulation dominate. Therefore, in an informal sense, private security is heavily regulated by the state through political, ethnic, and kinship ties; thus, "regulation" occurs not in the imagined ways of a (itself imagined) Global North perspective. The literature, therefore, does not sufficiently account for the interlinkages and hybridity of the state and non-state in contexts where, for instance, a high-level public official (or relative thereof) is also the owner of a private security company winning tenders to protect state assets of which that public official has some benefit.

Conclusion: revising understandings and regulatory frameworks

In light of the examples we provide above, what are the implications for how regulation is conceptualised where the private security are, or buy into, "the private networks of the shadow state" (Abrahamsen and Williams, 2011, p. 223). We acknowledge that the blurring of public and private interests, politics, and business is by any means a new phenomenon – it has long been identified that personal connections are necessary to conduct business with the state (not only in Africa, but in developed contexts too). It has also long been known that political actors, especially in contexts of transitional or weak state governance, may become intertwined with private interests and often corrupt or criminal elements. There is, for instance, a well-developed literature on the "informalisation [or personalisation] of politics," the interconnections and codependencies of political elites and the informal and formal economies (Chabal & Daloz, 1999, p. 1). However, there is a need to engage with this phenomenon as it pertains to the regulation of private security in situations described above. As we highlighted previously, one of the ways in which to conceptually engage with the reality of "simultaneous authority" is to employ the concept of hybridity. This framing leads one to a very different normative endpoint, one in which focus is shifted from a concern with analytically distinct entities to one which focusses on the networks of actors and relationships which intersect in the production of different outcomes. The most desirable of these outcomes remains deceptively simple to articulate: that security in all its manifestations – regardless of who provides it – should be effective, accountable, and orientated *for* the public good or at least align *with* the public good. The way forward in terms of achieving this in contexts where hybridity is the norm, and where the state cannot or perhaps should not be the primary regulator, remains open to debate. Some have suggested that those involved in providing security could be regulated or held accountable through a hybridisation of civil society and transnational institutions (Dupont, Grabosky, & Shearing, 2003). This would essentially constitute a system of state-like, "public" regulation but provided by other (non-state) entities. In this way, the state is not normatively favoured, and regulation is potentially shifted to entities without a vested interest. But of course there is also the danger that these entities, too, exhibit shadow state-like qualities where they "draw authority from their ability to control markets and resources rather than territory or coercive agents" (Hills, 2000, p. 165). This is especially true in contexts where, as mentioned, personal contacts with the state are imperative – this is particularly true for businesses, as Hönke (2013) articulates, but it holds for other entities as well.

In light of this, a way in which the regulation of private security could be conceived in hybrid situations is to tie it into a complex networked system where political accountability (which is held up as the normative ideal) is intertwined with public accountability, market accountability, and incentivised self-regulation, for instance. By implication, this means that the positive effects of one system may mitigate the negative effects of another system. In other words, rather than relying on one system of political accountability, within a hierarchical system of regulation (such as account-ability to a public regulator through licencing and so forth), a hybrid system of accountability could be an option. In the words of Braithwaite (2006, p. 39): "The biggest problem with hierarchical accountability is that it is hierarchical." It ties too much into one system of regulation and does not factor into account the hybridity of relations between entities and individuals. In other words, by holding public regulation or political accountability as the normative ideal, state-centric notions of democratic accountability prevail, leading scholars to call for a bigger role for government, which may not be appropriate.

How does one develop a hybrid system of regulation? In line with the suggestion of hybridity scholars, an empirical approach is vital to understanding how regulation works in hybrid systems of governance (Albrecht & Moe, 2015). It is also to engage with the reality of the competing incentives or motivations that currently drive or govern the industry in various contexts and to identify those incentives that may align it to a public good. For instance, in the context of hybridity, could security companies be motivated by public opinion or sentiments, corporate social responsibility, personal morality, or perhaps desires for legitimacy? Are there innovative regulatory tools that could be used to drive these incentives towards a public good – perhaps the use of rating agencies or other systems of public accountability that does not rely on public regulation? The fact remains that there is a need to adopt analytical tools to be able to engage with shifting forms and applications of regulation, particularly in light of bottom-up developments and the hybridity of practices being employed. There is also a need for more engagement with the nature of regulatory deficits, without making normative or analytical assumptions about how regulation happens or should happen. It is also to acknowledge that, in light of rapid advances in governance systems and the continued blurring of authorities, regulation cannot be understood in isolation of its functioning within hybrid systems of governance. In other words, scholars need to avoid the tendency to investigate the regulation of entities in isolation of their involvement in systems of power and codependency.

References

Abrahamsen, R., & Williams, M. (2009). Security beyond the state: Global security assemblages in international politics. *International Political Sociology, 3*(1), 1–17. doi:10.1111/j.1749-5687.2008.00060.x

Abrahamsen, R., & Williams, M. (2011). *Security beyond the state: Private security in international politics.* Cambridge: Cambridge University Press.

Abudu, A. M., Nuhu, Y., & Nkuah, J. K. (2013). Bridging the security gap in Ghana: The role of private security actors. *Developing Country Studies, 3*(10), 11–30. Retrieved from http://www.iiste.org/Journals/index.php/DCS/article/view/8153/8247

Albrecht, P., & Moe, L. (2015). The simultaneity of authority in hybrid orders. *Peacebuilding, 3*(1), 1–16. doi:10.1080/21647259.2014.928551

Ashkenazi, M., & von Boemcken, M. (2011). Liberia. In M. von Boemcken (Ed.), *Brief 45: Commercial security and development – Findings from Timor-Leste, Liberia and Peru* (pp. 35–48). Bonn: Bonn International Center of Conversion.

Bearpark, A., & Schulz, S. (2007). The private security challenge in Africa: Problems and options for regulation. In S. Gumedze (Ed.), *Private security in Africa: Manifestations, challenges and regulation.* Johannesburg: Institute of Security Studies.

Berg, J. (2003). The private security industry in South Africa: A review of applicable legislation. *South African Journal of Criminal Justice, 16,* 178–196. Retrieved from http://heinonline.org/HOL/LandingPage?handle=hein.journals/soafcrimj16&div=21&id=&page=

Berg, J., & Nouveau, J. (2011). Towards a third phase of regulation: Re-imagining private security in South Africa. *South African Crime Quarterly, 38,* 23–32. Retrieved from http://www.ajol.info/index.php/sacq/article/viewFile/101429/90616

Black, J. (2008). Constructing and contesting legitimacy and accountability in polycentric regulatory regimes. *Regulation & Governance, 2*(2), 137–164. doi:10.1111/j.1748-5991.2008.00034.x

Bowling, B., & Sheptycki, J. (2012). *Global policing.* London: Sage Publications.

Braithwaite, J. (2006). Accountability and responsibility through restorative justice. In M. Dowdle (Ed.), *Public accountability: Designs, dilemmas and experiences* (pp. 33–51). Cambridge: Cambridge University Press.

Brodeur, J.-P. (1983). High policing and low policing: Remarks about the policing of political activities. *Social Problems, 30*(5), 507–520. doi:10.2307/800268

Brooks, D. (2000). Messiahs or mercenaries? The future of international private military services. *International Peacekeeping, 7*(4), 129–144. doi:10.1080/13533310008413867

Button, M. (2007). Assessing the regulation of private security across Europe. *European Journal of Criminology, 4* (1), 109–128. doi:10.1177/1477370807071733

Button, M., & Stiernstedt, P. (2016). Comparing private security regulation in the European Union. *Policing and Society,* 1–17. doi:10.1080/10439463.2016.1161624

Chabal, P., & Daloz, J.-P. (1999). *Africa works: Disorder as political instrument.* Bloomington, IN: Indiana University Press.

de Waard, J. (1999). The private security industry in international perspective. *European Journal on Criminal Policy and Research, 7*(2), 143–174. doi:10.1023/A:1008701310152

Diphoorn, T. (2015). *Twilight policing: Private security and violence in urban South Africa.* Oakland, CA.: University of California Press.

Dupont, B., Grabosky, P., & Shearing, C. (2003). The governance of security in weak and failing states. *Criminal Justice, 3*(4), 331–349. doi:10.1177/146680250334001

Ferguson, J. (2005). Seeing like an oil company: Space, security, and global capital in neoliberal Africa. *American Anthropologist, 107*(3), 377–382. doi:10.1525/aa.2005.107.3.377

G4S. (2017). Where we operate. Retrieved from http://www.g4s.com/en/Who%20we%20are/Where%20we%20operate/

Gichanga, M. (2015). South Africa. In S. Gumedze (Ed.), *Promoting partnerships for crime prevention between state and private security providers in Southern Africa* (pp. 147–210). Pretoria: The Private Security Industry Regulatory Authority.

Goodley, S. (2011, October 31). G4S bid for Danish rival ISS meets a chorus of disapproval. *The Guardian,* p. 3.

Grant, E. (1989). Private policing. In T. W. Bennett, D. J. Devine, D. B. Hutchison, I. Leeman, & D. Van Zyl Smit (Eds.), *Acta Juridica* (pp. 92–117). Cape Town: Juta.

Gumedze, S. (Ed.). (2015). *Promoting partnerships for crime prevention between state and private security providers in Southern Africa*. Pretoria: The Private Security Industry Regulatory Authority.

Hills, A. (2000). *Policing Africa: Internal security and the limits of liberalization*. Boulder, CO: Lynne Rienner.

Hönke, J. (2013). *Transnational companies and security governance: Hybrid practices in a postcolonial world*. Oxford: Routledge.

Ibbotson, J. (1994, February). *Repositioning the security industry in a changing South Africa*. Paper presented to the South African Security Association Annual Conference, Johannesburg.

Johnston, L. (1999). Private policing in context. *European Journal on Criminal Policy and Research*, 7, 175–196. doi:10.1023/A:1008753326991

Kushner, K. (2015). Nonstate security and political participation: Reinforcing ruling party support in South Africa. *Africa Today*, 62, 107–135. doi:10.2979/africatoday.62.1.107

Loader, I., & White, A. (2015). How can we better align private security with the public interest? Towards a civilizing model of regulation. *Regulation & Governance*. Online version. doi:10.1111/rego.12109

Luckham, R., & Kirk, T. (2012). *Security in hybrid political contexts: An end-user approach* (Justice & Security Research Programme Paper 2). London: Justice & Security Research Programme.

Millar, G. (2014). Disaggregating hybridity: Why hybridity institutions do not produce predictable experiences of peace. *Journal of Peace Research*, 51, 501–514. doi:10.1177/0022343313519465

Minnaar, A. (2007). Oversight and monitoring of non-state/private policing: The private security practitioners in South Africa. In S. Gumedze (Ed.), *Private security in Africa: Manifestation, challenges and regulation* (pp. 127–149). Pretoria: Institute for Security Studies.

Mkutu, K., & Sabala, K. (2007). Private security companies in Kenya and dilemmas for security. *Journal of Contemporary African Studies*, 25(3), 391–416. doi:10.1080/02589000701662442

Molomo, M., & Maundeni, Z. (2015). Botswana. In S. Gumedze (Ed.), *Promoting partnerships for crime prevention between state and private security providers in Southern Africa* (pp. 45–94). Pretoria: The Private Security Industry Regulatory Authority.

Musah, A.-F. (2002). Privatization of security, arms proliferation and the process of state collapse in Africa. *Development and Change*, 33(5), 911–933. doi:10.1111/1467-7660.t01-1-00254

Nakueira, S. (2015). *The political economy of private security: Uganda* (Research report for the Centre of Criminology, University of Cape Town). Cape Town: UCT.

Nakutta, J., Duminy, N., & Simamuna, B. (2015). Namibia. In S. Gumedze (Ed.), *Promoting partnerships for crime prevention between state and private security providers in Southern Africa* (pp. 95–146). Pretoria: The Private Security Industry Regulatory Authority.

Noor, H., & Wagacha, D. W. (2015, June 1). Kenya desperately needs mechanisms to monitor and regulate the growing private security sector. *ISS Today*. Retrieved from https://issafrica.org/iss-today/does-private-security-mean-better-security-in-kenya

O'Brien, C. (2008). The dynamics of private security in Senegal. *Review of African Political Economy*, 35, 655–659. doi:10.1080/03056240802574078

Olawale, I. (2016, June). *Nigeria*. Paper presented at the meeting of "The Private Security Industry in Africa: The Opportunities and Challenges", Johannesburg.

Omotoso, O., & Ader, A. (2016). Challenges of providing security in Lagos State: The case of corporate private security organizations. *African Journal of Criminology and Justice Studies*, 9(1), 1–18. Retrieved from http://search.proquest.com/openview/0b5e4b879e3d0ad09a9cfbf50b38fd62/1?pq-origsite=gscholar&cbl=55089

Owusu, G., Owusu, A., Oteng-Ababio, M., Wrigley-Asante, C., & Agyapong, I. (2016). An assessment of households' perceptions of private security companies and crime in urban Ghana. *Crime Science*, 5, 1–11. doi:10.1186/s40163-016-0053-x

Palmer, A. (2015). *The new pirates: Modern global piracy from Somalia to the South China Sea*. London: I.B. Taurus.

Private Security Industry Regulatory Authority. (2016). Annual report 2015/16. Retrieved from http://www.psira.co.za/psira/images/Documents/Publications/Annual_Reports/PSIRAAnnualReport2015-16.pdf

Scott, C. (2000). Accountability in the regulatory state. *Journal of Law and Society*, 27(1), 38–60. doi:10.1111/1467-6478.00146

Shadrack, J. (2011). *The private security industry in Tanzania: Challenges, issues and regulation* (LL.M dissertation). University of Dar es Salaam, Dar es Salaam.

Shearing, C. (2016). Reflections on the nature of policing and its development. *Police Practice and Research*, 17, 84–91. doi:10.1080/15614263.2015.1109390

Simelane, H. (2008). Security for all? Politics, economy & the growth of private security in Swaziland. *Review of African Political Economy*, 35, 599–612. doi:10.1080/03056240802569276

Simelane, H., & Maziya, W. (2015). Swaziland. In S. Gumedze (Ed.), *Promoting partnerships for crime prevention between state and private security providers in Southern Africa* (pp. 211–261). Pretoria: The Private Security Industry Regulatory Authority.

Simelane, S. (2016, June). *Swaziland*. Paper presented at the meeting of "The Private Security Industry in Africa: The Opportunities and Challenges", Johannesburg.

Small Arms Survey. (2011). Small Arms Survey 2011: States of security. Retrieved from http://www.smallarmssurvey.org/publications/by-type/yearbook/small-arms-survey-2011.html

South African Police Service. (2016). Annual report 2015/2016. Retrieved from http://www.saps.gov.za/about/stratframework/annual_report/2015_2016/saps_annual_report_2015_2016.pdf

Spearin, C. (2001). Private security companies and humanitarians: A corporate solution to securing humanitarian spaces? *International Peacekeeping, 8,* 20–43. doi:10.1080/13533310108413877

Staff reporter. (2015, October 17). Rent-a-cop: Private security is hollowing out Nigeria's security forces. *The Economist.* Retrieved from http://www.economist.com/news/middle-east-and-africa/21674811-private-security-hollowing-out-nigerias-security-forces-rent-cop

Stenning, P. (2000). Powers and accountability of private police. *European Journal on Criminal Policy and Research, 8,* 325–352. doi:10.1023/A:1008729129953

Stenning, P. (2009). Governance and accountability in a plural policing environment – The story so far. *Policing, 3* (1), 22–33. doi:10.1093/police/pan080

United Nations Office On Drugs and Crime. (2014). State regulation concerning civilian private security services and their contribution to crime prevention. Retrieved from https://www.unodc.org/documents/justice-and-prison-reform/crimeprevention/Ebook0.pdf

Von Boemcken, M. (2012). *Dealing with private security companies: Options for development co-operation in Timor-Leste, Liberia and Peru.* Bonn: Bonn International Center for Conversion.

White, A. (2010). *The politics of private security: Regulation, reform and re-regulation.* Basingstoke: Palgrave Macmillan.

White, A. (2012). The new political economy of private security. *Theoretical Criminology, 16,* 85–101. doi:10.1177/1362480611410903

Williams, M. (2016). Global security assemblages. In R. Abrahamsen & A. Leander (Eds.), *Routledge handbook of private security studies* (pp. 131–139). London: Routledge.

Reforming security industry training standards: an Australian case study

Tim Prenzler, Rick Sarre ⓘ and Dae Woon Kim

ABSTRACT

This article critiques recent developments in training in the Australian security industry. Regulation of the industry is state- and territory-based, with eight jurisdictions enacting purpose-built legislation. Training was a key area of reform in the 1990s and early 2000s, but standards remained fragmented until 2008 when the Committee of Australian Governments agreed on a national competency framework to be implemented by 2010. However, despite the adoption of a common curriculum for core security tasks, the project derailed spectacularly in terms of consistency of standards, as revealed by a number of major inquiries and associated sources. This article analyses the reasons for this situation and recommends an alternative model to optimise competency standards in security work that includes much greater specificity in hours of instruction and in teaching and assessment methods. The lessons from this study have wider application given that deficits in security training appear to be a common problem internationally.

Background

The growth of the security industry since the 1960s has been a worldwide phenomenon and a major feature of the evolution of a broadening policing complex (Bayley & Shearing, 2001). This "securatisation" process has meant that security personnel and technology are now deeply enmeshed in people's everyday lives (van Dijk, 2008). Police security personnel ratios have been used as one measure of the sector. Surveys have shown that security personnel outnumber police by as many as 2-to-1 in many jurisdictions (Small Arms Survey, 2011; van Dijk, 2008). This means that people are much more likely to encounter security personnel than police officers at work sites, shopping centres, transport hubs, and around leisure activities. Security technology is now also ubiquitous in people's employment and personal lives.

The enlargement of security has been a major contributing factor to reductions in crime since the 1990s (van Dijk, 2008). At the same time, there has been a dark side to securatisation. Increasing numbers of people have been exposed to fraudulent contractors, harassment and violence, and suffered intrusions into their privacy. Various scandals, inquiries, and survey research have contributed to a broad ethical risk profile for the industry, summarised in the following 11 categories by Prenzler and Sarre (2008, pp. 266–269):

(1) Fraud
(2) Incompetence and poor standards

(3) Under-award payments and exploitation of security staff
(4) Corrupt practices
(5) Information corruption
(6) Violence and associated malpractice
(7) False arrest and detention
(8) Trespass and invasions of privacy
(9) Discrimination and harassment
(10) Insider crime
(11) Misuse of weapons

None of these problems is unique to security work. Each one can be seen across a range of occupations, including policing (Prenzler & Sarre, 2008). Consequently, there has been a strong case for basic controls to protect clients and third parties, as is common in any area of work that requires individuals to meet core competencies and maintain ethical standards.

Internationally, from the 1970s, as the industry rapidly expanded there was also growth in the adoption of basic licencing schemes, although there was often resistance from governments to even the most basic elements. For example, it was not until 2001 that security licencing was introduced in England and Wales (Weber, 2002). Nonetheless, by the 1990s, there was a standard model apparent in most democracies that provided a minimal form of government control over security personnel and their activities. The system involved licensing of the core functions of mobile and static guards, crowd controllers ("bouncers" or "door security"), bodyguards, and investigators. Licencing was managed by a specialist regulator through integrity checks – mainly character references and disqualifying criminal offences – and minimal training requirements – varying between a few hours and three days in many cases (Button & George, 2006; CoESS, 2013). Within the basic model, the regulator engaged in monitoring through spot checks on operators to ensure they were licensed and investigated and adjudicated complaints. In federal systems, where licencing is controlled by state or provincial governments, there was a recognition that national consistency was needed to prevent excessive compliance costs for companies operating across borders, and to prevent the creation of "safe havens" for shady operators in jurisdictions with low standards. More advanced regulatory systems licensed all security occupations and expanded training periods beyond a few days.

Button and George (2006) proposed criteria for evaluating regulation in terms of "width" and "depth". Width is concerned with coverage of the range of security-related occupations. Depth refers to the adequacy of criteria around competency and integrity. An assessment of regulatory systems in Europe, North America, and a number of other countries found enormous variation across the two criteria, although most systems lacked both breadth and depth (Button & George, 2006). European countries appeared to be the most sophisticated, with some having basic training requirements up to 200 hours (5–6 weeks). Many states in the United States required only eight hours of basic training or none at all.

One example of an attempt to generate consistency in training standards across jurisdictions involved the EPSSET's (1999) *European Vocational Training Manual for Basic Guarding*. The 164-page document, developed by a group of industry stakeholders including CoESS and the European Commission, sets out minimum standards for security guard competency and training, and sought voluntary compliance from European countries. However, regulatory surveys indicate that the goal of regional consistency has not been attained. CoESS (the Confederation of European Security Services) periodically publishes data on private security regulation. The most recent report, for 2013, across 34 countries, showed considerable depth in training. The average required basic training period was 98 hours (approximately three weeks). Fifty-eight percent of countries had "mandatory specialist training (requirements) (by law) for private security managers" (CoESS, 2013, p. 254). However, there was extensive variation within these figures. Some countries had unspecified hours or very low training hours, and others had quite significant requirements. For example, Sweden required 288 hours of basic training for guards (approximately 2 months) and 44 hours for managers. Hungary required 320 hours basic training. Seven countries were classified as "very strict" in terms of overall regulation, including training (p. 250).

In a more recent review, Button and Stiernstedt (2016) enlarged the Button and George (2006) framework, deploying a 100-point scale across 22 criteria. The criteria included staples such as licence-based coverage of security occupations and mandatory training; along with extensions to neglected areas such compulsory codes of conduct, the use of exams in training and employment conditions. The framework was applied to 26 of the 28 member states of the European Union by integrating data from diverse sources, including CoESS, the European Commission, and the United Nations. As with the previous studies above, wide variation in regulatory quality was identified, with Belgium scoring the highest number of points at 94, with Spain close behind with 88 points. Italy had the lowest score at 46, behind the Netherlands with 62.

The security regulation literature includes very few systematic evaluations of mandated training programmes. Available studies have been largely confined to practitioner surveys, with some variation in findings broadly related to depth of training – although the totality of studies is extremely limited in scope. Cobbina, Nalla, and Bender (2016) in the US and Manzo (2009) in Canada surveyed security operatives who had experienced between a few hours and a few days of mandated training. Respondents felt that training did not prepare them for initial duties and that most of their learning was on-the-job or drawn from previous experience. In the Australian state of Queensland, a survey of security managers found that opinions were divided over the adequacy of operative training programmes of 3–5 days, with only a third agreeing that training was adequate (Prenzler & Hayes, 1999). In contrast, a recent survey of security officers in Turkey by Cihan (2016) assessed a system with 120 hours (approximately three weeks) of mandated pre-service training, including 90 hours of theory and 30 hours of practical instruction. A small majority (56% of respondents) felt that the training was adequate for them, compared to 44% who felt it was inadequate. Similar practitioner surveys to these were conducted in the UK by the Security Industry Authority (2010a, 2010b). The results showed majority support for the training regime in place, although the hours were not specified in the reports.

More generally, there appears to be very strong public and practitioner support for the principle of pre-service mandated training for both operatives and managers (Prenzler & Sarre, 2014). There is also fairly clear support for elements of training that include such things as basic security procedures, law, communication, and force tactics (UNODC, 2014). There does not, however, appear to be a clear consensus around the issue of appropriate hours of prescribed training. For example, a recent review of security industry regulation by the United Nations Office on Drugs and Crime supported mandated training and noted enormous variation in hours between jurisdictions but failed to describe a model system that included minimum hours (UNODC, 2014). In addition, there is very little to be found in the literature on appropriate forms of instruction and assessment.

Study site and method

This article examines issues around security industry training standards through a case study of developments in Australia following major reforms initiated by the Committee of Australian Governments (COAG). As noted in the "Abstract" section, Australian security industry regulation is a state- and territory-based function. This situation derives from the federal constitutional structure in which state and territory governments are given responsibility for most justice functions, including police, courts, and corrections. Only when law enforcement extends into areas of national interest (such as cybercrime, terrorism, people smuggling, drug importation, and customs fraud) is the national government involved, through, for example, the Australian Federal Police or federal courts.

What this means is that the regulation of private security is primarily a concern of the eight states and territories: The Australian Capital Territory, New South Wales, the Northern Territory, Queensland, South Australia, Tasmania, Victoria, and Western Australia. The regulatory agencies operate largely independently of each other, with significant variation between jurisdictions. For example, there are differences in disqualifying offences and disqualification periods for security licence applicants; differences in regulatory agencies (some located in police departments, some in justice or fair trading departments); and differences in regulatory strategies in areas such as inspections, investigations and prosecutions, and auditing of training providers. Despite these arrangements, the Commonwealth has an interest in security industry regulation, in part through its interest in critical infrastructure protection; and all Australian governments attempt to work together on common problems and issues of national consistency through COAG. Federal mutual recognition legislation is also meant to ensure common standards by requiring acceptance across the country of qualifications issued in each state or territory.

Changes to security industry regulation in Australia have been driven largely by scandals, and repeated failures of regulation have forced enlargements to systems (Prenzler & Sarre, 2012). The first wave of minimalist industry-specific regulation began with the New South Wales *Security (Protection) Industry Act 1985* which introduced licensing of security firms, guards, and consultants. Training for operatives was set at two days, with one additional day for firearms accreditation. There was also some enlargement of controls on private investigators. The changes were driven by wider reforms of weapons legislation following concerns about gun crime, an industrial dispute which highlighted poor standards in the cash-in-transit industry, and issues of harassment and breaches of privacy by private agents (Prenzler & Sarre, 2012).

Violence associated with crowd controllers was also a major driver of change in the 1980s into the 1990s, directly influencing the promulgation of industry-specific legislation in the early 1990s in Victoria, Queensland, and the Australian Capital Territory. Other issues included fraud in contracting, infiltration of the industry by criminals, substandard skills, and illicit trading-in-information. New regulatory regimes were introduced in South Australia, the Northern Territory and Western Australia in the mid 1990s; and New South Wales introduced a tougher set of requirements with a new Act in 1997. By the end of the 1990s, there was a fairly common set of regulatory mechanisms focused on training for core operatives – notionally involving several days' instruction – and disqualifying offences for operatives and owners of firms.

The recurrence of old problems and a set of new problems forced a second wave of reform in the 2000s (Prenzler & Sarre, 2012). High-profile scandals – some exposed through major investigations – included deaths and numerous injuries caused by security officers, thefts of firearms from security firms, prisoner escapes, security breaches at major government sites, lax airport security, the involvement of security officers in smuggling at major airports, and infiltration of the industry by organised crimes gangs involved in extortion and drug supply. These crises, essentially involving integrity and competency issues, led to a variety of regulatory responses including innovations, on a piecemeal basis, in areas such as fingerprinting of applicants, criminal associate checks, targeted illicit drug testing and psychological tests, and enhanced training curricula (Sarre & Prenzler, 2011). Table 1 lists the main legislation in Australia as it stood at the end of the research period for this article in December 2016. The Acts refer to completion of "approved" training courses as a pre-condition for a licence for most operative categories.

The present study documents and critiques the reforms in security industry training in Australia based on the watershed COAG agreement of 2008, which introduced a comprehensive nationally consistent model. The study is focused on three major sources: (1) the report of a major investigation into corruption in security officer training in New South Wales, (2) the results of a national survey involving security managers and owners of security firms, culminating in (3) the 2016 report of a national assessment of security training by the peak federal training authority.

Table 1. Main security industry legislation, Australia, December 2016.

Jurisdiction	Legislation
Australian Capital Territory	Security Industry Act 2003
New South Wales	Security Industry Act 1997
Northern Territory	Private Security Act 1995
Queensland	Security Providers Act 1993
South Australia	Security and Investigation Industry Act 1995
Tasmania	Security and Investigations Agents Act 2002
Victoria	Private Security Act 2004
Western Australia	Security and Related Activities (Control) Act 1996

Source: Australian Legal Information Institute (http://www.austlii.edu.au/).

The COAG reforms

The issue of inconsistent security training standards within a federal system has been a live issue in Australia for decades (Sarre & Prenzler, 2011). A major step forward to address the problem occurred in July 2008 when COAG (2009) agreed to common basic standards. Concerns around national security and protection of critical infrastructure in the post-9/11 environment were key drivers (see COAG, 2005). The ability to mobilise large numbers of security officers for special events, as occurred with the 2000 Sydney Olympics, was also a consideration, as was the need to reduce barriers to interstate commerce. The Council commissioned a major report which recommended broad regulatory "harmonisation" (Centre for International Economics, 2007). The initial focus was placed on operative training for the "manpower sector" – covering "security officers", "crowd controllers", and "investigators" – with the introduction of common Certificate level courses (COAG, 2009, p. 5). Further stages of development were envisaged for the technical and consulting sectors, leading to an eventual comprehensive national licencing system (pp. 7–8).

Development of the new standards was delegated to a "Security Industry Regulators Forum Working Group", which drafted the "CPP07 Property Services Training Package", set within the Australian Qualifications Framework (COAG, 2009). The package appeared to provide for comprehensive coverage of the targeted "manpower sector", with the following certificates required for a pre-employment licence (with no provisional conditions nor workplace assessment requirement) (COAG, 2009, Attachment C):

Certificate II in Security Operations

- Security Officer Static Guard, Mobile Patrol
- Security Officer Control Room/Monitoring Centre
- Security Officer Guarding with a Dog
- Crowd Controller Licensed Premises and Places of Entertainment

Certificate III in Security Operations

- Armed Security Officers within the Cash in Transit industry
- Armed Security Officers (protecting property with a firearm)
- Unarmed Bodyguard

Certificate III in Investigative Services

- Investigators

The curricula attached to these certificates included key competences and associated units of study. For example, the Certificate II in Security Operations for crowd controllers included seven core units (COAG, 2009, p. 47):

- Communicate effectively in the security industry
- Maintain workplace safety procedures
- Work effectively in the security industry
- Respond to security risk situation
- Work as part of a security team
- Provide security services to customers
- Provide first aid

Five specialist units were also required:

- Protect safety of persons
- Control access to and exit from premises
- Monitor and control individual and crowd behaviour
- Manage conflict through negotiation
- Control person using empty hand technique

The national framework had all the hallmarks of a great leap forward, but its effectiveness depended on compliance and monitoring by the various regulators in each jurisdiction. Responsibility for specifying key requirements – such as minimum hours of training, methods of instruction and methods of assessment – was devolved to state and territory Vocational Education and Training Accreditation Boards (VETABs), which regulated Registered Training Organisations (RTOs). This was despite the fact that VETABs were notorious for a "hands off" approach to regulation of security training providers, and had contributed to the problem of poor and/or inconsistent standards that COAG had sought to address (Sarre & Prenzler, 2011). Security industry licencing authorities in each jurisdiction were considerably hamstrung by the division of labour between themselves and the VETABs.

The New South Wales Independent Commission against corruption investigation into corruption in security industry training

In October 2008 – at the same time as the signing of the COAG agreement – the Registrar of the New South Wales security industry regulatory agency – the Security Industry Registry – submitted a report to the Independent Commission Against Corruption (ICAC) concerning possible fraud by a security guard training firm, Roger Training Academy. The report followed complaints and allegations of fraud by former students and staff. "Roger" was a major player, with 26 percent of the training market in New South Wales – Australia's largest state. The Commission initiated a full-scale investigation including the seizure of documents, interviews, compulsory hearings, covert surveillance, and telecommunications intercepts.

The investigation report was made available in December 2009 (ICAC, 2009). The Commission identified extensive fraud and corruption at the Roger Academy. In many cases, individuals paid fees and were issued certificates of competency without any training nor testing. In other cases, students were provided answers to questions in exams. Students with poor English language skills paid additional money to pass. There was also an illicit trade in credit for previous training and/or experience, involving Roger and some other firms, and in the issuance of false certificates for First Aid, Responsible Service of Alcohol, and Responsible Conduct of Gambling. These certificates could be bought by candidates for AU$100 or AU $150 without training nor testing.

The scam involved 10 perpetrators and approximately AU$1.3 million between 2008 and 2009, although it had begun years before. The ICAC emphasised the potential for harm from the employment of untrained or inadequately trained (but ostensibly qualified) persons:

The security industry in New South Wales is responsible for providing security in significant ways – for example at airports, hotels and concerts, and also at government facilities, including army bases. The Commission's investigation found that corrupt conduct in connection with the certification of security officers resulted in a significant number of those officers engaging in security activities, some of which posed risks to their own and public safety, without having undertaken appropriate levels of training. (ICAC, 2009, p. 10)

Primary responsibility for the problem lay with the state regulator for training – the VETAB – which had failed to properly audit the companies involved and had failed to act on indicators of fraud.

The scandal overlapped the introduction of the COAG package, and the aftermath provided a crucial test of the new system. The ICAC report made 16 recommendations to improve the training system, including immediate review of all questionable qualifications and the possible re-testing of licence holders. It also recommended closer auditing of trainers, more stringent investigations of suspect practices, and more dynamic enforcement by a better resourced regulator. There was also a fairly radical recommendation that the Security Industry Registry "independently test and assess applicants prior to granting a security license" (ICAC, 2009, p. 59).

The ICAC initially committed to ongoing assessment of reform, which took the process well past the implementation of the COAG reforms. In the first (and, as it turned out, final) review, the ICAC (2011) claimed that most recommendations had been implemented. There was a procedure in place to check and upgrade qualifications issued by the corrupt trainers; although the recommendation relating to independent testing remained under development (and was never implemented). In June 2010, the Security Industry Registry – renamed the Security Licensing and Enforcement Directorate (SLED) – was enlarged with an increase in allocated staff from 40 to 73 (ICAC, 2011; Sexton, 2012). The SLED took on primary responsibility for the enforcement of training standards (overriding the VETAB), including through more intensive auditing and random onsite inspections of trainers. Its approach has most likely been the toughest, or at least "among the most stringent", in Australia, including the requirement for successful completion of an approved language, literacy, and numeracy test prior to commencing a training course (ASQA, 2016c, p. 26).

The 2009–2011 Australian Research Council linkage project

In 2008, the Australian Research Council funded a large "Linkage" cooperative research project covering key aspects of the work of the security industry in Australia. The project involved the Australian Security Industry Association Limited (the largest industry association in the country) and two universities (Sarre & Prenzler, 2011). The study included a large survey of security firm owners and security managers, conducted in 2010 – two years after the COAG agreement. The response provided insider answers to questions regarding experiences with, and perspectives on, the regulatory system, including a large number of questions about training.

The survey obtained 170 responses from across Australia, with the majority in New South Wales. The results identified strong support for the basic elements of existing licencing systems, but with mixed views on specific aspects (Sarre & Prenzler, 2011, pp. 53–81). A significant majority (67%) felt that the system was effective in "ensuring practical competencies for individuals entering the industry"; 66% believed the system had reduced assaults by security personnel, and 60% believed regulation had reduced injuries to security personnel. Overall, however, 67% felt that compliance with standards was not effectively monitored, and 59% thought the system was highly ineffective in removing disreputable operators. Only 36% agreed that there was adequate scope for input from the industry into the administration of the legislation, while 79% thought that communication between the regulator and licence holders was inadequate, and 68% thought that current legislation had been developed without sufficient consultation with the industry.

A number of additional questions were asked specifically about training (Sarre & Prenzler, 2011, pp. 60–71). Forty-eight percent of respondents thought the new national training competencies were appropriate, 39% thought they were not and 12% were unsure. Forty-eight percent thought that training standards had improved over the last five years, while 41% thought that they had not and 10% were unsure. Opinions were also divided about specific security competencies. Majorities felt that courses were adequate in teaching basic security procedures (83%), occupational health and safety (78%), and knowledge of law (60%). At the same time, skills training was considered inadequate for self-defence (75%), communication (73%), conflict resolution (69%), and physical restraint (69%). Fifty-eight percent thought training in security management should be mandated.

Opinions were also divided about skills development in specific security occupations. Majorities thought that mandated pre-licence training under current legislation was appropriate for the following (p. 71):

- 57% for unarmed guards,
- 55% for armed guards,
- 53% for the work of cash in transit guards,
- 51% for crowd controllers, and
- 57% for firearms carriage.

However, there was a strong division of opinion over the adequacy of training for the following areas of work, including large numbers in the "don't know" category:

- Only 38% agreed in the case of consultants, while 37% disagreed and 25% replied "don't know";
- 39% agreed for investigators, 24% disagreed, and 38% replied "don't know";
- 40% agreed for bodyguards, 26% disagreed, and 34% replied "don't know";
- 42% agreed for trainers, 30% disagreed, and 28% replied "don't know";
- 32% agreed for locksmiths and installers of physical security, 22% disagreed, and 46% replied "don't know";
- 40% agreed for dog handlers, 17% disagreed, and 43% replied "don't know";
- 43% agreed for loss prevention officers, 27% disagreed, and 31% replied "don't know";
- 41% agreed for electronic security installers, 30% disagreed, and 29% replied "don't know";
- 35% agreed for security salespersons, 38% disagreed, and 28% replied "don't know"; and
- 36% agreed for in-house security providers, 32% disagreed, and 32% replied "don't know".

The 2014–2016 Australian Skills Quality Authority (ASQA) investigation

In January 2016, the ASQA (established in 2011) released the long-awaited results of an investigation into security training, which had begun in 2014 (ASQA, 2016c). The initiation of the investigation was influenced by coroner reports which found that deficient training was a factor in a number of deaths associated with interventions by security staff at licenced premises. Most of the training packages for operatives agreed by COAG were at the level of Certificates II and III. The Australian Qualifications Framework set training periods for a Certificate II at between six months and one year, and Certificate II at one to two years. However, ASQA found there were too many "extremely short courses (i.e., five days or less)" in security, which could not possibly allow time for adequate skill acquisition (2016c, p. 8). Trainees also evidenced inadequate language proficiency, literacy, and numeracy; standards and instruction around restraint techniques were inadequate; and in some areas training did not align with specific tasks. The findings simply mirrored what the industry associations, investigative journalists, and academic researchers had been saying for years, including in highlighting the problem of trainees obtaining substandard qualifications in one state and then working in another (ASQA, 2016c, pp. 24–70; Harvey, 2012;

Sarre & Prenzler, 2011). The problem of inconsistent standards was facilitated by the Australian *Mutual Recognition Act 1992*, which requires states and territories to accept qualifications issued in other states and territories (Section 17). Consequently, it only required one "weak" jurisdiction for the whole security industry training framework to be undermined, and the situation forced ASQA to conclude that "[d]espite the decision of Australian Governments in July 2008 to harmonise job skills requirements for the security industry, this is yet to occur" (p. iv).

The scale of the problem of trainees bypassing specific jurisdictional requirements was enormous. The flows were primarily into New South Wales (which had more stringent enforcement arising from the ICAC inquiry) from Queensland, Victoria, Western Australia, and the Australian Capital Territory. In 2013–2014, for example, New South Wales was forced by law to provide 2623 licences to applicants with interstate licences. This amounted to 77% of all licences issued nationally that year under the *Mutual Recognition Act*. The imbalance was also illustrated in the following skewed numbers (ASQA, 2016c, p. 66):

> In May 2015, there were approximately 51,400 Security Officers and Guards employed in Australia. The largest proportion were employed in New South Wales – 16,500 (32.1 per cent). However, in the 2013-14 year (the latest figures available), New South Wales issued only 4,489 (10.7 per cent) of the total number of licenses issued across the country (the third lowest of all jurisdictions). Hence, while New South Wales has the largest employment share, it trains and licenses a much lower number of people.

In 2013–2014, Queensland had 22% of security employees but was responsible for 32% of "licences issued via training"; Victoria had 14% of security employees but issued 24% of licences; and the Australian Capital Territory had 4% of employees but issued 12% of licences (p. 67). Bizarrely, in Queensland, it was possible to obtain a security consultant licence without undertaking any training at all.

As part of its investigation, ASQA audited 67 of the 121 RTOs delivering basic security training in Australia. The audit found that 81% were non-compliant with at least one component of the 2015 *Standards for RTOs*, mainly in the area of "training and assessment strategies" (ASQA, 2016c, p. 102). In response to the audit, in 2015, non-compliant trainers were given 20 working days to rectify deficiencies. A follow-up assessment found the following (ASQA, 2016c, p. 3):

- 57 RTOs (85.1 per cent) were able to demonstrate full compliance with all of the standards required for registration.
- 10 RTOs (14.9 per cent) remained not compliant with one or more of the required standards.
  ASQA continued regulatory action against the 10 RTOs that were unable to demonstrate compliance after the 20 working day rectification period. As at 1 December 2015, six of these RTOs have been able to demonstrate compliance; three RTOs have not achieved compliance and are no longer registered training organisations on the national training register. One RTO has sought a review of ASQA's decision to cancel its registration at the Administrative Appeals Tribunal, and the matter is not yet finalised.

Subsequently, in 2016, in the aftermath of the report, ASQA de-registered a Queensland-based trainer – "Peacemakers" – due to "its failure to meet the national training standards... issuing qualifications and statements of attainment with almost no training being provided" (ASQA, 2016a, p. 1). It subsequently placed 236 graduates on notice to show they had adequate skills. In November 2016, it took further action, announcing it planned to "cancel a further 1,947 security and related qualifications and statements of attainment (SoAs) issued to 1,020 people by Peacemakers Security Pty Ltd (Peacemakers)" (2016b, p. 1).

The ASQA (2016c) report included a workforce review which found that low entry standards and short training periods meant that security work attracted large numbers of poorly educated applicants and persons from non-English-speaking backgrounds with poor communication skills.

In addition, low wages and often difficult working conditions led to high turnover of staff. This meant there was a continuing high demand for training places. Predicting future trends was difficult, but it was expected that government requirements around crowd controllers at major events and licenced premises would see increased demand for security staff in this high-risk area.

The ASQA report made eight recommendations to fix the problems it identified, and to complete the COAG reforms. However, it recognised the fundamental confounding problem of attaining appropriate nationally consistent standards within a fragmented jurisdictional framework. A key part of the solution, if there was ever going to be one, was for the provision of a much more specific set of standards that all parties would sign up to via COAG. With that in mind, it recommended the engagement of a "training package developer" to revise the security industry training package. Crucially, this included setting training periods; establishing clear language, literacy and numeracy standards; specifying physical skills requirements and acceptable restraint techniques; and mandating workplace assessment and refresher training.

Discussion

An effectively regulated security industry is essential both to ensure optimal crime prevention and to ensure that no harm is done through unethical, negligent, or incompetent conduct by security providers (UNODC, 2014). Australia has gone through an evolutionary process in attempting to address integrity and competency issues in the industry and ensure minimum standards. In that regard, Australia should have served as a useful laboratory for regulatory methods, with positive lessons for other countries and jurisdictions grappling with similar problems, including the issue of national consistency in federal systems. Unfortunately, however, Australian governments have, on the whole, repeatedly sought to apply a vague and minimalist model of regulation to the industry. This process has then backfired repeatedly, most recently in the attempt by COAG in 2008 to introduce appropriate and consistent standards across the country. The framework for qualifications, based upon the articulation of core curriculum content, was good in principle. However, devolution of responsibility for the details allowed for deep inconsistencies in practice. The problem was then exacerbated by the operation of mutual recognition legislation, which facilitated interstate portability and a trade in substandard qualifications.

The 2016 report on security industry training by ASQA provided the most recent and most systematic evidence of inter-jurisdictional regulatory failure in Australia. The report provided a stinging judgement of the national system of qualifications for security operatives in terms of quality assurance related to the "depth" of training and assessment, particularly where federal legislation facilitated the interstate portability of licenced operatives (cf., Button & George, 2006). The whole imbroglio illustrated the futility of relying upon vague standards in security regulation and training in key areas such as minimum hours (cf., Cobbina et al., 2016; Manzo, 2009), as well as instruction and assessment methods.

Unfortunately, the ASQA recommendations were themselves highly problematic. There was a clear articulation of the need for specificity in training but, as with the COAG reforms, this was delegated to another body with potential for significant dilution. Arguably, some areas required development through specialist input, such as details about physical skills training, but even here there should have been a clear articulation of essential processes, such as the place of simulations and practice-based assessment. It was also essential that ASQA come out and state a clear standard in other key areas. ASQA staff are supposed to be the experts on vocational training. In that regard, hours of training was a critical issue. COAG had agreed to Certificates II and III for most security licences. The ASQA report noted that the Australian Qualifications Framework set training periods for a Certificate II at between six months and one year and Certificate III at one to two years. This was contrasted with security training courses of a week or less. The simple solution was to set minimum hours for a Certificate II in security at 6 months and a Certificate III at 12 months. If that was too large a bite to swallow at once, leading European countries provide models in the range 1–2 months (Button & Stiernstedt, 2016; Cihan, 2016; CoESS, 2013) – perhaps approximating a Certificate I in Australia.

In addition, ASQA needed to apply current research-based best practice principles on assessment, particularly in relation to integrity. For example, the fact that online assessment was referred for review is a major concern. It should have been ruled out completely because of the potential for cheating, unless reliable authentication protocols could be established and proven. In addition, there was no specification across a range of further key topics, including refresher training and skills maintenance, auditing processes for training firms, and training in security management. ASQA also failed to address the general deficit in transparency and accountability regarding security regulation and training in Australia. Comprehensive data on complaints and allegations, case dispositions, litigation, audit findings, and other indicators of regulatory impact from all jurisdictions need to be published annually.

Conclusion

This article documented the rise and fall of plans to implement common national standards in security training in Australia, using three major reports. Australia is an example of a wealthy democracy that has repeatedly failed to properly manage the relatively simple matter of security provider training. In that regard, it provides an object lesson for other countries and jurisdictions about what not to do in developing a best practice system for competency and integrity at the entry level of security work. The research for this article showed that clear and very specific detail is essential to stop trainers and regulators failing to deliver to the intended standards. The issue is particularly important wherever there is diversity in training, including through federal systems, in that ambiguity or weak enforcement can create alternate substandard pathways into security work. This issue is critical given the fact that so many people are now dependent on the security industry for protection. It should be a matter of grave concerns that a sizeable proportion of the population continues to remain vulnerable to mistakes or misconduct by poorly trained and managed security providers.

ORCID

Rick Sarre ⓘ http://orcid.org/0000-0001-6268-1313

References

ASQA. (2016a). ASQA cancels qualifications issued by Queensland security trainer. Retrieved from http://www.asqa.gov.au/news/3163/asqa-cancels-qualifications-issued-by-queensland-security-trainer.html
ASQA. (2016b). Further Peacemakers security qualifications to be cancelled. Retrieved from http://www.asqa.gov.au/news/3303/further-peacemakers-security-qualifications-to-be-cancelled.html
ASQA. (2016c). Training in security programs in Australia. Melbourne: Australian Skills Quality Authority.

Bayley, D., & Shearing, C. (2001). *The new structure of policing.* Washington, DC: National Institute of Justice.

Button, M., & George, B. (2006). Regulation of private security. In M. Gill (Ed.), *Handbook of security* (pp. 563–585). Houndmills: Palgrave Macmillan.

Button, M., & Stiernstedt, P. (2016). Comparing private security regulation in the European Union. *Policing and Society*, Pre-print online. 1–17. doi:10.1080/10439463.2016.1161624

Centre for International Economics. (2007). *Harmonisation of private security industry regulation.* Canberra: Author.

Cihan, A. (2016). The Private security industry in Turkey: Officer characteristics and their perception of training sufficiency. *Security Journal, 29*(2), 169–184. doi:10.1057/sj.2013.4

COAG. (2005). *Special meeting on counter-terrorism, 27 September 2005.* Canberra: Council of Australian Governments.

COAG. (2009). *COAG harmonisation of the private security industry: Stage one; Manpower sector of the security industry.* Canberra: Council of Australian Governments.

Cobbina, J., Nalla, M., & Bender, K. (2016). Security officers' attitudes towards training and their work environment. *Security Journal, 29*(3), 385–399. doi:10.1057/sj.2013.34

CoESS. (2013). *Private security services in Europe: CoESS facts and figures 2013.* Wemmel: Confederation of European Security Services.

EPSSET. (1999). *European vocational training manual for basic guarding.* Brussels: European Private Security Services – Education & Training.

Harvey, A. (2012, September 24). False security. *7.30 Report* (Television). Sydney: Australian Broadcasting Corporation.

ICAC. (2009). *Report on corruption in the provision and certification of security industry training.* Sydney: Independent Commission Against Corruption.

ICAC. (2011). *Plan for implementation of recommendations, Operation Columba.* Sydney: Independent Commission Against Corruption.

Manzo, J. (2009). Security officers' perspectives on training. *Canadian Journal of Criminology and Criminal Justice, 51*(3), 381–410. doi:10.3138/cjccj.51.3.381

Prenzler, T., & Hayes, H. (1999). An evaluation of the Queensland security providers act: Implications for national regulation of the protective security industry. *Australian & New Zealand Journal of Criminology, 32*(1), 79–94. doi:10.1177/000486589903200107

Prenzler, T., & Sarre, R. (2008). Developing a risk profile and model regulatory system for the security industry. *Security Journal, 21*(4), 264–277. doi:10.1057/palgrave.sj.8350064

Prenzler, T., & Sarre, R. (2012). The evolution of security industry regulation in Australia: A critique. *International Journal for Crime and Justice, 1*(1), 38–51. doi:10.5204/ijcjsd.v1i1.72

Prenzler, T., & Sarre, R. (2014). Regulation. In M. Gill (Ed.), *Handbook of security* (pp. 857–878). Houndmills: Palgrave-Macmillan.

Sarre, R., & Prenzler, T. (2011). *Private security and public interest: Exploring private security trends and directions for reform in the new era of plural policing.* Sydney: Australian Security Industry Association Limited.

Security Industry Authority. (2010a). *The impact of regulation on the door supervision sector.* London: SIA.

Security Industry Authority. (2010b). *The impact of regulation on the security guard sector.* London: SIA.

Sexton, J. (2012, February 5). Security firm crackdown. *Sunday Telegraph*, Sydney, p. 27.

Small Arms Survey. (2011). *States of security.* Geneva: The Graduate Institute of International and Development Studies.

UNODC. (2014). *State regulation concerning civilian private security services and their contribution to crime prevention and community safety.* Vienna: United Nations Office on Drugs and Crime.

van Dijk, J. (2008). *The world of crime.* Thousand Oaks, CA: Sage.

Weber, T. (2002). *A comparative overview of legislation governing the private security industry in the European Union.* Birmingham: ECOTEC Research and Consulting.

The Taming of the Japanese Private Security Industry

NAOKO YOSHIDA

With the number of crimes climbing to over 2.5 million per annum and a 50% surge in the number of juvenile crimes, Japan is no longer a society secure in the knowledge that it is immune to crime rate inflation. One consequence of this is that the private security industry is increasingly gaining social recognition in Japan. However, the Japanese seem to retain high levels of confidence in the police and voices demanding 'open police' remain muted. The Japanese police has established itself as the supervisor of the private security industry. This paper sets out to answer a number of questions. How has this partnership between public and private police evolved? What is the constitutional position of the private security industry in Japan? And what is the long-term strategy of the Japanese police with regard to the emergence of private security provision?

INTRODUCTION

The myth of Japan's 'secure society' has collapsed. Once it seemed that the myth might last forever. 'Forces of Order' seemed to prevail in Japan. The crime rate has been historically low and the Japanese themselves regard their society as being an extremely safe one. Until 1994, the 'Shakai Ishiki ni kansuru Yoron Chosa, Sorifu', or the national poll on perceptions about society (conducted by the Prime Minister's Office), consistently showed that what Japanese were most proud of was their 'safe society'. This feeling of security dropped to the fourth position in 1995 after the AUM cult attack on the Tokyo underground and the Kobe earthquake. Although it quickly returned to the top in 1996's poll, confidence in security is now qualitatively different that in the pre-1995 level (Keisatsucho 1997, Preface).

The Japanese public is no longer content to leave security issues to the police. As in other countries, community policing has been introduced and private security providers have emerged offering supplementary police services. We might ask: what have the Japanese Police done to regain society's trust? Of course, they have attempted to improve their own capacity to tackle crime, or at least the impression of crime fighting ability. At the same time, the police have encouraged private policing, indeed in some instances they hav&even initiated it. This does not mean that the police have surrendered their role, or even part of it, to the public. The police have been trying to subsume the two new movements – community policing and private security businesses – under their supervision and the National Police Agency (hereafter referred to as the 'NPA') has attempted to impose its presence on both movements.

The NPA efforts were encapsulated in a large-scale reorganisation in 1994, which resulted in the creation of the 'Community Safety Bureau'. This bureau is in charge of the establishment and promotion of sound community policing, and supervising the private security industry is considered part of this task. This re-organisation led to a much greater emphasis on private policing and raises questions about the source of its impetus. Is it because the NPA was urged to do so by the Japanese public?

The answer cannot be simply in the affirmative since the Japanese generally assumed that their society was largely safe until 1993 as is confirmed by the polls. And yet, private policing has grown so significantly that the Japanese police have had to make concerted efforts to monitor it. In discussing this subject, this paper focuses on the private security business because it is a lesser known and more recent development than community policing, and yet plays a substantial, and largely unrecognised, role in Japan and elsewhere.

Debates about the rise of private policing in the USA and UK have focused on several factors that led to the development of private policing. Bayley and Shearing have pointed out that one of the features of the Anglo-American culture is the deep distrust in government itself and this distrust is thought to be one of the factors that have allowed the private policing to grow (Bayley and Shearing, 1996:595). It is difficult to maintain that there is an equally intense distrust of government in the Japanese culture, as Bayley correctly points out, so this explanation can be discounted in the Japanese context at the outset (Bayley, 1991). Other Western scholars have argued that fiscal constraint is the driving force in the growth of private security business (Jones and Newburn, 1998: 98). However, in Japan, until very recently, there has been little indication that the government budget was in such a crisis, so we can also discount this as an explanation of what is demonstrably a longer term trend. Shearing and Stenning suggest that the rapid growth of the private security industry is linked to the drastic increase in 'mass private property' such as shopping centres and private residential estates (Shearing and Stenning, 1983: 526). A focus on this phenomenon has some limited application in the Japanese context, although the North American style out-of-town shopping centre surrounded by acres of parking lot is not yet common in Japan, nor are 'gated communities'. Having said this, it is clear that 24 hour retailing is on the increase and this has been accompanied by a rise in the percentage of retail shops owned and operated by large corporations.

According to the Ministry of International Trade and Industry, the number of retail outlets employing four or less shop clerks fell from 80.1% in 1988 to 74.6% in 1997, while the percentage of shops employing ten or more clerks rose from 6.7% in 1988 to 10.5% in 1997. In 1994 there were some 45,388 retail outlets opened in excess of 16 hours per day (3.1% of the total), by 1997 this had risen to 53,764 (4.5% of the total). Meanwhile the number of privately owned retail outlets has fallen from just over 1 million in 1991 to about 833 thousand in 1997, while the number of corporately owned shops has risen from 571,182 to 586,627. These changes are not of great magnitude, but do seem to indicate something of a shift. The significance for the topic being pursued here is that the corporately owned shop with long opening times and large staff is quite likely to be furnished with CCTV surveillance and security personnel. It seems plausible that this is one of the factors promoting private security in Japan. Moreover, the rise of the 24 hour economy has re-configured the way Japanese people live their lives. Late night shopping may expose more people to risk of criminal victimisation, or at least heighten their perception of risk. Fear of crime seems a very plausible explanation for the growth in the private security sector, as Sheptycki has pointed out, 'the marketization of insecurity is changing the shape of some of the world's major cities as they are carved up into zones of risk suppression' (Sheptycki, 1998: 490). Private security guards are, like their public police counterparts, agents of risk suppression and their number is increasing.

Having explored some of the background features that may have influenced the rise of private security agents I would like to move on to discuss the Japanese private security business itself. Firstly, I would like to examine the industry's current situation. Secondly, this paper analyses the changes in the attitude of the NPA as a supervisor of the private security business and the relations between the two parties. In the course of the analysis, this article will detail some important points of the Security Business Act which give a greater control over security firms to the police.

THE CURRENT SITUATION OF THE PRIVATE SECURITY BUSINESS

In trying to describe the private security industry in Japan, it should be made clear that the definition of 'private security business' used here is the same as that used in the Japanese Security Business Act, which states that a 'private security business' is one that provides guarding services for persons or goods. The act also includes within it road traffic control. Although the Act does not relate to the manufacture of the alarm or CCTV systems, it does pertain to the security guards in charge of such equipment. Significantly private detective work is excluded. This definition is adopted here because almost all writings on this area are publications of the Japanese government or are based on them. As far as I am aware, there is no independent research which extends beyond this. Therefore, it is safe to assume that this definition is widely accepted in Japan for the time being.

The private security business field is prosperous in Japan although it is a very young industry. According to Miyazawa, the first private security firm was established in 1962 (Miyazawa, 1991: 250–251) at a time when the Japanese economy had suddenly started to boom. The increase in production levels required an increase in manpower, something which companies had difficulty in procuring. Faced with such difficulties, companies moved in-house security staff onto the production line. This move was facilitated by a characteristic of the production labour force in Japan at that time. Generally speaking, in-house security guards were not people specially trained for this purpose; companies would assign anyone to this task and security guards could be transferred to other departments after a certain period. Therefore, it was quite possible to position them on the production line. As companies moved in-house security guards to productive positions private security firms stepped in to offer services that would fill the vacuum. This growth trend was accelerated by events such as the Olympic Games in Tokyo in 1964 and the Osaka International Exhibition in 1970. In 1972, there were 775 companies employing 41,146 guards in Japan (Keisatsucho, 1974: 71). In 1996, these figures increased to 8,669 and 377,140 respectively (NB: these figures include part-time and temporary employees) (Keisatsucho, 1997: 113). In a quarter of a century, the security industry has increased by almost 820%. In 1971 approximately 70% of private security companies were rather small-sized in terms of their capital (less than 5 million yen) and 66% employed less than 50 guards (Sato, 1971: 108). Although it is still true that most private security firms are quite small, there are now some very large ones. For example, Sogo Keibi Hosho is one of the leading companies in this industry and its capital is over 2.5 billion yen. This company is categorised as being in the top 0.3 percent of all Japanese companies in terms of capital. According to the National Police Agency, in 1995 there were 6,752 security firms employing less than 50 staff, 1,388 employing between fifty and one thousand staff and 14 which employed over 1,000 personnel. The industry was regarded with some apprehension when, in 1971, it was found that 20 out of 321 presidents of security firms had criminal records (Sato, 1971:109). Among the 20 were two former members of crime organisations. This situation has much improved and the Security Business Act now stipulates that a criminal conviction can lead to disqualification in running such a business.

'Sales' of private security companies' services have been constantly growing. In 1987 they stood at 826.51 billion yen but 8 years later, the figure had doubled to 1775.85 billion yen. Comparison of these figures with the government budget for the public police highlights the increasing demand for private security services. In 1987, the government budget for the police was 2418.68 billion yen (Okurasho Insatsu Kyoku, 1988:86). The Japanese public thus paid a 35% additional fee for police services from private providers. By 1995 the budget for public police had increased to 3658.10 billion-yen (Keisatsucho, 1996: 331), at the same time the public had increased their spending on private police such that it amounted to an additional 48.5% security tariff.

Clearly the Japanese have become accustomed to the idea of private security provision. Indeed, Japan has more private security guards than policemen. In 1996, 377,140 security guards, including part-time employees, were working in Japan while there were only 224,985 police officers in total. Although the ratio of private security guards to public police remains smaller than in either the USA or UK, in Japan private security guards are becoming more visible (Bayley and Shearing, 1996: 587). Such guards provide a variety of services. In 1996, according to the NPA, in excess of 183,000 were employed in 'securing institutional sites' (e.g., shopping malls, businesses and factories), while some 15,300 were involved in policing 'corridors of security' (Sheptycki, 1997), that is transporting cash, and nuclear and other dangerous substances. The NPA figures indicate that bodyguards are not very common in Japan (at least officially), with only 432 people registered as performing that function.

THE ATTITUDE OF THE NATIONAL POLICE AGENCY TOWARDS THE PRIVATE SECURITY BUSINESS AND THE RELATIONSHIP BETWEEN THE TWO PARTIES

The position of the National Police Agency in 1971

This section describes the history of the supervision of private security firms by the Japanese police, the officially expressed position of the police and the legal framework. It will then consider the general attitude of regulating security businesses held by elite police administrators. It will draw on the content of a paper by Sato, a senior police administrator in 1971, in order to analyse the initial attitude of the Japanese police towards private security businesses. The essay is of great interest because in the following year the first Security Business Act was passed in the Diet, the Japanese Legislature. In Japan, both the Diet and the Cabinet have power to propose new legislation. If the Cabinet proposes an act, it is most likely that it has been drafted by senior government administrators and so could be said to reflect their goals and opinions. In addition, the more highly technical the legislation is, the more likely senior government administrators dominate its drafting process, due to their monopoly over the knowledge of the process of legislation. Given the fact that the Cabinet proposed the Security Business Act and it is highly technical legislation, one should pay particular attention to the opinion of senior police administrators. I would like to reiterate that Sato, the author of the essay, was one of the senior police administrators at that time.

The tone of Sato's essay on private security businesses was forceful. He felt that the police must regulate this industry. There were two reasons for this. Firstly, the business had caused some problems in society. This is not to deny that private security businesses had gained a relatively good reputation, indeed, they had earned wide recognition after co-operating with police in solving a serial murder case in 1969. In 1970, private security guards helped the police in 72 cases (Sato, 1971: 109). In spite of this, police maintained negative attitudes towards the business on the grounds that private security guards brought about problems in society. There was evidence that private security businesses harboured some people with an active connection to crime organisations as well as people with criminal records. In addition, private security companies undertook 'dirty' jobs that resulted in actual injuries to innocent citizens. The most famous instances include the Narita Airport case where private security guards hit protesters with wooden batons; the Naka-Minato municipal office case where guards were recruited to end industrial action by the use of physical force; the Chisso company case where guards inflicted injuries on minor shareholders at a shareholder meeting; and another instance where guards took advantage of their similar uniforms to that of police officers and tried to issue traffic fines to drivers (Zenkoku Keibigyo Kyokai, 1996: 6–7). These notorious cases cast a negative light on the industry as a whole.

Secondly, Sato suggested that perceived similarities between the police force and private security businesses might impair the authority of the police and he argued that private security guards should have no special police powers under any circumstances. Having argued this, he contended that there was a possibility that security guards might perceive themselves as having quasi-police authority. This was, according to him, a possibility because their uniforms and equipment were modelled on those of the police and their service was similar to that of the police and this led to the possibility of confusion amongst the public at large. People in the street might not be able to differentiate between the police and private security guards due to their similar appearance and Sato asked rhetorically: 'Under such circumstances, what would happen if private security guards' misbehaviour or criminal acts became more prevalent?' Thus, Sato appealed urgently for regulation of this young and apparently problematic industry emphasising that the police are the one and only organisation in Japan that exercise power authorised by public law, not by private contract. The police could not, in his view, confer any power on the private security business. The conclusion drawn was that the business should play only an auxiliary role to that of the public police.

However, it was evident to Sato that the private security business would not stop expanding since a substantial demand for this business was clearly evident, and that furthermore, the only impediment to its expansion that had been encountered up to that time had been a short-age of new recruits.

He put forward the view that the 'private security business emerged due to the demands of society and is now gaining notable importance ... We cannot ignore the usefulness of the private security business.' (Sato, 1971:107). He did not analyse this 'demand of society', neither would he depart from his presumption that the private security business should not be the main player in policing in Japan. This led to some twists or contradictions in his position paper.

Sato avoided two issues in his essay. Firstly, he did not address the question as to whether the Japanese police force provided an adequate policing service to the public or how this could be assessed, nor did he grapple with the question about the degree to which the private security business could be expected to fill any possible gaps. These omissions are significant and meaningful in analysing the attitude of the police towards the private security business. Sato himself admitted the ambiguity of the position of private security in society and he insisted that private security guards should not be vested with any special power concerning policing activities. However he also conceded that 'the private security service is different from other businesses', in that it may have a direct influence on life, body and property (*ibid.* p. 107). Therefore, he was forced to conclude that private police should be given limited powers to exercise coercive force, albeit limited to strictly defensive measures. His rationale for this was that, while private security guards were legally no more competent to exercise coercive force than any other citizen, in the case of catching criminals in *flagrante delicto* (i.e. red-handed), private security guards could be reasonably expected to deal with the situation in a more appropriate manner than a private citizen since, presumably like the police, they should be well versed in the rules of due process. In his opinion, private security guards should have the kind of training that would allow them to deal with criminal incidents properly. In spite of his admittance of the special nature of security guards, Sato would not go so far as to equate private security guards with police. He put forward a clear view of the two parties – police and private security guards – in which private security ranked as junior-police officers and played a supplementary role only. Therefore, he concluded, the private security business should operate along proper guidelines laid down by the police in order to ensure the business's sound development. The blue-print drawn up by Sato became public knowledge upon publication of his position paper. In the event, however, its realisation was not an unmitigated success for the NPA.

The major revision of 1982

In 1972, the first Private Security Business Act came into effect and with it the NPA secured its position as the supervisory agency of the private security business. However, the Act itself was no more than a documentation of administrative guidelines (Zenkoku Keibigyo Kyokai, 1996: 8). The failure to install strong institutional control over the business through the Act can plausibly be explained as being partly due to the overwhelming importance at the time of the fight against violent left-wing movements. The activities of groups such as the Japanese Red Army absorbed much of the NPA's attention. Another, perhaps more salient, reason for this inadequacy could have been the NPA's inexperience with this kind of legislation.

The 1972 Security Business Act was amended ten years later to strengthen the control of the police over private security businesses. Since 1982, there have been no major alterations to the Act. According to the police the need to amend the Act arose from five considerations (Zenkoku Keibigyo Kyokai, 1996: 8). Firstly, the focus of the industry had widened considerably beyond the scope of the original legislation. For example, it had started to provide its service at airports and to guard the transportation of nuclear substances. With such important new tasks being undertaken the NPA considered it an urgent need to establish proper guidelines for private security providers in order to establish lines of accountability.

Secondly, a large number of security companies continued to be overshadowed by an association with criminal organisations. Some firms were thought to be owned by persons with significant criminal records, others by persons thought to be connected to criminal organisations. Several cases came to public attention. For example, one security company employed someone for several months who was under 18 years old. A person under 18 years old is specifically disqualified from being a security guard under the Act. Having learned of the breach, the Public Security Commission of the Prefecture where it occurred issued an administrative disposition to the company which was openly ignored. It later emerged that the president of the company was a leading member of a crime organisation. It seemed evident that without sweeping such people out of the business, it would remain unfeasible for the business to develop soundly, let alone be accommodated as a 'junior partner' of the police.

Thirdly, misdemeanours and crimes committed by private security guards remained widespread. In 1982, there were as many as 362 ordinary penal offences committed by security guards, of which 55 were committed while on duty. On top of this, another 371 special penal offences involved security guards, of which 92 were committed while guards were on duty (Zenkoku Keibigyo Kyokai, 1996: 9). The crime rate among security guards in 1982 was about 54.7 per million whilst that of the general population was 128.8 per million (Homusho, 1996: 402), so it could be argued that the crime rate was actually very low in the industry. For the NPA however, these facts merely indicated that the existing legislation and supervisory system was not working.

Fourthly, many companies did not supervise or train their employees properly. In the view of the public police, adequate supervision and training could prevent problems such as the misconduct of security guards. However, many companies did not fulfil the requirements of the Act. In 1981, 36.1% of the offences against the Security Business Act concerned inadequacies of supervision and training. Companies often argued that training was not worthwhile and that their non-compliance was, there-fore, understandable (Zenkoku Keibigyo Kyokai, 1996: 9). It was resolved that both stringent control and clear guidelines would be necessary to improve the situation.

Lastly, a new security method, principally burglar alarm systems, had come into common usage by that time. These alarm systems were widely perceived to be one of the most efficient methods of crime prevention, especially in metropolitan areas. According to the Keisatsu Hakusho (1997) (White Paper on Police), there were almost 650,000 systems in operation in 1992, rising to over 800,000 in 1996 and this had implications for the number of back-up personnel as these security systems required private security providers to deploy more security guards. It also enabled security guards to report incidents to police without physically attending the crime scene. However, the use of this device was beset with difficulties not least of which were the increased number of false reports. This was partly blamed on poor technical standards and some companies were said not to have estab-lished an efficient system of evaluation of technical quality. As a whole, the alarm system did not work as designed and there was a perception that things could be improved by more careful regula-tion (Zenkoku Keibigyo Kyokai, 1996: 9–10). The time was ripe and, enabled by these justifications, the amendments to the 1972 Act were passed in 1982 and came into effect in 1983.

For a long time before the amendment the NPA appeared to be dismissive of private security companies' importance. However, subsequent to the amended Act, the NPA began to look upon the private security business as coming under its sphere of influence. This change in the NPA's policy was crystallised in the large-scale reorganisation conducted within the NPA in 1994.[1] The highlight of this event was the emergence of the 'Community Safety Bureau' (Seikatsu Anzen Kyoku).[2] This Bureau succeeded the former Safety Department and had expanded duties. One of its aims was to establish sound community policing in the daily lives of private citizens and make them conscious of community security problems. Among the activities included under the rubric of community policing were the profit-making activities of private security companies.

THE CONTENTS OF THE SECURITY BUSINESS ACT

The regulatory power of the police was strengthened with the 1982 amendment to the Security Business Act, which stated that new private security companies can only be established with the approval of the Public Security Commission of the Prefect, and must be re-approved every five years. All private security companies are obliged to obtain separate permission to provide an alarm system monitoring service and can only employ personnel specifically qualified to supervise alarm security systems. The amended Act extended police regulatory power over the daily operations of private security businesses as well. The training given to security guards was made more demanding and Public Security Commissions at Prefect level began to operate qualification examinations in 1986. This amended Act made private security a 'junior partner' of the Japanese police. This is evident in specific points in the amended Act.

The role of the private security firm in society and its supervisory body

The Act clearly states that a private security company is no more special than any other business. The issue of a license to establish a private security company does not result in the transfer of any policing power from the police force to the private security company. However, it was argued that since the service provided by the private security business is identical to that of the police for their service is to protect life, body and property or the like, this business should be supervised by the police force (Keisatsucho, 1997: 113). Although the official regulating body mandated by the Act is the Public Security Commission, which is a supervisory body of the police force as well, the Commission cannot physically sanction any on-site investigation without the police force at hand. Since the NPA was in charge of drafting and amending the Act it is clear from the outset that the public police was determined to supervise and regulate the private security business.

Sanctioning powers of the police over the private security business

In fact, the Act bestows on the police force *de facto* regulating control over the private security business. The police use their powers where the Act is violated. The result of provoking such sanctioning power can be severe. In addition to suspension of business for not less than 6 months or termination of business (Article 15), penalties of one year's imprisonment or fines of not greater than 500,000 yen (approx. £2,500 or US $4,500) are also possible (Article 17). Breach of the Act does not lead to criminal charges in every instance but breach of any article of the Act during the reapproval process, which takes place every five years, could lead to disqualification.

The training system for security guards

The system of supervision, training and certification of security employees has become much more demanding and is worth looking at in some detail. To begin with, there are six kinds of qualifications for security guards in Japan. Every prefectural Public Security Commission administers specific qualifications for airport guards, traffic guards, nuclear substance transportation guards, valuables transportation guards, alarm system administrators and the supervisors and trainers of security guards. The first four are not essential in order to undertake guarding tasks. The qualification for an alarm system administrator or supervisor is essential in executing this task. Each private security company must post a qualified person in each alarm system station. However, even if it is not compulsory to be qualified in executing the first four tasks, it is gradually becoming a *de facto* obligation. Some local governments provide in their regulations that private security companies have to station a minimum number of qualified security guards when executing guarding tasks entrusted by local governments (Keisatsucho, 1994: 49). According to the Keisatsu Hakusho of 1997 the number of qualified security guards stood at 23,464 in 1992 (just over 8% of the total number of employees in the industry) and stood at 38,451 in 1996 (just over 10% of the industry total). The National Police Agency reported in an Internal Newsletter in 1996 that there were 963 qualified security guards at airports, with 27,092 undertaking road traffic duties, 5,732 qualified personnel doing guarded transport, and 225 specially trained to guard the transportation of nuclear materials.

In addition to these qualifications and training courses for candidates, virtually all security guards, whether full-time or part-time, have to attend semi-annual lectures put on by someone who is qualified as a supervisor and trainer of security guards. This means that the company can entrust all of the training to another company or a public service corporation, such as prefectural Security Business Association, who will conduct it in accordance with the supervisor's and trainer's suggestions. The training course has two aspects. The first concerns the content of the Security Business Act, including how to make a report to the police and so on. The latter has four courses for the respective first four qualifications mentioned above and pertains to various skills and situations concerning security guard's duties. Therefore, although the first four qualifications above are not necessary conditions for the execution of guarding tasks, security guards have to be trained for their tasks.

Failure to provide training for security guards need not lead to criminal charges. However, this does not minimise the importance of the regulations since neglecting training can have grave consequences for business. Firstly, Article 3 subsection 7 of the Security Business Act stipulates that a person who is considered unable to provide a qualified supervisor and trainer of security guards in each branch of his (future) company will not be allowed to establish a company. Therefore, employing a qualified supervisor and trainer is necessary for the actual establishment of a private security company. Secondly, it is possible that re-approval of the license will be rejected on the grounds that the company is not in compliance with these sections of the Act. The conditions for re-approval are the same as those for the first approval and Article 3 subsection 3 provides that a person who has violated the Security Business Act and related regulations within five years can be disqualified. Thirdly, the prefectural Public Security Commission can issue an administrative guidance or disposition which amounts to *de facto* compulsion. Generally speaking, in order to avoid harsh sanctions being imposed upon activities, a private security company will keep in constant touch with the regulatory agency or Ministry in order to be able to predict what is expected of it and prepare to deal with anticipated problems. Consequently, the issuing of an administrative disposition or guidance is relatively rare and the receipt of an administrative guidance or disposition amounts to a strong censure.

Information required to be disclosed to the government

According to Article 12, a security company has to provide a list of its security guards containing the following information; name, photograph, registered address, current residence, date of birth, date of employment, training course attended, guarding task engaged in, qualifications possessed, a written oath signed by the security guard verifying that there is no reason why he should be disqualified from duty, a document signed by the trainer and the supervisor verifying he has received the proper training, the content of the particular contract executed and the number and kind of 'self-defence' tools possessed. With this information, the police can directly manage private security guards not only as a collective, but also as individuals. The company has to retain this information for one year after a guard leaves their employ and a violation of this provision may lead to criminal charges.

Control over use of coercive force by security guards

Through the requirements of Article 12 above, the police learn of the number of 'self-defence' tools in a security guard's possession and control of the coercive power of security guards is thus facilitated. Article 10 is more important in this context. The prefectural Public Security Commissions can prohibit or limit the use of specific self-defence tools or devices by security guards. Security guards cannot utilise any device or tool other than for self-defence purposes; self-defence tools include helmets, shields, wooden batons, tear gas, handcuffs and the like. Although these devices are regarded as implements for self-defence purposes, their use can threaten or cause fear among civilians. Consequently, their use can be prohibited or restricted accordingly. Normally, the prefectural Public Security Commission regulations ban the use of metal shields and metal batons which are longer than 60 cm, with diameters of more than 3 cm or weighing more than 320 grams. This standard is the same as that of batons commonly used by the police. However, even the use of metal batons which conform to the above standard may be further restricted when security guards form a unit. Through this move, the police have succeeded in keeping private security guards in an inferior position in terms of physical strength (Zenkoku Keibi Kyokai, 1996: 51–56). It seems that this legislation is a natural outcome of the phobia about weapons in Japanese culture. As an aside, it is worth pointing out that a license for a firearm such as a rifle is rarely issued to non-professionals. Private security companies have to report their possession of self-defence tools, even very basic ones like wooden batons under Article 12. The obvious tension here is not unlike the situation in the United Kingdom (South, 1988: 124–125) although arguably the legal situation is more clearly stipulated and finely delineated in the Japanese context.

Security Guards' Uniforms

Article 9 provides that private security companies should report to the prefectural Public Security Commission on the design, colour and emblems of the uniforms of guards and that these must be clearly distinguishable from those of the police. The Public Security Commission has the power to request an alteration if necessary. Normally, the production of uniforms at all similar to those of civil servants constitutes a minor offence that can lead to a fine. However, there is a tacit admission by police that it is necessary for security guards to be somewhat similar in appearance to the police, and that it is therefore unreasonable to fine security firms for issuing uniforms which are similar to those of the police force.

BUREAUCRATIC EXPANSIONISM IN THE NATIONAL POLICE AGENCY

I shall now discuss another interest of the police, especially one held by elite police administrators, which was referred to earlier in the paper. The term police 'elite' refers to a group of people who join the NPA through the National Public Service Examination First Category. Every year, the NPA recruits around 15–20 people through this channel. These are police officers, but they are more akin to civil servants who just happen to hold rank in the police force. There are two reasons for saying this. Firstly, such officers have little practical experience as operational police officers on the street during their career in the NPA. At most they are assigned beat and street detective work for approximately 9 months in the first year of their career and they rarely wear police uniform after that. Secondly, they are frequently transferred to other ministries, for example an economic regulatory ministry like the Ministry of Finance. Therefore, they regard themselves not so much as police officers but as government administrators.

What are the benefits for the police elite in establishing supervision over security businesses? There are two: a second career opportunity after leaving the NPA and a fund provided by these businesses that can be used at their discretion. According to Miyazawa:

> It is clear at this moment, at least, that the national association of the private security industry is staffed with many retired officers and its money provides the police with a large amount of discretionary funds. (Miyazawa, 1991: 255–256)

This raises profound questions about the uses to which these discretionary funds are put. To take one illustrative example, suppose that the NPA plans to draft legislation. The NPA needs to do thorough research before drafting but there is often no budget for that purpose. In this event, the association, with the expectation for maintaining a good relation with the NPA, would fund such research. It seems that the senior police administrators take it for granted that such associations will offer funds when the NPA needs it. Of course the purpose of the offer of funds should be read within the purpose or the prospectus of the associations since they are the public corporations.

Unfortunately there is little publicly available information which would allow researchers to trace the flow of money into the NPA from these sources and these matters remain obscure. Therefore this essay focuses on second issue: career opportunities for retired police elite members. Evidently, this is a compelling reason for members of the retired police elite to strengthen their control over the private security business. According to the Naisei Kankeisha Meibo, in 1996 ten people working in private security businesses were former members of the NPA who had retired from their posts. This number rose to 13 in 1997, while some of the original ten had died. It is apparent that these senior police administrators, the police elite, are actively pursuing second careers in the private security business.

To appreciate the significance of this interest of elite police administrators, it is necessary to understand that highly ranked government officers are compelled to resign from their posts to make way for younger colleagues. This ritual 'pat on the shoulder' (Bayley, 1991: 56) is supposed to happen at about age 55 but sometimes occurs at the age of 52, while the average retirement age in Japan is about 60. The NPA is no exception to this Civil Service rule, although it is not a legal obligation. The police elite are strongly encouraged, indeed expected, to resign, albeit with the tacit understanding that they will have opportunities for second careers in other organisations. Government officers rarely get fired, because the National Public Service Law provides that public servants can only be fired for inability or misconduct and this seldom occurs. Without the unspoken rule that senior officers should resign when they are offered second career opportunities, it would be difficult to keep the NPA running as an efficient organisation. It is vital for the NPA to ensure that these opportunities for retired police elite exist in order to promote the smooth replacement of personnel.

However, in order to have a second career in a private security company or a public service corporation funded by private security business, it is imperative that the business be prosperous. Thus, there is a somewhat contradictory responsibility for the police elite. The NPA needs to ensure the private security business is financially secure, otherwise it cannot absorb retired officers or generate funds. In order to keep the private security business prosperous, it is necessary to raise the public's confidence in the business. However, this cannot be at the expense of the NPA itself. The NPA has had to be seen as more trustworthy and, in a sense, more powerful than the private security providers in order to maintain its legitimacy and its vested interests. With these structural concerns the subordinate status of the private security industry, vis-à-vis the public police, has been assured.

POLICING POWERS OF THE PRIVATE SECURITY BUSINESS

There seems little doubt that the NPA attaches much importance to the private security industry's financial success but how do they evaluate the effectiveness of the policing power of the private security business in Japan? On the one hand, there are commonly held views about the crime prevention capacity of the private security business, an important recent example being the private security providers great utility amid the confusion during and after the Kobe earthquake. Indeed, some prefectural police forces have since concluded support agreements with prefectural private security business associations in the event of natural disasters. By the end of May 1997, 25 prefectures out of 47 had this sort of agreement (Keisatsucho, 1997:113–114). Regular statistics are produced which show the number of criminal cases solved with the help of private security providers. According to the Keisatsu Hakusyo for 1996 (p. 99) 116,652 incidents were solved by reference to information brought forward by citizens, often victims or other bystanders. Among them 7,531 incidents were successfully dealt with as a result of information coming from private security guards or through the firms that employ them. Such figures give no indication of the crime prevention capacity of a visible deterrent such as a uniformed security guard. What we do know is that, according to a National Police Agency Newsletter, a total of 331 security guards were awarded commendations for their actions in 1996, 154 of which had helped police in the arrest of suspects and 121 of which had apprehended suspects on their own. However, it seems that the NPA has shied away from the possibility that part of their duties could be better executed by the private sector either on the grounds of cost or efficiency. While virtually all the recent White Papers on Police refer to the importance of the private security business as one of the self-help measures on the part of the public, this is done with great circumspection so as not to undermine the perceived value of the NPA. At every turn the private security business is depicted as a 'junior partner' which should be supervised. This golden rule seems unquestionable. The picture thus painted is presumably reflected by the Japanese public's confidence in the public police. Even if it is not, this balance of responsibility is incorporated into Article 8 of the Act which specifically states that it 'does not grant private security companies or guards any special power'.

CONCLUSION

With the current legislation, control of the private security business in Japan by the public police has been affirmed. The fact that the Security Business Act protects Japanese citizens from sub-standard security service should not be undervalued. It certainly has raised the apparent standard of service provided by security guards. However, there is little doubt that one of the principal aims of the Act is simply to hold the role of the private security business in Japan to that of a 'junior partner' to the police. At the same time, while the NPA needs an obedient and loyal policing partner, this 'junior partner' has to be a prosperous and strong business enterprise in order that it provides a discretionary fund and a second career opportunity for retired police officers, as well as policing services for the public. This is very intriguing. It could be an extremely difficult task to keep an organisation economically powerful but at the same time politically and institutionally weak. However, this is just what the NPA has accomplished. The crime rate has not risen drastically, and in light of Japan's current economic problems, little attention has been paid to security problems. It seems unlikely that the Japanese people will begin to doubt the police's accountability, as is happening in the USA and the UK. It is too simplistic to explain this by reference to a 'culture of authoritarianism' in Japanese society because it overlooks the NPA's very deliberate policy toward the private security business which aims to limit private parties' policing services and to secure its position as a supervisor over such businesses. It is not in doubt that the private security business continues to improve its service as demanded by consumers while the NPA remains shackled with many obstacles such as budgetary limitations and institutional restrictions. Even now, the private security business has become a huge industry exceeding the police force, at least in terms of the number of people in the security workforce. How long it will remain possible for the NPA to maintain its position as supervisor of the private security business remains something of an open question. The answer partly depends on whether the public police force is seen to be efficient and effective in the provision of policing services. However, an independent evaluation of the public police has never been conducted. The ongoing 'marketisation of insecurity' (Sheptycki, 1998) seems to show that the Japanese public is anxious about the provision of policing services. It seems safe to say that, in the near future, the NPA will have to reconsider the position of the private security business in society as well as its own role in policing in Japan.

NOTES

1. The NPA, under the supervision of the Commissioner-General, has five Bureaux and a Commissioner-General's Secretariat. There are two departments in the NPA under a Bureau and a Secretariat. A department is between a Bureau and a Division in terms of size. Each Bureau has 4 to 8 Divisions.
2. It has six divisions, the Community Safety Planning Division, the Community Police Affairs Division, the Juvenile Division, the Consumer and Environmental Protection Division, the Firearms Control Division and the Drug Enforcement Division.

REFERENCES

Bayley, D. H. (1991) *Forces of Order: policing modern Japan*. California: University of California Press.
Bayley, D. H. (1994) *Police for the Future*. New York: Oxford University Press.

Bayley, D. H. and Shearing, C. D. (1996) 'The future of policing' in *Law and Society Review*. **30**(3).

Homusho (1996) *Hanzai Hakusho* (White Paper on Crime) (in Japanese). Tokyo: Okurasho Insatsu Kyoku.

Jones, T. and Newburn, T. (1998) *Private Security and Public Policing*. Oxford: Clarendon.

Keisatsucho (1994) Keisatsu Hakusho (White Paper on Japanese Police) (In Japanese), Tokyo: Okurasho Insatsu Kyoku.

Keisatsucho (1996) *Keisatsu Hakusho* (White Paper on Police) (in Japanese). Tokyo: Okurasho Insatsu Kyoku.

Keisatsucho (1997) *Keisatsu Hakusho* (White Paper on Police) (in Japanese). Tokyo: Okurasho Insatsu Kyoku.

Miyazawa, S. (1991) 'The Private Sector and Law Enforcement in Japan' in Gormeley, W. T. Jr., ed., *Privatisation and Its Alternatives*. Wisconsin: The University of Wisconsin Press.

Naisei Kankeisha Meibo Hensan Kai (1996) *Naisei Kankei-sha Meibo* (in Japanese). Tokyo: Zaidan Houjin Chiho Zaimu Kyokai.

Okurasho Insatsu Kyoku (1988) *Nihon no Hakusho* (White Paper of Japan) (in Japanese). Tokyo: Okurasho Insatsu Kyoku.

Sato, M. (1971) 'Keibi-hosho eigyo wo meguru mondai-ten' (The problems in private security business) (in Japanese) in *Keisatsu Gakuron Shu*. Tokyo.

Shearing, C. D. and Stenning, P. C. (1983) 'Private Security: Implications for Social Control' in *Social Problems*. **30**(5).

Sheptycki, J. W. E. (1997) 'Insecurity, risk suppression and segregation: some reflections on policing in the transnational age', *Theoretical Criminology*, **1**(3). pp. 303–315.

Sheptycki, J. W. E. (1998) 'Policing, Postmodernism and Transnationalization' in *British Journal of Criminology*. **38**(3), pp. 485–503.

South, N. (1988) *Policing for Profit*. London: Sage Publications.

Zaidan Houjin Chiho Zaimu Kyokai (1997) *Naisei Kankei-sha Meibo* (in Japanese). Tokyo: Zaidan Houjin Chiho Zaimu Kyokai.

Zenkoku Keibigyo Kyokai (Private Security Business Association) (1996), ed., *Keibigyo Hou no Kaisetsu* (The handbook of the Act of Security Business) (in Japanese). Tokyo.

The evolution of security industry regulation in the European Union

Mark Button and Peter Stiernstedt

ABSTRACT

The European private security sector has grown from a handful of small companies at the end of the Second World War into a multibillion Euro industry with thousands of firms and millions of security staff. In Europe, the demands for security is not just expressed notionally but also officially in The European Agenda on Security stating the European Union (EU) aims to ensure that people live in an area of freedom, security, and justice. This article will begin by exploring the role of private security in society. It will then move on to consider the main phases in the development of private security regulation in Europe. Following on from this, some of the main areas of policy development will be considered, such as European bodies, initiatives, and standards. Finally, the article will explore some of the potential options for the future in better regulating the European private security sector. From a historical perspective, the evolution of private security regulation can be divided into three phases: the laissez-faire, the centrifugal, and the centripetal era – each with its own distinct characteristics and impact on the concurrent industry. In the EU where there is the legal framework for the development of a single market in services, the key social partners have been at the forefront of developing a series of standards and guidance documents which promote standards across borders at the European level. However, the institutions of the EU have been reluctant to intervene at a European level in setting minimum standards of private security regulation. Thus, the changing terrain of the EU relating to security, regulation, and the private security industry means the current trajectory may be in need of an injection of more radical thought and consideration.

Introduction

The European private security sector has grown from a handful of small companies at the end of the Second World War into a multibillion Euro industry with thousands of firms and millions of security staff. Indeed the Confederation of European Security Services (CoESS), which represents a significant part of the European manned guarding sector of the industry (but not all), claims to represent members covering over 60,000 security companies, 2.2 million employees with a turnover of over €34.2 billion in 19 European Union (EU) member states and a total of 24 countries within Europe (CoESS, n.d.). The breadth of activities undertaken by the private security sector in the EU also varies significantly between states, but in most the trajectory has been one of increasing movement towards tasks traditionally associated with state-provided security services. Some of the functions now popularly undertaken in the EU include the provision of security at major places of public gathering as well as the security of places of critical national infrastructure, and in some countries the sector even guards and transports prisoners, monitors prisoners under supervision with electronic tags, patrols residential streets, guards crime scenes, and undertakes some parts of police investigations (CoESS, 2011; United Nations Office on Drugs and Crime [UNODC], 2014; Van Steden, 2007).

To give an idea of the proliferation of private security personnel, this means a presence at locations such as shopping centres, leisure parks, transport hubs, pop concerts, sporting events, airports, government facilities, military bases, nuclear power stations, courts, and so on. The list goes on and on, resulting in daily interactions with the ordinary citizen of Europe more common than not. Further, in some states, security staff regularly carry arms or other non-lethal weapons (UNODC, 2014). The Weberian "totem" of the state as holding the "monopoly of legitimate use of force" has been significantly cracked by the rise of private security. Even the "arms length" control of the private security as contractors for the state has been accompanied with equally if not larger growth of "nodes" or pockets of governance, beyond the state in the private and voluntary sectors, in which private security plays a significant part, often using "legitimate force" amongst other strategies to secure compliance (Button, 2008; Johnston & Shearing, 2003). Such profound changes, combined with the increasing demands of states and citizens for greater security, have stimulated both national and European-level interest in shaping, controlling, and making accountable the private security sector.

In Europe, the demands for security is not just expressed notionally but also officially as set out in the Stockholm program (2010) and then reinforced in The European Agenda on Security (2015) stating the EU aims to ensure that people live in an area of freedom, security, and justice. With the complex and often asymmetrical threats faced by modern societies, this has increasingly meant the need for further synergies and co-operation at all levels. The new variables of international borderless threats, the dynamic nature of globalisation, and the ensuing decrease of importance of geographic location are changing the face of security worldwide. State-driven security with policing as one of its primary weapons of choice is no longer enough, and in many member states the private security industry has assumed a substantial position in the provision of policing (CoESS, 2011; Jones & Newburn, 2006; Ocqueteau, 2006; Van Steden & Sarre, 2007). Private security as a response to the recognition of globalisation as a cause for growing societal complexity spawning ever more intricate threat dimensions is not something entirely new. In their paper "Modern Private Security: Its Growth and Implications," Shearing and Stenning (1982) suggested that private security was moving in the direction of a new disciplinary society and raised fundamental questions with respect to sovereignty, justice, and individual liberty at the time almost entirely unrecognised. Today the questions are certainly recognised, often debated, and given high priority on the European political agenda. Nonetheless, interstate disagreement persists and supranational policy does not always align with national ones. It is even less so when comparing the ambitious rhetoric with actual achievements, with a largely varied level of private security regulation throughout Europe (Button & Stiernstedt, 2016).

Despite persisting regulatory variance, since the end of the Cold War, the privatisation of security in Europe is developing rapidly where the new security "fashion" is for developed nations to adopt a national security doctrine with increasingly specialised police functions, with non-core security functions increasingly outsourced to the private market. This development and growth of private security has consequently also been a key factor behind the expansion of security industry regulation. As more and more people have come into contact with security personnel or become dependent on security technology, there has been an increasing recognition of the need for better management of these encounters and relationships (Prenzler & Sarre, 2012). The response itself has evolved with the growth of the private security industry and now includes elements of regulation, and thereby cleansing the market of deviant providers, to efforts to communalise by equalising access to the security market. The most recent evolutionary step suggested is towards a civilising model with the regulatory goals being inclusive deliberation and social solidarity (Loader & White, 2015). Presented as a model, this final step is perhaps better viewed as another smaller, yet not insignificant, nonetheless chronologically subsequent – both in appearance and in implementation – piece of an increasingly fine-tuned regulatory melody harmonising throughout Europe.

Notwithstanding, the private security industry to this day is continuing to grow, an inexorable fact that has been attributed to a wide variety of factors (Jones & Newburn, 2006; Shearing & Stenning, 1982). Deliberate policies of privatising policing have not been particularly significant (Prenzler & Sarre, 2012). The evolution of private security and the regulation thereof is a noteworthy topic and has been investigated in different regions of the world such as Australia (Prenzler & Sarre, 2012) and Africa (Abrahamsen & Wiliams, 2005; Kasali, 2012). Also in Europe, the issue is being addressed by both academics and policymakers (Button, 2007a; CoESS, 2011; De Waard, 1999).

This article will begin by exploring the role of private security in society. It will then move on to consider the main phases in the development of private security regulation in Europe. Following on from this, some of the main areas of policy development will be considered, such as European bodies, initiatives, and standards. Finally, the article will explore some of the potential options for the future in better regulating the European private security sector.

The role of private security in society

The rate of growth in size of the private security sector is paralleled only by the concurrent expansion in role and responsibility. This inevitably leads towards an increase of importance (or at least relevance) of the issue, politically and practically, being elaborately weaved into the fabric of modern society. Currently, many of the functions traditionally assumed by the public police are now undertaken by private security (Button, 2007b; CoESS, 2011; Gimenez-Salinas, 2004; Hainmuller & Lemnitzer, 2003; Jones & Newburn, 1998; Ocqueteau, 2006; Van Steden, 2007). Further, as recent events have shown in failing states when law enforcement agencies are discredited, reformers turn to creating parallel private security structures (The Economist, 2015). Then, in a sense, completely replacing the traditional function of the police and state monopoly on, not only providing security but also enacting force and violence.

The sheer speed with which the private security industry is evolving puts a heavy strain on regulation to keep up. Although most countries in the EU have already put in place a range of legal, practical, and supporting mechanisms to underpin a Europe of, if nothing else, internal security. Some countries in the EU actually bear the hallmark of having implemented some of the most demanding regulatory systems in the world (Button, 2008; Prenzler & Sarre, 2008). Nonetheless, as many studies have shown, the systems vary considerably in content (Button, 2007a, 2012; Button & Stiernstedt, 2016; CoESS, 2011; De Waard, 1993). While covered by significantly less research, the same is arguably true for the level of actual efficiency, that is, societal impact of the regulation or lack thereof.

The expansion of private security is sometimes interpreted as a sign of economic growth and as an adjunct to more capitalistically influenced market economies. Together with rising crime rates, often appearing in tandem with economic growth, in turn pushing for further expansion of theprivate security market both in size and reach. As always, correlation does not imply causation, but it does make for a solid argument of private security and the regulation thereof evolving symbiotically with society as a whole. It is and will remain an ever more pressing concern on all levels of Europe, national as well as supranational, for governments and NGOs alike. So how has the private security regulation evolved throughout history to its meritorious place as an integral and essential part of modern society?

Method

A historical account of the phases of Private Security Regulation from a European perspective

Reviewing the literature available on the topic of private security regulation, the evolution thereof may be divided into at least three distinct phases. The extent to which various concepts within the discipline are adequately covered by extant literature varies and the diversity of sources called for a systematic methodology to map the territory. The method applied is informed by the rigorous system proposed by Wolfswinkel, Furtmueller, and Wilderom (2013), assuring in-depth analysis of empirical facts and related insights. The five-stage process of the method consists of define, search, select, analyse, and present and can be considered as a means by which central literature and underpinning research can be systematically mapped out for in-depth analysis. Having said that, the final methodology applied does not consist of totally rigid and sequential analysis, but actually rather moves away from such prescriptive constructs letting the analytical system act as a conceptual framework within which the qualitative analysis resides. This allowed the interrelationships, dependencies, and inconsistencies, in (and to some extent beyond) the particular topic to be explored. This produced a policy-piece-type result, formulated as follows: from a historical perspective the evolution of private security regulation can be divided into three phases – the laissez-faire, the centrifugal, and the centripetal[1] era – each with its own distinct characteristics and impact on the concurrent industry.

Laissez-faire Europe 1930s to mid-1970s

The antecedents of the private security industry can be traced back many hundreds of years if roles such as watchmen and locksmiths are considered (George & Button, 2000). The first private security companies in their modern form began to be formed in the early nineteenth century. The emergence and substantial growth in the private security industry, however, can be traced to the post-war period, particularly from the 1960s onwards (Jones & Newburn, 1996; George & Button, 2000). Regulation of private security, however, has some unexpected origins in this period. For example, in both Belgium and the Netherlands, legislation was passed in the 1930s to regulate fascist militias, which was sufficiently wide in scope to be used to regulate the emerging and fast-growing private security sector some years later (De Waard & Van Der Hoek, 1991 De Waard, 1996). For most of Western Europe, the early expansion was accompanied with industry self-regulatory measures to try and set and raise standards. This period was characterised by little European-level interest with states and national private security industry groups largely preoccupied with their own country and regulatory needs (De Waard & Van Der Hoek, 1991).

Centrifugal Europe mid-1970s to early 1990s

Rapid expansion of the private security industry, the important roles it was beginning to secure, along with a variety of problems associated with the sector triggered debates in many countries over whether statutory regulation of some form should be introduced. Some states used existing statutes, not specifically designed for private security, such as the Netherlands (De Waard, 1999); some introduced special regulation, such as Spain (various laws and regulations between 1978 and 1981); other resisted, for ideological reasons (UK) or simply because the industry had not developed significantly or did not exist (Greece, Eastern communist states). However, from the mid-1970s and during the 1980s, there was a group of Western European countries beginning to introduce statutory regulation. These countries, however, legislated according to their own needs with little reference for a common European approach. The forces for regulation were creating very different approaches to regulation of private security in the countries which were already part or destined to be part of the EU (De Waard & Van Der Hoek, 1991).

From centrifugal to centripetal Europe early 1990s onwards

In 1990, the EU consisted of 12 states and of these all bar Greece, the Republic of Ireland, and the UK had some form of regulatory system for the private security sector. However, in countries such as Germany, regulation was based upon general trade legislation and was minimal. In Belgium and the Netherlands, it was based upon laws designed for private militias and in Italy too on dated legislation from the 1940s. A report published for the Dutch Ministry of Justice in 1991 noted the significant variations across Europe in regulation, particularly upon training (De Waard & Van Der Hoek, 1991). The UK, Republic of Ireland, and Greece were still to regulate and relied to varying extents on self-regulatory measures. Most countries were looking towards their own regulatory needs with little reference to the rest of Europe. However, the report for the Dutch Ministry of Justice showed some countries were beginning to look at what other countries were doing and to consider wider European implications (De Waard & Van Der Hoek, 1991). Significant changes began to emerge from the early 1990s, however, with a variety of developments occurring, which have increased the needs for greater European co-operation and harmonisation, shifting the force from centrifugal to centripetal.

The creation of the European single market in the EU unleashed the foundations of free movement of labour, undertakings, and services within the EU. The former communist countries of Eastern Europe shook off their Soviet masters, many enthusiastically looking to and embracing their Western neighbours' ways of doing things and of course most eventually joining the EU, along with some of the remaining Western European countries who were outside. The expansion to Eastern Europe also substantially increased movement of citizens around the EU. For instance, over the last decade, 2.5 million have migrated to the UK, with a significant proportion of these from the EU and particularly Eastern Europe (Barrett, 2014). Indeed in 2011, there were estimated to be almost 700,000 Poles alone who had emigrated to the UK (Okolski, 2014).

Underneath these macro developments, a variety of security-level developments also emerged adding to the growing centripetal forces. Large global security companies have emerged operating in multiple states of the EU: G4S, Securitas, and Prosegur. For example, G4S has over 600,000 employees operating in 110 countries throughout the world generating £6.4 billion of revenue (G4S, 2016). Security risks have increased substantially, particularly vis-à-vis terrorism, organised crime, and increasingly cyber developments (Control Risks, 2016).

Acting as a barrier to some of these forces have been the regulatory systems for private security, which at the time of writing consists of 28 EU member states. These vary significantly in the standards that are applied to the private security industry. This is illustrated by, for example, CoESS facts and figures for private security services in Europe (2013), providing a rating on the strictness of private security legislation for each country. Here, a numerical value was allocated to each country on the basis of the answers to a questionnaire. Through a point allocation system, five judgment criteria were devised: very strict,[2] strict,[3] medium,[4] low,[5] weak, and non-existent, indicating the different levels of regulatory strictness on a national level.

Along the same lines, although applying a significantly more sophisticated and detailed analysis, Button and Stiernstedt (2016) have also assessed the regulatory systems based on a variety of criteria drawn from guidance such as the UNODC (2014) guidance on regulation, the ECORYS (2011) report on security regulation, as well as previous research by Button (2007a), amongst several others. A maximum of 100 points was possible, and of the 26 states that were assessed, the points ranged from 94/100 in Belgium to 22/100 in the Czech Republic. Broadly, the EU countries can be sorted according to the following regulator typology: super[6] (75+ points), strong[7] (50–74 points), weak[8] (25–49 points), and quasi[9] (24 points and below).

This distinction is purely based upon the points achieved by the country, with those with 75 points or more meeting the highest standards, hence "super regulators," those with 50–74 doing well, but not in the elite, nevertheless "strong regulators." Then there are the countries with significant gaps in their systems and hence "weak regulators" and finally the example of the Czech Republic, which is so weak that it could even be considered as a "quasi-regulator." To highlight this difference, a security officer in the Czech Republic has no mandatory number of hours of training to start working in the industry, which compares to one in Sweden who has to complete close to and in excess of 300 h depending on role.

Findings

European organisations and their relationship with Private Security Regulation

The need to turn the tide away from the centrifugal forces was identified in the late 1980s by some European security organisations, which culminated in structures and organisation being created to push for various harmonisation-related measures. This "turning of the tide" towards centripetal forces can be traced to the formation of a number of influential European bodies dedicated towards lobbying European institutions for actions more favourable to the European security industry. Notably CoESS was formed in 1989 bringing together the national trade associations for the manned guarding sector in the member states and candidate member states. CoESS, however, was not the first such European body and was preceded by several more security technically focused bodies such as EUROALARM (1970), EUROSAFE (1988), ESTA (1976), and EASEM in 1987. More recently, the European Organisation for Corporate Security (EOCS) was created in 2005 and the European Organisation for Security (EOS) in 2007. Some of these organisations had been created with a greater focus on standardisation bodies, such as EUROALARM, rather than the EU. In contrast, CoESS, followed some time later by EOCS and EOS, is predominantly orientated towards the institutions of the EU and as will be shown has engaged in a wide range of activities that have contributed towards centripetal forces on regulation. Parallel to the employer bodies, trade unions representing security officers across Europe had been working through UNI-Fiet (now Europa) to support centripetal initiatives. In 1991, for example, there was a motion to the European Parliament calling for European harmonisation of regulation (George & Button, 2000: pp. 182–183).

The turning point towards a period becoming concerned with the need for greater harmonisation, however, can be traced to the work of the European Commission Directorate General V in partnership with CoESS and Uni-Fiet conference in London in 1996, where CoESS and UNI/Fiet signed a joint agreement on vocational training. The declaration made very clear the first centripetal shift of thinking amongst the key social partners in the EU, stating:

> The social partners have been co-operating in a number of ways on the issue of vocational training. A project under the European Union's FORCE Programme was carried out during 1994. This European perspective provides the basis for deepening co-operation between the social partners on the subject of vocational training. It has allowed the defining of common occupational profiles described in terms of the tasks which security operatives carry out. This provides the basis for developing a common European approach to vocational training in the European security industry which highlights the best from each national context whilst respecting the diversity in national practices and training structures which exist. (COESS, 1996)

This has been followed by much more work between the social partners developing joint declarations and standards, which will be discussed in more depth shortly. However, the most significant development between the social partners was in 2001 when the social partners signed the "Joint declaration of CoESS and UNI-Europa" on the European harmonisation of legislation governing the private security sector (CoESS, 2001). The declaration noted the problem of, amongst others:

> National regulations differ from one another and they prevent the sector from drawing on the full benefits of European integration.

And it went on,

> ...CoESS and UNI-Europa therefore call on the European ministers responsible to take the necessary measures so that the private security sector is governed by laws aimed at ensuring high quality standards and a high degree of professionalism in all countries of the European Union, and so that European harmonisation of the *following aspects* can be developed. (authors emphasis)

These aspects included authorisations to practice (workers), licences (companies), evaluation and supervision by public authorities, professional training, health and safety, working conditions, and the provision of cross-border services. This was a significant call for the institutions of the EU to create supranational structures to facilitate commons minimum standards across a wide range of areas.

A few years later, the EU did offer a centripetal initiative for the private security sector, but of a deregulatory flavour which was unpalatable to most of the European security industry. In January 2004, the European Commission published a draft Directive with the aim of creating a real internal market for services. The services covered amount to around 50% of economic activity of the EU and the Directive explicitly included security services. The Directive fuelled much debate over the future direction of Europe. In the context of private security, however, CoESS opposed the Directive seeking exemption for private security or significant changes to it. This rested on two concerns: first, the Directive's aspiration to get rid of "authorisation schemes," which would mean the licensing structures that exist in most countries and second, the "country of origin" principle, where a provider legally operating in one member state could market its services in another without having to comply with their regulations (CoESS, 2004).

These concerns were amplified at the time with the accession of Cyprus and the Czech Republic, who at that time had no or virtually no regulation. Unchanged the Directive could have resulted in companies from countries with lesser regulatory systems moving to those with higher standards and undercutting them, returning the security sector to the old downward spiral in standards, which is what regulation was introduced to address in most countries. However, after intensive lobbying of members of the European Parliament, by CoESS and other organisations, the Directive was amended to exclude the security sector (amongst others) in a vote on 16 February 2006 (CoESS, 2006).

European standards

In the EU, where there is legal framework for the development of a single market in services, the key social partners have been at the forefront of developing a series of standards and guidance documents which promote standards across borders at the European level. The key partners, CoESS (security company trade associations) and Uni-Europa (trade unions), have developed the following, which seek to set standards for private security regulators, companies, and operatives across the EU:

- European Vocational Training Manual for Basic Guarding (1999)
- Code of Conduct and Ethics for the Private Security Sector 2003
- Preventing Occupational Hazards in the Private Security Sector (manned guarding and surveillance services) 2004
- European Educational Toolkit for three Private Security Activities 2006

The training manual, code of conduct, and educational toolkit are all voluntary standards, although they do carry status in many states in the EU around the creation of basic standards. The document on preventing occupational standards brings together much of the wider health and safety regulations of the EU and directs how they apply to the private security sector.

European regulations

The institutions of the EU have been reluctant to intervene at a European level in setting minimum standards of private security regulation. However, the single market has impacted upon how some states regulate private security. There have, therefore, been decisions in the European Court of Justice which have influenced what EU states can and cannot do in regulating private security. Under Articles 39 (now 48), 43 (now 49), and 49 (now 56) of the EU single market, it provides for

- Free Movement of Persons, Services, and Capital: Workers
- Freedom of Establishment
- Freedom to Provide Services

Several members of the EU have sought derogations for private security regulation on the grounds that the sector contributes to public security, which is possible for activities which in themselves are directly and specifically connected with the exercise of official authority. However, the European Court of Justice has found this does not apply to security undertakings and security staff, as merely making a contribution to the maintenance of public security, which any individual may be called upon to do, does not constitute exercise of official authority (Button & Dalda, 2014). As a consequence, there are a number of states in the EU which have been found not to be compliant with the single market regulations in their regulatory systems for private security, effectively inducing deregulation. These include Spain, Italy, Portugal, the Netherlands, Belgium, and Hungary. Some of the requirements which have required reform include the following:

- Nationality requirements (restricting licences to one country requirement).
- Residence requirements (requiring licence holders to live in one state).
- Minimum share capital (requiring a minimum share capital for owners).
- Requiring authorisation (without accepting authorisations from other member states).
- Licences linked to territorial area or sub-district in state, which means multiple licences would need to be sought to operate across a state.
- Not recognising other states' training/professional qualifications.
- Operators must be a legal person (company), rather than individual.
- Setting minimum standards for number of workers in undertaking.
- Securities/guarantee must be with home country.
- Requiring swearing oath of allegiance to home country.
- Price approvals by local regulator.

These illustrate that in a negative way EU institutions have been influencing the regulation of private security. However, it is this framework in an enlarged EU with increasing flows of workers, undertakings, and services which poses a threat to the regulatory systems of some EU countries. Those established and working in the lowest (Czech Republic) can work in the highest (Belgium). In the price-driven world of private security purchases (Goold, Loader, & Thumala, 2010), this opens up the possibility for the unscrupulous to use lower regulating countries to enter higher ranking. It provides for an advantage for those in lower ranking countries to use their lower standards and costs to expand into higher ranking. Ultimately, it also undermines the "security blanket" by providing holes which can be exploited.

Discussion

Coming to terms with the centripetal forces: options for the EU

The EU, a political creature now over 60 years old, founded on an underpinning idea of institutional organisation much older than that, coming to life after the Second World War. Often attributed as the architect of the European integration project is Robert Schuman, French Foreign Minister between 1948 and 1952, who sought and brokered a consensus between the six founding countries. This consensus was codified in a treaty, the European Coal and Steel Community, in Paris in April 1951. The idea was to put some of the responsibilities to a specific entity – the European Commission (at the time the high authority) – the only supranational institution that pursues the public interest of its constituents. Over time, the European integration project, now known as the EU, has expanded and been modified by new treaties and amendments. Most recently, the Lisbon treaty represents a paradigm shift in the way in which the EU developed over the years, shifting away from being primarily driven by an economic engine to a more encompassing process including citizens in the process. Simplifying the legislative process, giving more power to the union, but also to the EU parliament the only institution that is directly elected. The central theme is to ensure democracy and transparency, particularly the legislative process that is arguably more transparent than the one that exists in most member states. With the strict adherence to the principle of competence, where the actions of the EU heavily depend on the desire of the member state of actually having the EU coming up with new policies, the legislative harmonisation of the private security industry is absent. Moreover, with the EU only being able to act insofar as it has received competences of the member states, once the competence has been received, there is still a due process to reach agreement for a new policy. Historically, the road to any policy coordination is quite long and regulation of the private security industry will probably not be an exception to that rule.

Juxtaposed to the need for the regulation of private security are the increasing integration of the EU and the creation of a single market. The private security industry is treated as a major business services sector, and this is despite some attempts by member states to secure a similar status to state security apparatus (CoESS, 1998). As such, the private security industry would be exempt from these provisions, which the state security apparatus already is. However, as discussed, such attempts have failed, which means the private security industry is treated like any other business service industry and a private security company or operative legitimately operating in one member state can do so in another based upon the home country authorisation. Some European countries have already developed very detailed and high-quality legislation. It is these kinds of legislations and regulations that must serve as a basis for any future European harmonisation in order to enhance the overall level of the industry. But national regulations are sometimes non-existent, inadequate, and do not guarantee the professionalism the sector needs. By differing from one country to another, they are preventing the sector from drawing on the full benefits of European integration. This, however, requires a clear desire to have more Europe in the first place, a notion to which there is many perspectives and differing opinions. Adding to the complexity, even if the citizens of a member state show that desire, the political elite of the same country may be conceptually as well as ideologically against this. Because every time there is more Europe, there is less national state – giving the political rulers something rather significant to lose and little to gain. Thus, unless there would be an electorate space where the leaders presented themselves in front of a European electorate, the supranational politics of the EU is still very much an affair of nation states where national politics dominate over EU politics. Thus, the conditions to have a political debate must be created and stimulated, in part by articles like this, to if, why and how private security regulation should be European and not national – as the foundation for any change from a supranational level.

Conclusion

The future of European private security regulation

It is within this challenging context to which we now turn. The changing terrain of the EU relating to security, regulation, and the private security industry means the current trajectory may be in need of an injection of more radical thought and consideration. A radical question might be whether a supranational regulator for private security regulation is necessary for the whole EU? On the one hand, this might be seen as the most simple solution to the new terrain, ensuring the same minimum standards across the EU. On the other hand, however, such an approach would be radical, unusual (at least from a historical perspective), and politically disagreeable to many member states. Indeed, even federal states such as the USA, Canada, and Australia have not felt this necessary.

More palatable would be a directive that sets out the basic minimum requirements for all member states of the EU. Such European-level regulation has already touched a number of business service sectors, such as banking, insurance, and air travel, to name some. Such an approach has some precedent with what has happened in Australia relating to some standards for the private security sector across states and territories, where the Council of Australian Governments has sought to create greater harmonisation across the federal states and territories, although with limited success (Sarre & Prenzler, 2011). A directive could set basic requirements for the licensing of individuals and firms and draw out some of the minimum standards they should meet. Nevertheless, even this in the current politics of the EU, with some states such as the UK (and others) pursuing less European-level intervention, combined with the strains on some common security apparatus such as the borderless arrangements of the Schengen area would be unlikely.

In the absence of such an initiative, the current non-binding approach of building more of the infrastructure of European-level standards and structures should be the priority for the policy-makers and social partners of the European private security industry. Greater investment in the development of common model European standards around the building blocks of an effective regulatory system should be developed with member states encouraged and incentivised to embrace them. Such standards could include the following:

- Model regulatory systems
- Training standards for all of the common roles
- Model licensing requirements for firms and individuals
- Standards for significant security infrastructure, such as control rooms and training centres
- Guidelines for the use of force, lethal, and non-lethal violence
- Codes of conduct and industry ethics policies

Thus, it is the view of the authors that the most effective way to underpin more effective pan-European private security regulation is a directive mandating minimum standards, which member states then implement. At the same time, the authors are also realistic about the political land-scape, and the acceleration of more and demanding voluntary standards is the most achievable and likely policy in the short and medium term in the current politics of the EU.

The European private security sector has grown into a multibillion Euro industry with thousands of firms and millions of security staff. The rate of growth in size of the private security sector is paralleled only by the concurrent expansion in role and responsibility. This inevitably leads towards an increase of importance of the issue, both politically and practically, and also provides a notion of its being elaborately weaved into the fabric of modern society. Where increasing demands of states and citizens for greater security have stimulated both national- and European-level interest in shaping, controlling, and making accountable the private security sector. Although, when comparing the ambitious rhetoric with actual achievements, there is a highly varied level of private security regulation throughout Europe (Button & Stiernstedt, 2016).

This article has explored the role of private security in society and established that it is and will remain an ever more pressing concern on all levels of Europe, national as well as supranational. It then moved on to consider the main phases in the development of private security regulation in Europe. The phases as described are the *laissez-faire Europe 1930s to mid-1970s* followed by the *Centrifugal Europe mid-1970s to early 1990s* and finally *From centrifugal to centripetal Europe early 1990s onwards*. Following on from this, some of the main areas of policy development were considered. Where the institutions of the EU have been reluctant to intervene at a European level in setting minimum standards of private security regulation. Further, those services that have been regulated have, if anything, effectively induced deregulation. As there are a number of states in the EU which have been found not to be compliant with the single market regulations in their regulatory systems for private security. Changing this is not a simple task as, at least historically, the road to policy coordination is quite long and regulation of the private security industry will probably not be an exception to that rule. With the supranational politics of the EU is still being very much an affair of nation states where national politics dominate over EU politics.

In conclusion, the article explored some of the potential options for the future in better regulating the European private security sector. Given the challenging context and perhaps most notably constantly changing terrain of the EU relating to security, regulation, and the private security industry mean the current trajectory may be in need of an injection of more radical thought and consideration. The simplest solution of a supranational regulator established by the EU does not seem feasible in the short or midterm. Consequently, the only realistic alternative is a directive that sets out the basic minimum requirements for all member states of the EU. Being conscious of the pace of which the institutions of the EU work, in the absence of awaiting such an initiative, the current non-binding approach of building more of the infrastructure of European-level standards and structures should be the priority. The European harmonisation of the private security services sector is the ultimate goal and the reference for any concrete initiative. Thus, it is the view of the authors that the most effective way to underpin more effective pan-European private security regulation is a directive mandating minimum standards.

Notes

1. Centrifugal denotes a force directed outwards from an orbital centre as opposed to centripetal force directed inwards. The nomenclature is used to conceptualise, and no distinction is made insofar that in reality centripetal force is an *actual* force and centrifugal force is an *apparent* force.
2. Serbia, Hungary, Belgium, Sweden, Portugal, Spain, Luxembourg.
3. Turkey, Greece, Macedonia, Romania, Bosnia and Herzegovina, Croatia, Slovenia, Slovakia, Italy, Switzerland, The Netherlands, Estonia, Lithuania, Denmark, Norway, Finland, Malta.
4. Ireland, UK, France, Germany, Bulgaria, Latvia, Cyprus.
5. Austria, Czech Republic, Poland.
6. Belgium, Spain, Slovenia, Greece, Portugal, Sweden.
7. Ireland, Finland, Romania, Luxembourg, Germany, Malta, France, The Netherlands, Estonia, Poland, Denmark, Latvia, Bulgaria, UK, Slovakia.
8. Italy, Cyprus, Lithuania, Austria.
9. Czech Republic.

References

Abrahamsen, R., & Williams, M. (2005). *The globalisation of private security: Country report: Nigeria*. Aberystwyth: University of Wales.
Barrett, D. (2014) Immigration from eastern Europe was massively underestimated, says official report. Telegraph online. Retrieved from http://www.telegraph.co.uk/news/uknews/immigration/10757336/Immigration-from-eastern-Europe-was-massively-underestimated-says-official-report.html
Button, M. (2007a). Assessing the regulation of private security across Europe. *European Journal of Criminology, 4*, 109–128. doi:10.1177/1477370807071733
Button, M. (2007b). *Security officers and policing*. Aldershot: Ashgate.
Button, M. (2008). *Doing security: Critical reflections and an agenda for change*. Basingstoke: Palgrave.
Button, M., & Dalda, Y. (2014). FACT FINDING REPORT ON PRIVATE SECURITY IN TURKEY Improvement of Civilian Oversight of Internal Security Sector Project. Brussels: United Nations Development Programme.
Button, M. (2012). Optimising security through effective regulation: Lessons from around the globe. In T. Prenzler (Ed.), *Policing and security in practice*. Basingstoke: Palgrave.
Button, M., & Stiernstedt, P. (2016). Comparing private security regulation in the European Union. *Policing and Society*, 1–17. doi:10.1080/10439463.2016.1161624
CoESS. (1998). Case C-114/97. Retrieved from http://www.coess.eu/?CategoryID=325
CoESS. (2001) Joint declaration of CoESS and UNI-Europa on the European harmonisation of legislation governing the private security sector. Retrieved from http://www.coess.org/_Uploads/dbsAttachedFiles/Joint_declaration_on_European_harmonisation_of_legislation_EN.pdf
CoESS. (2004). Annual report. Retrieved from http://www.coess.org/documents/annual_report_2004.pdf
CoESS. (2006). News. Retrieved from http://www.coess.org/
CoESS. (2011). *Private security services in Europe*. Brussels: COESS.
CoESS, (n.d). About COESS. http://www.coess.org/
COESS. (1996). Vocational training in the European security industry. http://www.coess.org/_Uploads/dbsAttachedFiles/Vocational_training_in_the_private_security_industry_EN.pdf
CoESS. (2013). *Private security services in Europe - CoESS facts and figures 2013*. Wemmel: Confederation of European Security Services (CoESS).
COM. (2015). *185.(2011). Communication from the Commission to the European Parliament, the Council, the European Economic and Social Committee, and the Committee of the Regions - The European Agenda on Security*. Strasbourg: European Commission.
Control Risks. (2016). *Riskmap Report 2016*. London: Control Risks.
De Waard, J. (1993). The private security sector in fifteen European countries: Size, rules and legislation. *Security Journal, 4*(2), 58–62.
De Waard, J. (1996). The private security industry in The Netherlands: Developments and future perspectives. *Security Journal, 7*, 227–234. doi:10.1016/0955-1662(96)00176-2
De Waard, J. (1999). The private security industry in international perspective. *European Journal on Criminal Policy and Research, 7*(2), 143–174. doi:10.1023/A:1008701310152
De Waard, J., & Van Der Hoek, J. (1991). Private security size and legislation in the Netherlands and Europe. The Hague: Dutch Ministry of Justice.
Economist, T. (2015, September 26). Mr Saakashvili goes to Odessa. Retrieved October 13, 2016, from http://www.economist.com/news/europe/21667967-georgian-reformer-tackles-ukraines-real-public-enemy-number-one-corruption-mr-saakashvili-goes
ECORYS. (2011). *Security regulation, conformity assessment & certification* (Vol. *Final Report – ume I: Main Report*). Brussels: European Commission, DG Enterprise & Industry.
European Private Security Services Education and Training. (1999). *European vocational training manual for basic guarding*. Retrieved February24, 2015, from http://www.eesc.europa.eu/resources/docs/138-private-act.pdf
G4S. (2016). Who are we? Retrieved January 15, 2016, from http://www.g4s.com/en/Who%20we%20are/
George, B., & Button, M. (2000). *Private security* (Vol. *1*). Leicester: Palgrave Macmillan.

Gimenez-Salinas, A. (2004). New Approaches Regarding Private/Public Security. *Policing and Society, 14*, 158–174. doi:10.1080/1043946042000228906

Goold, B., Loader, I., & Thumala, A. (2010). Consuming security? Tools for a sociology of security consumption. *Theoretical Criminology, 14*, 3–30. doi:10.1177/1362480609354533

Hainmuller, J., & Lemnitzer, J. M. (2003). Why do Europeans fly safer? The politics of airport security in Europe and the US. *Terrorism and Political Violence, 15*, 1–36. doi:10.1080/09546550390449863

Johnston, L., & Shearing, C. D. (2003). *Governing security*. London: Routledge.

Jones, T., & Newburn, T. (1996) 'Policing and disaffected communities'. In *21st Report of the Standing Advisory Commission on Human Rights 1995-96*. London: HMSO.

Jones, T., & Newburn, T. (1998). *Private security and public policing*. Oxford: Clarendon Press.

Jones, T., & Newburn, T. (Eds.). (2006). *Plural policing*. Abingdon: Routledge.

Kasali, M. A. (2012, September). Analyzing the evolution of private security guards and their limitations to security management in Nigeria. *African Journal of Criminology and Justice Studies, [S.L.], 5*(1 & 2). ISSN 1554-3897.

Loader, I., & White, A. (2015). How can we better align private security with the public interest? Towards a civilizing model of regulation. *Regulation & Governance*. doi:10.1111/rego.12109

Ocqueteau, F. (2006). France. In T. Jones & T. Newburn (Eds.), *Plural policing*. Abingdon: Routledge.

OJ C 115/1. (2010). The Stockholm programme — An open and secure Europe serving and protecting citizens. Brussels: European Union.

Okolski, M. (2014) Polish emigration to the UK after 2004. Why did so many come? Migration Research Unit. http://www.geog.ucl.ac.uk/research/transnational-spaces/migration-research-unit/discussion-papers/MOJS%20revise%20041114_accept.pdf

Prenzler, T., & Sarre, R. (2008). Developing a risk profile and model regulatory system for the security industry. *Security Journal, 21*, 264–277. doi:10.1057/palgrave.sj.8350064

Prenzler, T., & Sarre, R. (2012). The evolution of security industry regulation in Australia: A critique. *International Journal for Crime, Justice and Social Democracy, 1*, 1. doi:10.5204/ijcjsd.v1i1.72

Sarre, R., & Prenzler, T. (2011). *Private security and public interest: Exploring private security trends and directions for reform in the new era of plural policing*. Sydney: ARC Report.

Shearing, C. D., & Stenning, P. C. (1982). *Private security and private justice*. Montreal: The Institute on Public Policy.

United Nations Office on Drugs and Crime. (2014). *State regulation concerning the civilian private security services and their contribution to crime prevention and community safety*. Vienna: UNODC.

Van Steden, R. (2007). *Privatizing policing*. Amsterdam: BJU.

Van Steden, R., & Sarre, R. (2007). The growth of private security: Trends in the European Union. *Security Journal, 20*, 222–235. doi:10.1057/palgrave.sj.8350052

Wolfswinkel, J. F., Furtmueller, E., & Wilderom, C. P. M. (2013). Using grounded theory as a method for rigorously reviewing literature. *European Journal of Information Systems, 22*, 45–55. doi:10.1057/ejis.2011.51

Critiquing the regulation of private security in the United Kingdom: views from inside the sector

Rob Mawby and Martin Gill

ABSTRACT

The UK Private Security Industry Act 2001 provided the legal mechanism for the statutory regulation of parts of the private security sector with the explicit aim of reducing criminality in the industry and raising standards. It created the Security Industry Authority as the regulator which commenced operation in 2003. Since then, it has received mixed reviews, and proposals have been forwarded to change its status and the way it works. This paper provides insights from two groups most affected by regulation: security specialists who buy security, and managers and directors of security companies who are subject to regulation and work with its strengths and weaknesses. The paper reports on their views of both the existing regime and some proposed changes. It suggests that the regulator and the industry share similar views albeit there has been a lack of emphasis on what it takes to enhance the ability of the industry to support the public generally rather than just those who pay.

Background

In recent years, there has been a growth of research on private security with the identification of a range of agencies that help provide security nationally and internationally in "nodes" (Loader & Walker, 2007; Wood & Shearing, 2007). The very complex process of coordinating these agencies in the interests of the common or public good is made more difficult by the presence of a private security sector which is accountable to its paymaster and for this and other reasons is seen as a problematic partner in public securitisation (Gill, 2015; Loader, 1997; Loader & Walker, 2007; Shearing and Wood, 1983; White, 2014a; Zender, 2009). Moreover, in the balance between maintaining security and preserving liberty, some have highlighted how the scales have tipped too far in the direction of the former (see, Moss, 2009, 2011). Against a background where private security has been seen to play a crucial role in the crime drop witnessed by much of the Western world in recent years (van Dijk, Tseloni, & Farrell, 2012), and concerns about the effectiveness of regulation regimes, it is unsurprising that private security regulation should be viewed as a topic worthy of more research (Hoogenboom, 2010).

There are a multitude of different types of security regulators, and a similar variety of security regulation regimes around the world (Button, 2012; Button & George, 2006; see also Loader & White, 2015). Statutory regulation arrived relatively late in the United Kingdom but, despite some initial scepticism and debate about the details, was generally welcomed in principle (White, 2010). In the United Kingdom, only some parts of private security are subject to statutory regulation (principally, all manned guarding, close protection, door supervision, i.e., "bouncers," public space surveillance [PSS], i.e., "CCTV operators," and security guarding). The licencing of private investigators is being considered as part of a review of the Security Industry Authority (SIA) by the Home Office but it has not reported yet. It should be stressed too that regulation is fairly recent, following the passing of the Private Security Industry Act, 2001, which created the SIA. This came into existence in 2003 and required every individual conducting security operations in regulated sectors to possess a licence.

It is important to note that the activities of the security sector are vast (Button, 2002) as surveys of the sector in the USA (Collins, Cordner, & Scarborough, 2005) and Australia (Sarre & Prenzler, 2011) have also attested to, and the industry is increasingly multinational (Graham, 2012; Home Affairs Committee, 2012). Indeed, researchers have noted that there are no state security functions that are not also available for purchase privately (Button, 2008; Johnston, 1992). Yet, and perhaps because of this, standards of security service are perceived to be patchy, and some see security as a "tainted trade" (Thumala, Goold, & Loader, 2011). At least part of the reason why regulation gained appeal was the low standards practised by some in private security (George & Button, 2000). This was bad for business and so security company executives saw a need to align their own economic interests with those of the state, "in line with the public good" which included "lobbying vociferously for a system of statutory regulation" (White, 2010, p. 175; see also White & Gill, 2013). Despite the support that regulation had, post-regulation assessments suggest a somewhat mixed view as to whether it has been successful in raising the performance of the security sector (for discussion, see, White, 2015; White & Smith, 2009, 2014), while a focus on drawing out and enhancing the ways in which the private security sector contributes to the public good has not been central policy concerns (but see Loader & White, 2015; Lofstrand, Loftus, & Loader, 2015).

The UK coalition government (2010–2015) was sceptical, at least about the value of the SIA. Indeed, an internal government document leaked to the BBC on 22 September 2010 outlined plans to abolish the SIA as part of the so-called burning of the quangos. Oddly, the SIA was subject to a last minute reprieve which was actively supported by leading representatives of the security sector which quickly formed "The Security Alliance" to represent the industry. The Security Alliance proposed some key principles for a new regulatory regime which were largely supported by the SIA (Henig, 2010). And the SIA effectively supported the government's proposal that recommended its own abolition, or at least suggested that it should be reconstituted as a non-departmental public body as part of "a phased transition" to a new regulatory regime.

The principles of the new regime in England and Wales (but not Scotland and Northern Ireland where different regulations apply) were that the focus on licencing would move from the individual to the business, and with the business being licensed in certain and as yet unspecified areas of the security sector; it would be a criminal offence for these businesses to operate without a licence; and the reconstituted SIA (still to be called the SIA), having approved a company's processes for licencing individuals, would permit it to register its own employees against national standards. At least one idea floated was that they would then join a national register operated by the SIA. Those companies that did not have the desire or otherwise do not want to take in this work themselves could look to newly created mediated access providers to undertake the work for them. So the argument went, because the business would be licensed, it meant the regulator could be assured of minimum standards and so would not need the quality elements of an Approved Company Scheme. Instead, the functions it carried out could be taken over by what was widely referred to as a hallmark scheme and operated by the industry. It was always far from clear who precisely would run this scheme and the ways in which it would be a differentiator and attract the support of buyers. Moreover, there were unanswered questions as to how much responsibility to deploy staff would be permitted. Since the business was to be licensed, the costs would, for the most part anyway, be borne by the business. But what these were to be, how they would be calculated, and how they would be shared between individual and company were unknown.

At the time of writing and with the election of a new government in 2015, no progress has been made on changing the structure and powers of the regime; business licencing has never been introduced.[1] The general principles that received some industry support and which the SIA has been promoting may not be able to be brought about because government priorities rest elsewhere and are focused on a deregulation agenda. The aim of this paper is to understand what those in the industry feel the priorities of regulation to be, and to show that there is some interest within the security sector in looking beyond pecuniary advantage not least because good security, including for the public good, is also good for business.

The research

This paper sought to add some insight from those who were most likely to be affected by the legislative changes, i.e., people who were involved in the buying of security (clients of security companies who represent organisations in the purchasing of security), known herein as the procurers, and the directors and managers of security companies, herein the "managers." A third sample, comprising those who worked as security operatives, mostly guarding, but including those who specialised in public surveillance work and door supervisors, was included in the research but is not covered in this paper. The topics included in the survey were informed by a wide range of sources, including previous (published and unpublished) research in the area; policy documents; discussions with representatives from the security world; two group discussions, one in the United Kingdom with the Members of the Security Research Initiative and one in the USA with a small group of members of Chief Security Officers Roundtable; and four interviews with individuals actively involved in regulation, either of the security sector outside England, or of another business activity altogether. The questionnaire was then constructed, piloted, and distributed.

The questions that respondents were asked to address focused, *inter alia*, on the extent to which the SIA has met its primary aims of eliminating the criminal element and increasing public safety; the extent to which regulations should be extended to sectors not currently covered; views on what the priorities for regulation should be; attitudes towards the priorities that should be attached to key elements of any new regime; and some principles that should guide its operation including the perceived maturity of the security sector in being able to manage aspects of its own governance. Fundamentally, the aim was to better understand how those who worked in security viewed statutory regulation as it then existed and in the context of recent and imminent changes.

The samples were selected via a variety of routes. Unfortunately, there are no databases that contain details of all security personnel from which to draw a sample. Even in the regulated sector, the licencing authority does not have a usable database of officers that are licensed since they have to opt in to be included in mailings and only a minority do so (personal communication). The following outlets were therefore used: the main security media were asked to advertise the study and the key publications did so, sometimes including details in the publications and on their website too; the representative and membership associations were asked to notify members and again the key ones did so, indeed the British Security Industry Association (BSIA) invited its members to participate and encouraged them to involve colleagues; the SIA advertised the study and invited participation via its website and by including a feature in its newsletter, indeed details about participation in the study found its way into various organisational newsletters.

Questionnaires were distributed in early 2012. Replies were received from 209 of those involved in the procurement of security services and 509 managers and directors from security suppliers. Of those involved in the procurement of security, most (77%, $n = 151$) described themselves as security specialists, that is, they managed the security section within the company, and these are the focus of the following section.

By far, the majority were male (88.7%) and white (88.1%). Most were middle aged, with 42% aged 45–54 and 26.7% aged 35–44. In terms of academic qualifications, 34.3% had a postgraduate qualification, 24.3% a degree, 24.3% A levels, and 17.1% GCSEs. Less than a quarter (23.8%) held an SIA licence, although most were members of at least one security-related organisation (82.1%), the most commonly mentioned being the Security Institute (49%), and 27.2% were members of ASIS. More than half (54.3%) worked for companies employing at least 500 staff. Asked in which sectors their company operated, respondents gave a broad range of answers, indicating that no one sector predominated.

Of the 509 managers and directors from security suppliers who took part in the survey, 41.8% described themselves as directors, 26.3% as senior managers, and 31.9% as managers. Here, these are together described as managers unless there are differences between them. Most were middle aged, with 36.6% aged 45–54 and 30.8% 35–44, making them on average slightly younger than security purchasers. Again, though, by far, the majority were male (88.9%) and white (91.6%). In terms of academic qualifications, 20.9% had a postgraduate qualification, 20.9% a degree, 22.2% A levels, and 35.9% GCSEs. Most held an SIA licence (72.5%) and they or their companies were usually members of at least one security-related organisation (69.7%), most commonly BSIA (24.5%), the Security Institute (19.8%), and ASIS (12.4%).

Combined, they demonstrated a wealth of experience in the security industry, with 14.1% reporting over 30 years in the industry, 25.3% 21–30 years' experience, and 37.6% 11–20 years. Most were based in large organisations, with 31.7% based in companies employing at least 3000 staff. Most companies (69.2%) were Approved Contractor Scheme (ACS) accredited, and this was especially so for the largest companies.

Their companies covered a broad spectrum of the work of the security industry, although by far, the most common was the provision of security guards. At least a quarter also described PSS, supplying, installing or maintaining security equipment, and security consultancy as main areas of their business. Not surprisingly, companies providing security guarding, door supervision, PSS, and cash-in-transit services, as well as those involved in the supply, installation or maintenance of security equipment were especially likely to be ACS accredited.

Our two samples reflect a broad range of security service-related senior managers. However, assessing how representative they are of those working in the industry is fraught with difficulty. There are no national databases for any of the samples. Moreover, because the work of the security sector is so varied, the characteristics of workers will vary considerably. Similarly, security companies undertake such a wide variety of work in so many different contexts, what is "typical" or "average" is not easy to determine. Unsurprisingly, therefore, research which has been conducted, typically on small samples, has tended to confirm the variety rather than offer guidance as to what is "typical" or "average." In order to make progress, we obtained details from several sources to compare those who took part in the survey with other populations. For example, a major national security company supplier provided a breakdown of its staff and these were compared to the sample we obtained. Additionally, we sent details of our sample to approximately 20 different people/groups for comment. While any conclusions must be treated with caution, it appears that our samples were not atypical of those working in senior positions in the industry, albeit, males and better qualified staff are overrepresented and our samples are possibly slightly older than might be expected.

Research findings: the clients' perspectives

Managers/Purchasers of security for companies provide a unique perspective on the quality of the services on offer and staff engaged in security. Their views demonstrate a positive assessment of many aspects of the industry but concerns about others. For example, their assessments varied, with close protection services viewed most positively and commercial investigation least positively. Second, in-house services were consistently viewed more positively than contract services. Third, and despite this, the extent to which in-house services were rated more positively varied. It was most pronounced in the case of PSS operators, least for door supervisors.

In the light of these concerns, what solutions are available? Security can be enhanced in a number of ways. In particular, staff performances can be improved through training and better supervision, the industry can be better monitored though regulation and inspection, and buyers and providers can take more care to enter into contracts where the needs of both side (including financial ones) are met.

Security specialists were asked for their views on the adequacy of the training received by the security staff they deployed. With the exception of guards, a large number were unsure. Excluding these, a majority felt that training was at least adequate. However, in the case of guards, and to a lesser extent door supervisors, a large number saw more training as desirable.

The general level of dissatisfaction is illustrated in the following quotes:

> Regulation of minimum standards of training must be widened to include in house staff. Many companies are providing little if any training.

> Ongoing training for officers. Clear progression path. More autonomy for talented officers to support their contract and advise and support clients.

> The perception will never change until there is a standard level of training and development for all security teams both in house and contractors.

> Training has become another way of making money out of the operatives and is being run by companies that don't care on quality. The training side should be taken away from companies and given directly to colleges, universities or security academies.

Training requirements form a part of the requirements built into a regulatory system, but regulation is much broader than this. Regulation and inspection are key issues within the security industry, with proposals to modify and extend the current system vigorously debated. In the light of this, it is no surprise that security specialists presented a variety of perspectives on the ways in which services are – and should be – regulated and inspected, in some cases demonstrating a collective viewpoint, in others uncertainty and disagreement.

For example, asked how successful the SIA had been on three levels, security specialists were extremely ambivalent. Only 35.2% felt that it had eliminated the criminal element from working in the industry, 35.2% that it had ensured that the legal requirements for working in the industry had been enforced, and 29.8% that it had increased public safety. Table 1 illustrates replies in terms of the average scores on 5-point scales, where 1 indicates that the SIA had been successful and 5 unsuccessful.

Criticisms of the SIA and the regulatory system are illustrated in the following quotes:

> Any future regulator should have more teeth than the current SIA and be more proactive in pursuing those who fail to comply.

> Whatever form of regulation is decided on, it must have teeth and must drive up standards in the industry. The only thing worse than poor regulation is ineffective regulation.

> It is important that the priority for security is fully realised and that companies HAVE to be properly licensed in order to operate.

> I think for licensing to be effective it must be backed up by rigorous enforcement and a system of sanctions with real bite. A system of excellence must be just that. Currently the security industry is awash with ex-military personnel (of which I am one) who have no security based qualifications but tout themselves as experts or professionals. They are neither.

Table 1. Security specialists' views of the success of the SIA, where 1 indicates that the SIA has been successful and 5 indicates unsuccessful ($n = 124–125$).

Impact of the SIA	Mean
Eliminated the criminal element from working in the industry	2.92
Ensured that the legal requirements for working in the industry have been enforced	2.93
Increased public safety	3.15

Nevertheless, as Table 2 illustrates, security specialists were convinced of the need for regulation. Regarding four key sectors of the industry that are not currently regulated, over 80% felt that installing security equipment, private/commercial detective work, and security consultancy should be regulated, and over 70% also considered regulation necessary for the manufacturing of security equipment.

While security specialists had some reservations about the operation of the existing regulatory scheme, they were generally positive about the value of regulation. Building on this, security specialists were then asked about the aims of regulation. Table 3 shows that they were very clear that the main aims of regulation should include the development of minimum standards to which companies should operate. They also concurred that the aims of regulation should be to keep people safe, and that licencing organisations effectively would increase confidence in the security sector. However, they did not think that licencing should reduce the cost of security to buyers.

They were also asked for their feelings about how regulation might look in the future. Overall, 76% thought that representatives from the security sector should sit on the council of the regulatory body, and even more (93.6%) felt that all directors of security companies should be subject to a "fit and proper persons" check. However, barely a quarter felt that the security sector was as yet sufficiently mature to be able to manage aspects of its own regulation. Over two-thirds also agreed that the licence fee should include the cost of a strong enforcement scheme, and the same number thought that if the security sector became responsible for assessing competency, it was appropriate that the regulator had a power of veto over standards. A majority of security specialists also agreed that business licencing should provide considerable autonomy to security companies to deploy staff and be responsible for them and that public sector buyers should be required to specify attainment of industry hallmarks in contract awards.

Security specialists also viewed the introduction of a hallmark as a positive development. A large majority of those answering (85.5%) favoured the introduction of a "hallmark" that recognised quality in addition to the minimum standards required by business licencing. And three quarters favoured a scaled award scheme rather than one benchmark. Almost half (45.2%) thought that the introduction of a hallmark would increase public regard for licenced security companies, with only one respondent considering it would have a detrimental effect. However, as the following two perspectives illustrate, the introduction of a hallmark was seen as a positive step, but not in itself sufficient:

I think a Hallmark is a good idea however this would need to be used for every Supplier otherwise it would just become another (standards body).

Table 2. Security specialists' views on whether there should be regulation of the following organisations, on a scale of 1–5, where 1 indicates strong agreement and 5 indicates strong disagreement (n = 126).

Type of organisation	Strongly agree or agree (1–2) (%)	Mean
Private/Commercial detective work	81.8	1.61
Those installing security equipment	85.7	1.66
Security consultants	80.2	1.79
Manufacturers of security equipment	70.6	2.06

Table 3. Security specialists' views on the aims of regulation, on a scale of 1–5, where 1 indicates strong agreement and 5 indicates strong disagreement (n = 124–125).

Statement	Strongly agree or agree (1–2) (%)	Mean
A main aim of regulation should be to develop the minimum standards to which companies must operate	91.9	1.55
A main aim of regulation should be to keep people safe	72.6	1.95
Licencing organisations effectively will increase confidence in the security sector	55.2	2.43
Licencing organisations should reduce the cost of security to buyers	24.8	3.22

Hallmarks and other 'badges' do not increase the quality of the security guard; minimum training standards, rigorous background checks and widespread enforcement by the regulator will increase public confidence in the security industry.

While security specialists had clear ideas about the way regulation and licencing should be heading, they were somewhat lukewarm about the proposals that were in the pipeline, with 28.3% expressing approval and 15.7% negative views. Only 11.8% said they were unaware of the proposals.

In summary, security specialists are largely positive about the security services they procure/manage; over half felt that security added value to their business. They were more positive about in house than contract in terms of quality of service, but more felt that contractors offered better value for money.

But criticisms were also evident. Clients did not view security guarding companies as untrustworthy, but they did express concerns about levels of training. Just a quarter felt that the sector was sufficiently mature to manage its own regulation, indeed even if the sector becomes responsible for assessing competency, over two-thirds felt that the regulator should have a veto over standards. Only a little over a half felt that licenced businesses should have "considerable autonomy" to deploy their staff. Moreover, the verbatim comments of clients suggested an awareness that poor quality of security provided was in part as a result of the low pay levels for security operatives.

There was an ambivalent attitude as to whether the SIA had achieved its objectives, although they generally agreed with what it is seeking to achieve. They agreed that the main aim should be to enforce minimum standards and keep people safe and approved extending it to areas currently unregulated by statute. Similarly, there was support for a Hallmark, and only one person felt this could be detrimental. Moreover, most felt that once it existed, public sector buyers should be required to specify it.

Research findings: the suppliers' perspectives

As the directors and managers of security providers, a management perspective on the services on offer and staff deployed provides an invaluable counterpart to the views of their clients (and their staff). The questions asked of clients and suppliers overlapped considerably. In this section, the focus is on suppliers' views on the implications of regulation including proposed changes and managing staff. The following section highlights similarities and differences between the samples.

Suppliers were asked a series of questions about their views concerning inspection and enforcement, regulation, whether or not hallmarks were a positive step forward, financial constraints, and why they felt companies changed their security suppliers.

Asked how successful the SIA had been on three levels, suppliers – like clients – held mixed views, albeit they were somewhat more positive in each case. For example, 39.9% felt it had eliminated the criminal element from working in the industry (one of the SIA's key aims) and 41.7% that it had ensured that the legal requirements for working in the industry have been enforced. Less (27.8%) considered that it had increased public safety. Table 4 illustrates replies in terms of the average scores on 5-point scales, where 1 indicates that the SIA had been successful and 5 unsuccessful, with a midrange score of 3.00.

Nevertheless, verbatim comments demonstrate widespread unease with the present system:
The SIA are a joke and the sooner it's replaced by the new regulator the better.

SIA needs tightening up on standards in the field, also trainers need to be checked on, there are too many trainers who pass people to keep up the pass rate, the private security industry still has thugs who work on doors and keep the name of decent doorstaff down.
Need more enforcement and checks done by SIA, to force companies to close immediately if found to be doing illegal stuff.

Table 4. Suppliers' views of the success of the SIA, where 1 indicates that the SIA had been successful and 5 unsuccessful (n = 453–456).

Impact of the SIA	Mean
Increased public safety	3.05
Eliminated the criminal element from working in the industry	2.83
Ensured that the legal requirements for working in the industry have been enforced	2.76

There were, however, significant differences between different subgroups of directors/managers in their assessment of the SIA. Those who held an SIA licence were particularly likely to consider the SIA successful. Those involved in security guarding and PSS were also relatively positive, while those working for the smallest companies were more critical. Those working for ACS-approved companies were more likely to feel that it had ensured that the legal requirements for working in the industry have been enforced, but their views were no different to other directors/managers in other respects.

Nevertheless, as Table 5 illustrates, directors/managers were, like clients, convinced of the need for further regulation. Regarding four key sectors of the industry that are not currently regulated, over 80% felt that installing security equipment, private/commercial detective work, and security consultancy should be regulated, and almost two-thirds also considered regulation necessary for the manufacturing of security equipment. However, while clients put rather more emphasis on the need to regulate those installing security equipment, directors/managers prioritised the regulation of security consultants and detective work.

The desirability of further regulation was widely accepted, but it was significantly more likely to be favoured by those in ACS-accredited companies, whereas again those from the smallest companies were less convinced.

Like clients, suppliers were then asked about the aims of regulation. As Table 6 illustrates, they clearly agreed that two of the main aims of regulation should be to develop minimum standards to which companies should operate and to keep people safe and also endorsed the suggestion that licencing organisations effectively would increase confidence in the security sector. In each case, the mean score is well below the 3.00 scale midpoint. At the same time, they rejected the idea of an "elite club" of top end companies. In terms of the costs involved, they rejected both the suggestion that licencing organisations would have the effect of reducing the cost of security to buyers and that

Table 5. Suppliers' views on whether there should be regulation of the following organisations, on a scale of 1–5, where 1 means agree strongly and 5 means disagree strongly (n = 389–392).

Section 1

Organisation	Strongly agree or agree (1–2) (%)	Mean
Those installing security equipment	83.2	1.70
Manufacturers of security equipment	63	2.20
Private/Commercial detective work	86.4	1.52
Security consultants	88	1.55

Table 6. Suppliers' views on the aims of regulation, on a scale of 1–5, where 1 means agree strongly and 5 means disagree strongly (n = 402–407).

Section 2

Statement	Strongly agree or agree (1–2) (%)	Mean
The main aim of regulation should be to develop an "elite club" of top end companies	25.2	3.62
A main aim of regulation should be to develop the minimum standards on which companies must operate	82.3	1.74
A main aim of regulation should be to keep people safe	73.6	1.90
Licencing organisations effectively will increase confidence in the security sector	69.1	2.13
Licencing organisations should reduce the cost of security to buyers	26.9	3.14

businesses should be expected to pay more for their licence to ensure that a strong enforcement scheme was in operation. In terms of the burden of costs for regulation, there was ambivalence about whether or not the poorest performers should bear the majority of the costs for enforcement (27.7%, $n = 112$, in favour and 38.7%, $n = 157$, against) and whether those who had achieved the British/International Standards accreditation should pay proportionately less (33.6%, $n = 136$, in favour and 30.1%, $n = 122$, against). Notably, there were no significant differences between those whose companies were ACS accredited and other directors/managers on whether poor performers should pay more or companies that had followed British/International Standards less.

Suppliers were also asked for their feelings about who should be involved in regulation. As Table 7 demonstrates, the idea that representatives from the security sector should sit on the council of the regulatory body was strongly endorsed, as was acceptance of the fact that all directors of security companies should be subject to a "fit and proper persons" check. However, less than two in five felt that the security sector was as yet sufficiently mature to be able to manage aspects of its own regulation, and the mean score of 2.94, close to the scale midpoint, reflects a divided opinion among suppliers. A majority of suppliers, though, agreed

- that business licencing should provide considerable autonomy to security companies to deploy staff and be responsible for them (with SIA licence holders significantly more likely to agree);
- that public sector buyers should be required to specify attainment of industry hallmarks in contract awards (with directors/managers of ACS-accredited companies significantly in favour) and
- that if the security sector becomes responsible for assessing competency, it was appropriate that the regulator had a power of veto over standards (a widely held view across all subgroups).

Finally, almost three quarters (73.4%, $n = 295$) agreed that the key to the success of a security regulator was the effectiveness of its enforcement regime. However, views were divided as to whether the inspection procedures for the ACS were weak, with 27% feeling that they were, 26.5% disagreeing, and 29.2% undecided.

Suppliers also proffered their opinions on the desirability of hallmarks for the industry. A large majority (78.7%) favoured the introduction of a "hallmark" that recognised quality in addition to the minimum standards required by business licencing, and approval was high from all sectors surveyed, albeit slightly less than among clients. About two-thirds (66.3%) favoured a scaled award scheme rather than one (high or low) benchmark. Asked who should manage the hallmark, opinions varied, although, overall the "inspectorates and certifiers" was

Table 7. Suppliers' views on who should be involved in regulation, on a scale of 1–5, where 1 means agree strongly and 5 means disagree strongly ($n = 404$–407).

Statement	Strongly agree or agree (1–2) (%)	Mean
Representatives from the security sector should sit on the council of the regulatory body	86.3	1.70
If the security sector becomes responsible for assessing competency, it is appropriate that the regulator has a power of veto over standards	57	2.35
Public sector buyers should be required to specify attainment of industry hallmarks in contract awards	62.6	2.20
All directors of security companies including shadow directors should be subject to a "fit and proper persons" check	89.5	1.44
Business licencing should provide considerable autonomy to security companies to deploy staff and be responsible for them	69.2	2.07
The security sector is now sufficiently mature to be able to manage aspects of its own regulation	39	2.94

the most common choice, considered very appropriate by 44%, but there was no significant support for any other option.

Despite suppliers' concerns over quality, however, it was clear that costs were an equally important, and often overriding, concern. Thus, almost two-thirds (64.9%, $n = 262$) felt that "Low margins change the focus of contract security directors/managers from security to cost control." These views were common across the sector but particularly so among those working in PSS. About half (50.9%, $n = 205$) also accepted that, "Security is predominantly a grudge purchase" (more than among procurers), with only 23% ($n = 93$) disagreeing. The wider implications of this were noted:

> Absolutely support the drive to increase standards within the industry but the simple economics of the times we face almost make standards "a nice to have". We have always sought to maintain the highest levels of accreditations to demonstrate to clients and potential clients that we operate to the highest standards. In the current economic climate it is now a serious consideration as to which standards you strive for as the market is not supporting them. Clearly that sets a different conundrum for both suppliers and buyers – how cheap is too cheap and what do you really sacrifice for saving that 10p an hour? We are finding that a lot of new contracts not only minimise the margin but defer large chunks of risk too, so contracts are becoming more punitive as clients strive to get quality but build in claw backs to make sure budgets are hit.

> Main area for the security industry not providing standards of service that are required and can be achieved, is the continued pressure on pricing by most customers. The industry is capable of achieving and delivering way beyond current standards if end users accepted this comes at a price and stop commoditising the industry.

> The industry has greatly improved at all standards but is now severely hampered by cost saving initiatives driven by client procurement and budget management.

Suppliers were also asked for their views on the security staff they employed. In general, directors/ managers felt that training was adequate, although many were unsure, especially with regard to those working in close protection and cash and valuables in transit. However – as with clients – in the case of guards and door supervisors, considerably more thought that current requirements were less than was required.

Like security procurer, suppliers felt that training was particularly important where risky or conflict situations were involved. They were similarly more ambivalent about whether the level of training required should be left to the licenced company rather than the regulator for some tasks like those that did not involve public contact.

In summary, suppliers were able to see the benefits and drawbacks of the current regulatory regime but were more positive than clients. They too favoured regulation being extended to other parts of the security sector. For them, it had been partially successful in introducing important changes to the industry, but less so in generating a benefit that was linked to the overall aim of regulation, such as making people safer. An important caveat here is that those who held an SIA licence, and those who were employed by companies that were ACS accredited, and may be closer to the work of the SIA, were often more positive.

Overall, they agreed with the main aims of the SIA, to reduce criminality and raise standards, and felt that effective legislation increased confidence in the security sector. It is perhaps surprising that they did not feel an aim of regulation should include the desire to reduce costs to buyers. And while they saw merit in representatives from the security sector being involved strategically in regulation, they felt there were limits to what could be expected of a sector that lacked maturity.

A hallmark to identify quality was seen as a good thing, although it seems that the inspection regime will need to be better than the one that currently exists for the ACS (which the hallmark will replace). Suppliers too felt that public sector buyers should be required to demand the hallmark and, predictably, they favoured security companies being granted autonomy to deploy their staff.

Overall, they felt training could be improved. Those who were involved with door supervisors especially felt so. Those involved in managing guards were more positive about guard training even if others were not. The principle that those involved in risky or conflict situations should receive more training was supported, but trusting companies to determine training in other cases was, perhaps surprisingly, less enthusiastically supported. This may be a further reflection of the view that the sector was as yet insufficiently mature to manage too much itself.

Suppliers recognise turnover in the industry as high but felt that this was less so in the companies they worked for. It seems that the reasons rest less with the nature of the work in dealing with risky situations (as is sometimes supposed), and more in working conditions, specifically in terms of pay, limited personal development, and lack of appreciation. These are things at least that companies can control, especially – and perhaps only – with the support of clients.

Comparing perspectives

The preceding sections suggest a degree of common ground between the clients and providers of private security with regard to the need for regulation. Here, we draw these findings together, and where available include the views of security operatives.

The need for sufficient, and sufficiently robust, inspection and regulation is a core concern, both within the wider community and within the security industry. Yet, both clients and suppliers, and indeed operatives, expressed doubts about the current system. While there were differences in emphasis, a large majority of each sample agreed that the main aims of regulation included both developing minimum standards to which companies must operate and the need to keep people safe (Table 8).

However, asked about the success of the SIA, as Table 9 illustrates, the views of directors/managers were less enthusiastic, with clients especially sceptical.

Asked directly, almost three quarters (73.4%) of suppliers agreed that the key to the success of a security regulator is the effectiveness of its enforcement regime. However, views were mixed on whether the inspection procedures for the ACS were weak, with 27% feeling that they were and 26.5% disagreeing. If the new hallmark is to be based on the principles of the ACS, there are clearly lessons that need to be learned.

Most of those asked felt that it was important for the security industry to be involved in the regulatory process, but equally that outside scrutiny was crucial. For example, 72.9% of clients and 86.3% of suppliers felt that it was important that representatives from the security sector should sit on the council of the regulatory body. And 54% and 69.2%, respectively, agreed that business licencing should provide considerable autonomy to security companies to deploy staff and be responsible for them. But less than a quarter of clients and only around two-fifths of suppliers and

Table 8. Percentage of clients, suppliers, and operatives who agreed with the following aims of regulation.

	Clients	Suppliers	Operatives
To develop minimum standards	90.1	82.3	91.8
To keep people safe	73.5	73.6	88.3

Table 9. Clients' and suppliers' mean views of the success of the SIA on a 5-point scale where 1 indicates that the SIA had been successful and 5 unsuccessful.

	Clients	Suppliers
Ensure that legal requirements for working in industry enforced	3.23	2.96
Eliminate criminal element from working in industry	3.30	3.06
Increase public safety	3.43	3.27

Table 10. Views on whether there should be regulation of the following organisations, on a scale of 1–5, where 1 means agree strongly and 5 disagree strongly.

	Clients	Suppliers	Operatives
Those installing security equipment	1.81	1.73	1.67
Security consultants	1.90	1.63	1.67
Private/Commercial detective work	1.99	1.69	1.66
Manufacturers of security equipment	2.04	2.31	2.10

operatives considered the security sector sufficiently mature to manage aspects of its own regulation. Similarly, around nine-tenths of each sample thought that all directors of security companies, including shadow directors, should be subject to a "fit and proper persons" check.

As Table 10 illustrates, there was also widespread agreement that four aspects of the security industry not currently regulated – installers and manufacturers of security equipment, private/ commercial detectives, and security consultants – should be regulated, and operatives largely concurred with the views of clients and suppliers.

When asked, clients (85.7%) and security directors/managers (78.7%) were also firmly committed to the introduction of hallmarks for the industry, in each case expressing a preference for a scaled award scheme rather than one benchmark. Overall, there was considerable support for the principle of licencing and for the engagement of the private sector in it, albeit that some had reservations about too much independent action or action not guided by a worthwhile enforcement/inspection regime.

Discussion

It is evident from this review that for those working in the sector, an enhanced regulatory regime may have much to commend it (although the extent to which any change will be welcomed will always be dependent on price). That stated, there seem more pressing concerns than a focus on business licencing. Clients generally agreed with the aims of the SIA they were ambivalent as to whether it had achieved its objectives: indeed only a minority thought it had. There was widespread agreement that its main aim should be to enforce minimum standards, keep people safe, and to a lesser extent increase public confidence in the sector.

Looking to the future, the value of a strong enforcement regime emerged as important, indeed over two-thirds thought so, and that the regulator should have a veto over standards, while three quarters believed security sector representatives should sit on the council of a regulatory body, and over 9 in 10 that all directors should be expected to pass a "fit and proper persons" check. All this against a background where most felt that the security sector lacked maturity to manage aspects of its own regulation.

They were supportive of extending regulation to areas that were currently not regulated by statute. Similarly, there was support for an industry hallmark, and most felt that once it existed, public sector buyers should be required to specify it in tenders and that overall it would increase public regard for licenced security companies.

Suppliers saw the benefits and drawbacks of the current regulatory regime but were more positive than clients. They too favoured regulation being extended to other parts of the security sector. For them, it had been partially successful in introducing important changes to the industry, but less so in generating a benefit that was linked to the overall aim of regulation, such as making people safer. An important caveat here is that those who held an SIA licence, and those who were employed by companies that were ACS accredited, and perhaps closer to the work of the SIA, were often more positive.

Overall, they agreed with the main aims of the SIA, to reduce criminality and raise standards, and felt that effective legislation increased confidence in the security sector. It is perhaps surprising that they did not feel an aim of regulation should be to include the desire to reduce costs to buyers. Yet, they were not elitist. There was only minimal support for regulation being governed by an elite group and for the costs being borne by the poorest performers. And while they saw merit in representatives from the security sector being involved strategically in regulation, they felt there were limits to what could be expected of a sector that lacked maturity.

A hallmark to identify quality was seen as a good thing, although it seems that the inspection regime will need to be better than the one that currently exists for the ACS (which a hallmark would presumably replace) which was often seen as lacking teeth and operating at a level that enabled those who were unable to offer a quality service to operate within the law. Suppliers too felt that public sector buyers should be required to demand the hallmark and, predictably, they favoured security companies being granted autonomy to deploy their staff.

The private sector is now recognised as a key partner in protecting the public not least because so much of the national infrastructure is in private hands, and also because there is evidence that the private sector can be effective (see, e.g., White, 2014a, 2014b). What is less clear is what makes good security regulation (for discussion see Prenzler & Sarre, 2014). There is much to commend an approach that takes account of the views of those who work in the industry who are committed to the principle that a key aim is keep the public (at the very least, those whom they are charged with protecting) safe, and of models that facilitate looking at the private security sector as moral agents keen to act in the public interest rather than just economic ones seeking the best deal (see, Loader & White, 2015). This study gives some insights into the sorts of issues that will be important in raising standards.

There is of course much ore to be done. The debate about which areas of activity should be covered by different forms of regulations continues. And there is so much more that can be done to learn from the experiences of different countries. Indeed, despite the range of good work that has been done (see, Button & Stiernstedt, 2016), this is an area which merits a greater focus.

Conclusion

Perhaps, the most compelling point to make from this study is that the long-standing debate about whether statuary regulation is necessary has been replaced by an appreciation that the benefits outweigh the costs, even where it is recognised that the current regime has sometimes disappointed in its ability to deliver on its objectives. That said, there is a commitment to extending security provision to other areas and to ensuring that any new regime draws on the best of what exists but seeks to curb the excesses of those in the market who view poor performance as a business model characterised as it is by being able to charge lower prices.

At least some companies, and those closest to the workings of the current regime, recognise that acting in the public good is best for business (White, 2010). The security sector, including both buyers and suppliers, see value in regulation and see the need for higher standards than the government has hitherto been prepared to commit to. Earning the right to be a valued part of the nodes of security governance is as important as it is problematic when you are a private company in existence to pursue profit. In the case of private security, there is some evidence that companies have recognised this, perhaps more than regulators or government, and this represents a new challenge both to those who are sceptical that even a well-intentioned private security sector should play a part in protecting the public, and to others who have dismissed private security as a partner because it lacks credibility.

Note

1. As noted, in 2016, the Home Office undertook one of its regular reviews of the Security Industry Authority. All government arm's length bodies are subject to such periodic reviews and this has yet to be published.

References

Button, M. (2002). *Private policing.* Collumpton: Willan.

Button, M. (2008). *Doing security: Critical reflections and an agenda for change.* Basingstoke: Palgrave.

Button, M., & George, B. (2006). Regulation of private security: Models for analysis. In M. Gill (Ed), *The handbook of security.* London: Palgrave, MacMillan.

Button, M., & Stiernstedt, P. (2016). Comparing private security regulation in the European Union. *Policing and Society: an International Journal of Research and Policy,* 1–17. doi:10.1080/10439463.2016.1161624

Button, M. (2012). Optimising security through effective regulation: Lessons from around the globe. In T. Prenzler (Ed.), *Private security in practice: Challenges and achievements* (pp. 2012). Basingstoke: Palgrave.

Collins, P., Cordner, G., & Scarborough, K. (2005). *ASIS foundation security report: Scope and emerging trends: Executive summary.* Washington, DC: ASIS Foundation.

George, B., & Button, M. (2000). *Private security.* Leicester: Perpetuity Press.

Gill, M. (2015). Senior police officers' perspectives on private security: Sceptics, pragmatists and embracers. *Policing and Society, 25*(3), 276-293. doi:10.1080/10439463.2013.865736

Graham, S. (2012, 12 March). 'Olympics 2012 security: Welcome to lockdown London', *Guardian.* Retrieved from www.guardian.co.uk/sport/2012/mar/12/london-olympics-security-lockdown-london

Henig, R. (2010, 10 July). *A Common purpose – Raising standards in the private security industry.* SIA annual Conference. London.

Home Affairs Committee. (2012). *Olympics security: seventh report of session 2012-13, volume 1, report, together with formal minutes.* London: House of Commons. Retrieved from www.publications.parliament.uk/pa/cm201213/cmselect/cmhaff/531/531.pdf

Hoogenboom, B. (2010). *The governance of policing and security: Ironies, myths and paradoxes.* Basingstoke: Palgrave.

Johnston, L. (1992). *The rebirth of private policing.* Routledge: London.

Loader, I. (1997). Private security and the demand for protection in contemporary Britain. *Policing and Society, 7,* 143–162. doi:10.1080/10439463.1997.9964770

Loader, I., & Walker, N. (2007). *Civilianising security.* Cambridge: Cambridge University Press.

Loader, I., & White, A. (2015). How can we better align private security with the public interest? Towards a civilizing model of regulation. *Regulation & Governance, 22*(Dec). doi:10.1111/rego.12109

Lofstrand, C., Loftus, B., & Loader, I. (2015). Doing 'dirty work': Stigma and esteem in the private security industry. *European Journal of Criminology.* doi:10.1177/1477370815615624

Moss, K. (2009). *Security and liberty: Restriction by stealth.* Basingstoke: Palgrave.

Moss, K. (2011). *Balancing liberty and security: Human rights and human wrongs.* Basingstoke: Palgrave.

Prenzler, T., & Sarre, R. (2014). Regulation. In M. Gill (ed), *The handbook of security* (2nd ed.). London: Palgrave.

Sarre, R., & Prenzler, T. (2011). *Private security and the public interest: Exploring private security trends and directions for reform in the new era of plural policing.* Canberra: Australian Research Council.

Thumala, A., Goold, B., & Loader, I. (2011). A tainted trade? Moral ambivalence and legitimation work in the private security industry. *The British Journal of Sociology, 62,* 283–303. doi:10.1111/j.1468-4446.2011.01365.x

van Dijk, J., Tseloni, A., & Farrell, G. (2012). *Closing the doors: New perspectives on the international crime falls.* Basingstoke: Palgrave.

White, A. (2010). *The politics of private security: Regulation, reform and re-legitimation.* Basingstoke: Palgrave Macmillan.

White, A. (2014a). A crisis of regulation. In C. Hay, D. Richards, & M. Smith (Ed.), *Institutional crisis in twenty-first-century Britain* (pp. 198–217). Palgrave Macmillan.

White, A. (2014b). Post-crisis policing and public-private partnerships: The case of Lincolnshire police and G4S. *British Journal of Criminology, 54*(6), 1002–1022. doi:10.1093/bjc/azu063

White, A. (2015). The impact of the private security industry act 2001. *Security Journal, 28*(4), 425–442. doi:10.1057/sj.2012.53

White, A., & Gill, M. (2013, January). The transformation of policing: From ratios to rationalities. *British Journal of Criminology, 53*(1), 74–93. doi:10.1093/bjc/azs049

White, A., & Smith, M. (2014). The paradox of security regulation: Public protection versus normative legitimation. *Policy & Politics, 42*(3), 421–438. doi:10.1332/030557312X655495

White, A., & Smith, M. J. (2009). *The security industry authority: A baseline review.* London: Home Office.

Wood, J., & Shearing, C. (2007). *Imagining security.* Collumpton: Willan.

Zender, L. (2009). *Security.* London: Routlege.

Common past - different paths: Exploring state regulation of private security industry in Eastern Europe and post-Soviet republics

Mahesh K. Nalla and Anna Gurinskaya

ABSTRACT

In this paper, we explore the nature of the security guard industry with a focus on security guard employment relative to police officer, the diverse legislative guidelines pertaining to the scope of their functions, employment eligibility, training, and legal powers in the new independent and post-socialist countries in Eastern Europe and post-Soviet republics. Findings suggest that despite the rapid proliferation of private security industry in the post-socialist countries relative to the gradual growth experienced in the European continent in many of the new independent states, public police continue to play a critical role in the form of employees of state-owned security guard companies. Further, we find considerable disparity in the employment ratios of police officers and security guards in these countries though not much variation in the rigor of legislative framework for private security guard employment in the post-socialist nations appeared, which was minimal at best.

Introduction

Discussion of the private security guard (PSG) enterprise and issues surrounding the nature of the industry in terms of its growth, regulation, and accountability has been widely researched around the world. More specifically, the growth, demand, and the expansion of private security companies (PSCs) and PSGs in many of these developed and emerging markets were attributed to the neoliberal state policies in security governance, crime prevention, and law enforcement, resulting in privatization of many state functions and the emergence of new public management of security (Ortiz, 2010). In the European Union (EU), which includes some of the post-socialist states, first, PSGs outnumber police officers in at least six countries (Button, 2007), suggesting linkages to neoliberal ideology and market-driven policies. Second, the proliferation of mass private property (Shearing & Stenning, 1981) in the form of gated communities, shopping malls, and amusement parks raised the demand for private police. Third, the transformation of urban centers from office-centric central business districts into commercialised, youth-centric, consumption-driven, night-time economies drew awareness to risk, security, and liability and heightened the demand for security and private police (Hobbs, Lister, Hadfield, Winlow, & Hall, 2000; Loader, 1999).

The PSG industry is a flourishing enterprise, with over 20,000,000 documented security guards internationally (Evans, 2011; van Steden & Sarre, 2011) often hired by entities in both the public and private sectors. The expanding presence and the role of PSGs, acting either independently or in tangent with public police in regulating social life, is reflected in the changing nature of policing in many countries. PSGs engage in similar, if not identical, roles to that of public police, often bringing them in contact with the general public. For instance, PSGs assume special duties, exercise powers, use force, and, in some instances, undertake tasks similar to public police (Jones & Newburn, 1998; Rigakos, 2002; Stenning, 2000), raising concerns over industry standards as they pertain to licensing and training. Experience from the Americas (Nalla & Crichlow, 2017), Australia (Prenzler & Sarre, 1999), the United Kingdom (Button & George, 2001), and the EU (Button, 2007) suggests that states have developed and employed regulatory structures and standards related to regulating the PSG industry and that they are often considered minimal relative to expectations for public law enforcement.

Many countries in Central, Eastern, and South-eastern Europe, as well as some of the post-Soviet republics, have also experienced the emergence and expansion of PSG industries since the early 1990s. The adoption of a market-oriented philosophy after decades of the strict nonmarket economic system (Berend, 2009) with the collapse of the Soviet Union and the disintegration of some of the Balkan states were some of the contributing factors. Further, many post-socialist countries in this region had redefined their policing mission by restructuring their ministries of interior, resulting in the retrenchment of hundreds of personnel employed in state police bureaucracies. The result was the recognition of the rising insecurity and the consequent demand for law and order from its citizens generating the demand for private police. Many of the unemployed former police personnel either became entrepreneurs starting their own PSCs or found work in occupations that resembled their former occupation. Some post-socialist states have incorporated their own PSCs with their ministries of interior offering PSG services employing their former state police personnel (Nalla, Gurinskaya, & Dzmitryieva, 2015). Thus, the structure and functioning of police in the former socialist republics and other Central and Eastern European countries continue to influence the development of post-socialist social control of its citizens, particularly in the context of the emergence of private police.

While the need for PSG industry regulation is widely recognised with considerable attention given to the analyses of the nature, type, and rigor of legislative frameworks in many parts of the world, we know little about these issues in many transitional and emerging democracies in the post-socialist Eastern and Central Europe, Caucasus region, and Central Asia. There have been reviews of regulations on some of the former socialist republics that are currently members of the EU (Button, 2007, 2012) and former Yugoslavia (Sotlar, 2009; van Steden & Sarre, 2010a, 2010b, 2011). However, very little information is available on the nature and scope of private security, nor is the topic widely researched in the former socialist republics including former Soviet republics. One of the limitations is that data are not only not current or accurate but, for some countries, unavailable. Further, where information is available, the material is not available in English. Thus, the focus of this paper is a first step in covering some of these issues, to assess the nature of the security guard industry and regulations in these regions. In doing so, we pay additional attention to countries of the former Soviet Union as well as other former socialist states in Eastern and Central Europe, some of which are now members of the EU. We begin by assessing the employment trends of PSGs in these countries, comparing their strength with the public police, and assessing the legislative framework that governs PSGs' conditions of employment, training requirements, and statutory powers. We caution, however, that the data are limited and, as Button notes, "exploring different systems of regulation can be viewed at best as a snapshot"; and importantly, data are often unavailable or dated and it is easy to misinterpret legal regulations (2007, p. 113). In addition, the best available information for many of the countries in this region is either missing or simply not available. Where data are available it comes from country reports generated by nongovernmental organizations' sponsored research on varied issues peripheral to the PSG- and PSC-related concerns targeted for this paper. Additionally, to the extent possible, most recent non-English language PSG- and

PSC-related legislations were translated by country experts with the exception of Azerbaijan, where online Google translation was utilised as a tool to decipher-related matters on the subject.

PSG industry development in post-socialist Europe

With the fall of the Berlin Wall in 1989, which heralded the end of the Cold War and the dissolution of communist states in Central and Eastern Europe, many of the new republics with centralised planned economies transitioned to market-driven states. This resulted in the emergence of private property and the consequent demand for property protection. In some states, large police forces underwent reorganization and downsizing, resulting in an overnight market for many of the unemployed state police and military personnel (Juska, 2009; Taylor, 2014). The emergence and growth of the PSG industry in the post-socialist countries was not uniform and sustained. Some countries – particularly Poland, Latvia, Estonia, and Slovenia, among others who joined the EU between 2004 and 2007 – made significant strides in economic and political reforms to help transition from socialist modes of governance to market economies. These countries made significant efforts in aligning their PSG regulatory framework to other similarly situated members of the EU (Button, 2007). Similar coverage on the nature of the PSG industry in the other countries in the region was unavailable, particularly the Western Balkan states and some post-Soviet republics that had either a delayed start in shifting to market economies or were subject to civil and political strife.

The growth in private policing services in post-socialist countries has several explanations, some of which were noted above: the decrease of public security budgets, the overall tendency of privatization of previously public services, the introduction of new legal acts, requiring the provision of high standards of security in public spaces (transportation, schools, businesses, and shopping centres), and finally, public demand and increasing terrorist threats. Frye (2002) argues that in countries such as Russia and Poland, private security agencies mushroomed to offer protection to new businesses in the wake of liberalization and the emergence of market economies. Similarly, Volkov (2016) coined the term "violent entrepreneurs" to describe the role that the alliance of the newly emerged organised criminal groups, private protection and security services, and informal protective associations of state security employees played in the making of Russian capitalism. He called them rackets that were euphemistically referred to as private protection organisations. However, the private security industry gradually emerged from the shadows of an informal economy. The greatest gains in the PSG industry are likely to occur in countries that are experiencing growth spurts, as in Asia, Eastern Europe, Africa, and the Middle East, where the market for private security is not only underdeveloped but in great demand (Abrahamsen & Williams, 2005). Data on PSGs from some of these Eastern European, Asian, and African nations find support for this assumption (van Steden & Sarre, 2007).

In some countries, police personnel are allowed to work as PSGs. In the wake of extensive budget cuts and retrenchment of thousands of police personnel, Russia, in its early post-Soviet era, allowed its personnel to work at PSCs while in active service with the permission of their directors irrespective of the nature of the property they are assigned (Born, Caparini, Cole, & Scherrer, 2007; Volkov, 2016). This system was so prevalent that in the mid-1990s nearly 20% of the personnel had dual employment in both the Federal Security Service and PSCs (Volkov, 1999). Other examples of role conflict include instances where both PSCs and public police work at the same sites (e.g., sporting events) with each having their own responsibilities: private security for site security and public police for preventing riots as in countries such as in Croatia, Kosovo, and Bulgaria.

The supply side of security in response to the demand in some post-socialist countries was quickly taken over by organised crime (Volkov, 1999). But most countries in this region enacted legislation creating PSCs run by the state with former police and military personnel as employees. These developments resulted in the mushrooming of PSCs that were entirely private and independent of the state ownership. In other words, state-run PSCs became competitors, often bringing them in conflict with other privately owned guard companies. In some countries, such as Albania, in the formative years, the number of guards employed by PSCs in the country was limited to no more than 5% of the country's police personnel. Weak legislation, inadequate oversight of PSCs, and state-owned PSCs competing with regular PSCs may have contributed to a booming grey market in PSGs in these countries.

In the Balkan region, the early development of the industry witnessed PSCs' strong ties to organised criminal groups that not only provided protection to small businesses but also engaged in illegal activities such as extortion, shakedowns, and violence. For instance, in Serbia, tens of thousands of unlicensed armed guards, some of them with criminal records, work as security guards (Dojčinović, n.d.). These developments were further complicated by the fact that with the downsizing of national military and police security services, governments have created their own commercial PSCs who compete with government-regulated PSCs (Born et al., 2007). Kosovo, Macedonia, and Montenegro share similar historical origins of PSCs.

In Albania, PSCs emerged in 1993 and grew to 269 companies employing 4093 guards in 2004 (Born et al., 2007; Small Arms Survey, 2011). By 2015 there were 8911 compared to 10,998 Albanian Security Police officers: However, estimates of grey market employment puts the number at about an additional 1000 guards (Dyrmishi & Madhi, 2015). Initially, when Albania introduced PSCs, the law mandated that private security personnel could not exceed 5% of the size of public police (Born et al., 2007).

Bosnia and Herzegovina also experienced the growth of PSCs in the early 1990s with a very rigid localised regulation of the industry by local government that made the nationwide emergence of PSCs fraught with complications. In 2004, there were an estimated 41 companies employing about 2000 personnel (Head, SEESAC, & Brigada, 2005). In Serbia in 2015, there were 600 registered companies employing an estimated workforce of 40,000–50,000. Nearly 50% of the contracts were with public institutions or companies and 30% with unregistered personnel (Petrović & Milošević, 2015). Grey market demand for unauthorised and unlicensed guards or moonlighting police officers is relatively high in these counties because of the risky nature of jobs in specific industries (e.g., bouncers in bars, debt collection, etc.) and poor wages (Petrović & Milošević, 2015). Foreign PSCs such as Securitas and G4S are major players in the market and compete with state-owned PSCs (Petrović & Milošević, 2015).

Relative to other countries in the Balkan region, PSCs in Kosovo that began to emerge after the conflict ended in 1999 were largely unregulated. In 2009, the personnel employed in PSCs were 4500 relative to 8000 police officers, but by 2014 there were 109 companies employing 5041 for basic security services, cash-in transit, and electronic surveillance of property services which excludes an estimated 20–30% of the grey market (Emini & Vrajolli, 2015).

PSG employment

The Confederation of European Security Services (CoESS), a clearinghouse located in Belgium, compiles data from the 27 EU states, some of which are located in the post-socialist Central and Eastern Europe. CoESS's comprehensive data on private security include guard employment as well as legislative provisions for PSGs as they relate to minimum qualifications, special powers, and training requirements. In recent years, CoESS (2013) has also begun to gather data from seven other countries that include Bosnia and Herzegovina, Bulgaria, Croatia, Romania, and Serbia. In addition to the CoESS data, some details on the nature of the PSG industry in the former Yugoslavia are available through the efforts of the South Eastern and Eastern Europe Clearinghouse for the Control of Small Arms and Light Weapons (SEESAC) and other independent sources. Drawing off the work of SEESAC, employment trends of the industry in the former Yugoslavia are available (van Steden & Sarre, 2010a), but discussions on the legislative framework that guides the industry are lacking.

In general, PSG employment data were largely unavailable until the late 1990s and the subsequent data are rather sketchy. In a 1999 European survey, de Waard (1999) observed that approximately 592,050 personnel were deployed in the 27 participant countries. The only countries from Eastern Europe included in this study were Bulgaria (475 security personnel per 100,000 population), Lithuania (121/100,000), Poland (26/100,000), and Czech Republic (10/100,000). This survey was the most extensive research of its kind at the time. However, a later study on security guard employment in Europe (van Steden & Sarre, 2007) included data from eight Eastern European countries based on available data from the early 2000s. Included in this study were Czech Republic (N = 28,100; 1/363 [security guard per population]), Estonia (N = 4,900; 1/286), Hungary (N = 80,000; 1/125), Latvia (N = 5,000; 1/460), Lithuania (N = 10,000; 1/360), Poland (N = 200,000; 1/193), Slovakia (N = 20,840; 1/259), and Slovenia (N = 4,500; 1/444).

The employment data for the current study come from the CoESS (2013) report on EU member countries that include some post-socialist countries as well. But this information is not comprehensive as it does not include data for Albania, Georgia, Kosovo, Moldova, Montenegro, Russia, and Ukraine, among others. Data for these countries (Table 1) were compiled from independent sources for years ranging from Moldova (2000), Kosovo (2014), Georgia (2006), Montenegro (2007), Russia (2015), Ukraine (2006), and other single country reports. Employment figures were not available for Belarus as well as the six former Soviet republics in Central Asia with the exception of Kazakhstan. Table 1 provides information on the number of security guards, number of guards who can carry a firearm, security guards per population, police officer per population, and the ratio between police officers and security guards per population. The data come from sources that were collected between 2009 and 2015. Table 1 also shows the range in rate of PSG per population, providing an opportunity to identify countries with higher rates of guards per population as well as in comparison with police officers. Countries that have the highest number of PSGs (fewer than one per 200 residents) per population include Latvia (1/105), Hungary (1/125), Bulgaria (1/132), Poland (1/155), and Romania (1/176). Countries with one security guard per 200–300 residents are Czech Republic and Russia (1/199 each), Croatia (1/249), Serbia (1/240), Estonia (1/289), and Lithuania (1/294). Countries with one security guard per 300–500 residents are Albania (1/325), Macedonia (1/307), Slovakia (1/314), Slovenia (1/326), Moldova (1/339), Montenegro (1/347), Georgia (1/439), and Kosovo (1/662). Only two countries, Bosnia and Herzegovina (1/1,075) and Ukraine (1/1,418), have the smallest ratios of security guards per residents exceeding 1,000 residents. Independent reports suggest that Armenia has 1242 (Johannes, 2009) or one guard per 2415 residents and Kazakhstan has 77,500 (Marat, 2012) PSGs or one guard per 231 citizens. However, data for the number of police officers in Armenia are unavailable. Armenia had an estimated 1242 PSGs in 2009 employed by 18 PSCs (Johannes, 2009). Uzbekistan does not have any PSG legislation but PSCs operate openly, while Kyrgyzstan has 350 registered PSCs (Marat, 2012) while the chairperson of the Union of Security and Detective Agencies estimated 100,000 security guards working in the country (Sultanov, 2016). Data from Uzbekistan are unknown as the country banned private security agencies in 2014 (Azizov, 2014).

Data on PSG employment in some of these countries have to be carefully considered. Apart from the reliability, compared to the data from EU member states, including those from post-socialist nations, there appears to be a larger grey market for PSGs in the less developed countries in the region. Employment data for PSGs from CoESS data differ significantly from independent estimates. For instance, in Albania there are an estimated 1000 personnel engaged in similar work who are not counted as guards (Dyrmishi & Madhi, 2015). In Bulgaria, the National Statistical Institute data puts the PSG number at 67,800. However, the Ministry of Labor estimates are at 120,000–130,000 and the unions' estimates are around 180,000–200,000 (Dzhekova & Rusev, 2015). In Kosovo, the official PSG number does not account for nearly 20–30% who are part of the grey market (Emini & Vrajolli, 2015); in Serbia about 30% of

Table 1. Security guards versus police officer employment in post-socialist nations (2013).[a]

Country	Number of security personnel	Population per security guard	Population per police officer	Security guards per police officer
Albania[b] (2015)	8,911	325	263	0.81
Armenia[c]	1,242	2,415	NA	NA
Azerbaijan[d]	NA	NA	726	NA
Belarus	NA	NA	NA	NA
Bosnia and Herzegovina	3,576 [4,207]	1,075	217	0.20
Bulgaria	57,146	132	155	1.7
Croatia	±16,053	249	205	0.82
Czech Republic	51,542	203	238	1.72
Estonia (2007)	±6,000	224	419	1.87
Georgia[e]	10,000	439	147	0.34
Hungary	±80,000	125	380	3.04
Kazakhstan[f,g]	77,500	231	417	0.55
Kosovo[h] (2014)	5,041	662	296	0.48
Kyrgyzstan[f]	100,000	60	NA	NA
Latvia	21,500	105	300	2.86
Lithuania	11,000	294	290	0.99
Macedonia	2,878	734	213	0.29
Moldova[i] (2000)	10,000	339	252	1.59
Montenegro[i] (2007)	1,900	347	156	0.45
Poland (2007)	250,000	155	377	2.43
Romania	61,200	176	350	1.99
Russia[g] (2015)	715,600	199	187	0.94
Serbia[j] (2015)	40,000–50,000	240	240	1
Slovakia	±17,200	314	251	0.80
Slovenia	7,520	326	256	0.79
Tajikistan	NA	NA	NA	NA
Turkmenistan	NA	NA	NA	NA
Ukraine[k]	33,000	1,418	268	0.62
Uzbekistan	NA	NA	NA	NA

[a]CoESS (2013) data unless specified. Comprehensive employment data were not available for Belarus, Azerbaijan, Kyrgyzstan, Tajikistan, Turkmenistan, and Uzbekistan.
[b]Dyrmishi and Madhi (2015).
[c]Johannes (2009).
[d]UNODC (2005–2006).
[e]Hiscock (2006).
[f]Sultanov (2016)
[g]UNODC (2015a, 2015b).
[h]Emini and Vrajolli (2015).
[i]Small Arms Survey (2011).
[j]Petrović and Milošević (2015).
[k]Born et al. (2007).

guards are not registered (Petrović & Milošević, 2015); and, in Montenegro, there are about 500 unlicensed PSCs (Born et al., 2007) and about 2000 guards work without permits (Tomovic, 2015). The implications of unlicensed guards and the grey market raise concerns of safety and civility given the opportunities they encounter with regular citizens. Dojčinović (n.d.) notes that in Serbia, often these unlicensed guards are employed by criminal gangs and roam the streets without supervision or state oversight and are engaged in extortion, shakedowns, and violence with no deterrence for their behaviour. In Ukraine, the State Protection Service, a government police organization, had 51,000 officers, offering many of the services PSCs offered (Born et al., 2007) further complicating measurement issues. Comprehensive information for Azerbaijan, Belarus, Tajikistan, and Turkmenistan was not available for all categories listed in this table. However, data from independent sources suggest that while Azerbaijan has 726 people per police officer (UNODC, 2005–2006), research also suggests that shopkeepers pay protection money to local police, a service something akin to having PSGs (Gorta, 2009).

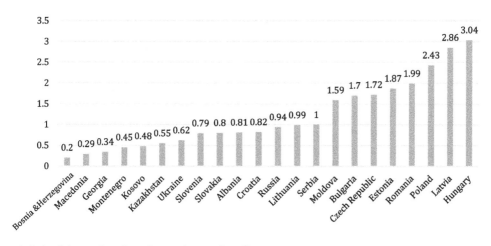

Figure 1. Ratio of the number of security guards per police officer.

Figure 1 provides data on comparisons between police officer and security guard ratios, that is, relative to the size of public police whether PSGs strength is higher or lower. The data demonstrate that post-socialist countries also vary in terms of the guards per police employment ratios. For instance, Hungary has the highest PSGs per police officer ratio of 3.04, that is, there are three security guards employed for every one public police officer. This is followed by Latvia (2.86:1), Poland (2.43:1), Romania (1.99:1), Estonia (1.87:1), Czech Republic (1.72:1), Bulgaria (1.70:1), and Moldova (1.87:1), where there are more security guards employed per public police officer. Countries where there are equal or fewer security guards versus police officers are Serbia (1:1), Lithuania (0.99:1), Russia (0.94:1), Croatia (0.82:1), Albania (0.81:1), Slovakia (0.80:1), Slovenia (0.79:1), Ukraine (0.62:1), Kazakhstan (0.55:1), Kosovo (0.48:1), Montenegro (0.45:1), Georgia (0.34:1), Macedonia (0.29:1), and Bosnia and Herzegovina (0.20:1). For Serbia, some estimates put security guard–police officer ratio at 1:1 (Petrović & Milošević, 2015), suggesting that, relative to the neighboring Balkan states, the country has witnessed a healthy expansion of the PSG industry. These regional differences in development draw attention to the need to further explore two possible scenarios that lead to demand for private protection. The first factor is governance deficit, which may occur when the state is unable to adequately provide safety and security to its citizens (fragile states), and the second relates to consequence of market liberalization policies, entrepreneurship, and shifts in property relations.

Regulatory framework for the PSG industry

In the following sections, we will evaluate the regulatory framework for PSCs and their employees on a range of issues that include minimum standards for employment, licensing, rights, privileges, and training requirements. Among the countries in the Balkan Peninsula, Albania passed its first PSC legislation in 2001. As the market expanded in 2014, a revised regulation was enacted for certification and licensing PSCs and PSGs (Dyrmishi & Madhi, 2015). However, there were no details available regarding requirements and restrictions for PSGs to be eligible for appointment. In Bosnia, the two laws that regulate PSGs are the Law on Agencies for Protection of People and Property in Federation of Bosnia and Herzegovina and the Law on the Protection of People and Property and Private Detective Work (Head, SEESAC, & Brigada, 2005). In Kosovo, the first regulatory framework for PSCs was enacted in 2000 by the United Nations Mission in Kosovo (UNMIK), with basic regulation of PSCs (Emini & Vrajolli, 2015). These regulations strictly prohibited PSCs from carrying firearms. The 2011 Law on Private Security Services was enacted based on the models of many Western European countries, which limited the responsibilities of

PSC employees to avoid infringement on mandates of Kosovo Police (Emini & Vrajolli, 2015). In Serbia, the Law on System of Social Self-Protection (1986) allowed for the operation of small PSC firms, employing no more than 20 personnel. These firms were primarily established by former Serbian police officers. To date, the growth has been rather haphazard, given lack of adequate regulations, which were not enacted until 2013 with the Law on Private Security and the Law on Private Detectives.

Through the 1970s in Bulgaria, several types of PSCs were available as State Police contractors. In the 1990s, such contracts were abolished (Born et al., 2007). The limited information that can be gleaned from the Law on Private Guarding Activity – 2004, suggests that PSCs must have a licence to operate (Dzhekova & Rusev, 2015). In Georgia, a regulatory framework for PSCs, which typically employed personnel to protect pipelines and guard property, appeared to be missing until 2008 as there were only 10 major companies in operation to that point that dealt with guarding property (Born et al., 2007). Both the PSCs and Georgian government run PSCs called Private Property Departments that do not have the right to carry firearms (Born et al., 2007).

Most countries in Eastern Europe require PSGs and/or companies to go through a licensing process and have rather similar standards regarding guards' age, citizenship status, absence of criminal record, and physical condition. The data from the CoESS report (2013), as well as from independent sources where available, are presented in Table 2. Most countries mandate that in order to become a PSG one must be of a minimum age of 18 years with the exception of Estonia and Moldova, where the required age is 19 and 21 years, respectively. Some countries, such as Estonia and Poland, require guards who work in specific areas, such as cash-in transit work, to be 21 years of age. Citizenship is a requirement for some countries, but those like Croatia and Czech Republic who are EU members require at least a valid identification card from any other member country. Some countries allow those who carry EU or European Economic Area (EEA) identification cards.

Details regarding minimum education standards are limited. Romania has the least educational minimum, requiring only a primary education. Bosnia and Herzegovina, Poland, and Serbia require secondary education; Croatia and Estonia refer to basic education; and Russia requires professional education. Information on minimum educational requirements for other countries is not available in current research. Georgia and Moldova specify that public security personnel are not allowed to perform the duties of a PSG (Born et al., 2007). With the exception of the Czech Republic and Slovakia, most of the countries of this region require security guards to have a licence. Moldova distinguishes between guards as employees of the PSC, which do not need a licence, and PSGs that require a licence. It has to be noted that in Russia, Georgia, Ukraine, Kazakhstan, and Moldova, a PSC must be licensed, not the guard. In Kazakhstan, a guard needs a separate licence only if he acts as an independent contractor. Information on these requirements for Croatia is not available. Russia is also the only country in the region that requires guards to be finger printed and photographed. Information on Tajikistan and Turkmenistan was not available. However, for Belarus, Generalov and Gorlov (2001) noted that a proposed bill, *On security guard business in the Republic of Belarus*, envisioned the PSG industry limited to personnel who could use special equipment to guard juridical persons as well as their property and staff. They add, however, that ordinary citizens could avail security services from the security guard association housed in the Ministry of Internal Affairs.

Background checks

All of the countries in the region mandate background checks. However, what constitutes a background check varies from one country to another. We identified at least eight types of background checks, which are presented in Table 3. Information on the specifics of background checks was not available for Albania, Kosovo, Montenegro, Tajikistan, and Turkmenistan. The most common form of background check is verification of criminal record, required by 16

Table 2. Minimum standards and restrictions for security guards in post-socialist Europe.

Country[a]	Citizen or resident	Minimum age (years)	Minimum education	Fingerprint and photo	Background check	Licence
Albania[b]	NA	NA	NA	NA	NA	NA
Armenia[c]	Armenia	NA	Professional training	NA	NA	No
Azerbaijan[d]	Azerbaijan	20	Basic	NA	Yes	Yes
Bosnia and Herzegovina	Bosnia and Herzegovina	18	Secondary education	NA	Yes	Yes
Bulgaria	Bulgaria	18	Middle school and above	NA	Yes	Yes
Croatia	ID card NA	18	Yes	NA	Yes	NA
Czech Republic	ID card	18	NA	NA	Yes	No
Estonia	ID card	19 or 21	Basic education	NA	Yes	Yes
Georgia[e]	NA	18	NA	NA	Yes	Yes
Hungary	EEA	18	Professional training	NA	Yes	Yes
Kazakhstan[f]	Kazakhstan	21	Professional training	NA	Yes	Yes
Kosovo	ID card	NA	NA	NA	NA	NA
Kyrgyzstan[g]	NA	18/21 (for firearms)	Professional training	NA	Yes	No
Latvia	NA	18	NA	NA	Yes	Yes
Lithuania	Lithuania, EU, or EEA	18	NA	NA	Yes	Yes
Macedonia	NA	NA	NA	NA	Yes	Yes
Moldova[h]	Moldova, immigrants with authorization from the Ministry of Interior	21	Professional training	NA	Yes	Yes
Montenegro	NA	NA	NA	NA	NA	NA
Poland	NA	18 or 21	Secondary Education	NA	Yes	Yes
Romania	Romania or EU	18	Primary education	NA	Yes	Yes
Russia[i]	Russia	18	Professional training	Yes	Yes	Yes
Serbia	Serbia	18	Secondary education	NA	Yes	Yes
Slovakia	EU, EEA, or Swiss	21	NA	NA	Yes	No
Slovenia	EU or EEA	18	NA	NA	Yes	Yes
Ukraine[j]	Ukraine	18	Appropriate education or training	NA	Yes	Yes
Uzbekistan[k]	NA	20	Appropriate education	NA	Yes	Yes

[a]CoESS (2013) data unless specified.
[b]Dyrmishi and Madhi (2015).
[c]The Law of the Republic of Armenia.
[d]The Law of the Azerbaijan Republic.
[e]The Law of Georgia.
[f]Law of Kazakh Republic.
[g]Law of Kyrgyz Republic.
[h]Law of the Republic of Moldova.
[i]Federal law No. 2487–1, "On private detective and security activity in Russian Federation."
[j]Law of Ukraine.
[k]Marat (2012).

Table 3. Background checks required for private security guards.

Country[a]	No criminal record and/or pending trial	Physical fitness and/or mental illness checks	Entrance exam and other restrictions	Language proficiency	Integrity/ reliability check
Armenia[b]	Yes	Yes	Yes		
Azerbaijan[c]	Yes	Yes			Yes
Bosnia and Herzegovina	Yes	Yes	Yes		
Bulgaria	Yes				
Croatia	Yes			Yes	Yes
Czech Republic				Yes	Yes
Estonia	Yes	Yes		Yes	Yes
Georgia[d]	Yes				Yes
Hungary	Yes		Yes		
Kazakhstan[e]	Yes	Yes	Yes		
Kyrgyzstan[f]	Yes	Yes	Yes		
Latvia	Yes	Yes			
Lithuania	Yes	Yes	Yes	Yes	
Macedonia	Yes				
Moldova[g]	Yes		Yes		
Poland			Yes		
Romania		Yes			
Russia[h]	Yes	Yes	Yes		Yes
Serbia	Yes		Yes		
Slovakia	Yes	Yes			Yes
Slovenia	Yes		Yes	Yes	
Ukraine[i]	Yes	Yes			
Uzbekistan[j]	Yes	Yes	Yes		Yes

[a]CoESS (2013) data unless specified.
[b]The Law of the Republic of Armenia.
[c]The Law of Azerbaijan Republic.
[d]The Law of Georgia.
[e]Law of Kazakh Republic.
[f]Law of Kyrgyz Republic.
[g]Law of the Republic of Moldova.
[h]Federal law No. 2487–1, "On private detective and security activity in Russian Federation."
[i]Law of Ukraine
[j]Marat (2012).

countries (Armenia, Bosnia and Herzegovina, Bulgaria, Croatia, Estonia, Hungary, Kazakhstan, Kyrgyzstan, Latvia, Lithuania, Macedonia, Russia, Serbia, Slovakia, Slovenia, and Ukraine). Nine countries have checks for physical fitness and/or mental health (Armenia, Bosnia and Herzegovina, Estonia, Kazakhstan, Kyrgyzstan, Latvia, Lithuania, Romania, and Slovakia), with 11 other countries imposing entrance exams and/or other restrictions (Armenia, Bosnia and Herzegovina, Hungary, Kazakhstan, Kyrgyzstan, Lithuania, Moldova, Poland, Serbia, Slovenia, and Russia). Five countries have minimum language proficiency requirements (Croatia, Czech Republic, Estonia, Lithuania, and Slovenia) and another six countries have strict policies on guard uniforms and identification cards that do not resemble police forces (Hungary, Latvia, Lithuania, Moldova, Poland, and Slovakia). Six countries require integrity and reliability checks (Croatia, Czech Republic, Estonia, Georgia, Russia, and Slovakia). It is not clear in all instances, however, what these integrity checks require and which institutions issue these certificates. Poland specifies establishing integrity from the chief of police of the relevant *Voidoeship* (police chief of the region). Georgian law prohibits employment of security guards who, according to the information provided by the Ministry of Interior, have connections with terrorists or terrorist organizations, illegal military groups, or criminal groups. In Russia, in the event that a state agency performs a background check and uncovers that an applicant is a member of a criminal, extremist, or terrorist organization, the applicant will be denied certification as a guard. In addition, Croatia and neighboring Slovenia require proof of prior work experience while Bosnia and Herzegovina is the only country that requires evidence of honorable discharge from the army. Kazakhstan, Moldova, Russia, and Ukraine require potential employees to prove they do not use narcotics. The countries that have the highest number of background checks are Croatia (5), Lithuania (5), and Russia (5). Most other countries have at least three to four varieties of background checks. Countries that did not have any available information were not included in Table 3.

Training requirements

Nearly 50% of all the countries in this group require anywhere between 21 and 100 h of training, while 18% of the countries require 20 h or fewer. Though most of the countries mandate training from certified training institutes and even specialist schools and colleges, the qualitative nature of the training was not available in our data. Relative to Western Europe, there is a wide disparity in terms of the number of hours of formal training required for security guards in East European countries. Among the countries that demand a higher number of hours (over 300) of training are Hungary and Romania. In the second tier, only two countries, Latvia (160 h) and Slovenia (94 h), appear on the list, while most of the remaining countries require about 50 h of training. In Russia, all security guards must undertake professional training at one of the licensed educational institutions. At least 98 h of training are required for the lowest category of security guards (they are not allowed to use special devices [e.g., batons, etc.]), 174 h are required for the middle category (allowed to use special devices and civil weapons), and 266 h are required for the highest (allowed to use firearms). The number of hours and general requirements for the training programme is approved by the Ministry of Education (2010). The training programme must include a legal component, special training in tactical aspects of protection services, the use of technical and special devices and firearms (including practical training), first aid, and physical and psychological training. Of all the countries in this region, only five countries require a refresher course (Armenia, Bosnia and Herzegovina, Russia, Serbia, and Slovenia), among which Russian security guards must attend refresher training every 5 years in order to prolong their security guard certificate. While some countries, such as Albania, mandate 5 days of training, there is no evidence of supervision to check if training ever occurs (Born et al., 2007). Data for these countries are compiled from CoESS (2013) for EU member states and specific laws for the remaining countries were incorporated either from the specific laws of respective countries or from data sources identified in footnotes of Tables 1–3. Countries that did not have any available information were not included in Table 3.

Firearms and firearm training requirements

A large number of countries in the region have provisions for guards to carry firearms under certain conditions. In Georgia, however, both PSCs and Governmental PSC guards are allowed to carry firearms (Law of Georgia, 2015) similar to Ukraine (Law of Ukraine, 2012). In Kosovo, the UNMIK prohibits guards to carry firearms unless for special assignments (Emini & Vrajolli, 2015). In Albania, weapons must be registered both to the company and to the individual employee, while in Russia firearms are limited to self-defence, or to prevent group or armed attack on persons or property under the supervision of the guard (Born et al., 2007). Further, in Albania, the provisions of Article 17 of the *Law on Weapons and Ammunition* applies directly to PSCs and requires guards must be medically fit, trained in firearms handling, and not have a criminal record (Born et al., 2007). There is a wide range in the number of mandated hours and modalities of training – anywhere from 4 h (Slovenia) to 245 h (Poland). Some countries specify that training be undertaken in police academies (Bosnia and Herzegovina, Estonia, Poland, and Serbia) or under the sponsorship of the Ministries of Interior (Kazakhstan, Lithuania, Moldova, Russia, and Slovakia). A few others such as Bulgaria and Hungary allow guards to receive training from licensed training institutes. Data for these countries are compiled from CoESS (2013) for EU member states and data for the remaining countries were incorporated either from the specific laws of the respective countries or from data sources identified in footnotes of Tables 1–3. Data for Albania, Azerbaijan, Belarus, Croatia, Kosovo, Montenegro, Tajikistan, Turkmenistan, Ukraine, and Uzbekistan are not available.

Special powers for security guards

Generally, the rights of PSGs in these instances do not differ from the rights of any citizen who is witnessing a crime and is determined to seize and deliver the offender to a police station or hold the offender until the police arrive. In some instances, PSGs have very limited power: guards are not allowed to perform any actions that are considered to be the prerogative of the law enforcement agencies: arrest, search and seizure, interrogation, etc. If a person commits a crime at the site where security services are provided or violates the law at the site, a PSG is required to apprehend the offender and immediately undertake all possible efforts in order to transfer the offender to the police. Many countries allow PSGs to use physical force.

Security guards in most countries in Eastern Europe have limited powers of search and seizure. Some countries specify the rights and responsibilities of security guards, spelling out duties, both prescriptive and proscriptive. For example, Slovenia's law states that security guards can issue warnings and request identification. Estonia notes that guards have the right to search and confiscate hazardous items and hand them over to police immediately. Romania allows security guards to act as first responders in cases of fire and disasters. Croatia notes that guards can search persons, vehicles, and objects entering the premises under their watch.

Some countries specify the circumstances. For example, Croatia authorises search and seizure but the search is limited to clothing and footwear conducted by the same gender (i.e., female guards search female suspects). Romania is unique in their allowance of security guards to perform a full search and seizure. Bulgaria, Latvia, Lithuania, Russia, and Poland do not permit security guards to search and seize evidence, while Georgia and Moldova require evidence to be guarded until police arrival. Details on special provisions, rights, and responsibilities are not available for Albania, Kosovo, and Montenegro.

All provisions in the legislation of the countries included in this study suggest rights and special powers proportional to the nature and type of the committed offence. Most countries provide for right to arrest; carry auxiliary equipment such as batons, handcuffs, and rubber and plastic truncheons (as is the case in Bulgaria); and use trained dogs (Georgia, Russia, and Ukraine). Some countries, such as Bosnia and Herzegovina, have more detailed and specific provisions. The law states that use of force is permissible under special conditions such as self-defence, protecting persons or property, or preventing escape of suspects. However, the suspects need to be warned before using force. The laws in Moldova provide similar regulations. Russia has a number of laws and sub-legislative acts that outline the use of force, special devices, and firearms, as well as responsibility for their misuse in great detail. The Criminal Code of the Russian Federation specifies that all actions performed when apprehending the criminals must be proportional to the nature and type of the committed offence and should not excessively harm the offender.

Security guards can typically also make arrests with limited use of force. Croatia, Estonia, Kazakhstan, and Poland give PSGs temporary arrest powers, but they have to report the matter immediately to the police. Kosovar PSGs have citizen's arrest powers with the provision that they also notify the police immediately. Armenia, Georgia, Latvia, Macedonia, Romania, and Russia allow PSGs the right to deny access or evict unauthorised persons from premises. Serbia authorises guards to proactively prevent crime or reactively prevent it if they witness a crime in progress.

Discussion

In this paper, we provide an overview of the PSG industry in post-socialist countries in Eastern Europe and former Soviet republics. More specifically, we provide a framework to compare the nature, size, and the regulatory mechanisms that govern the recruitment, selection, rights, powers, and responsibilities of personnel employed in the industry. Relative to countries in most Western European nations, the birth of PSCs in many Eastern European countries began with a "bang" and not as an evolutionary process. If shifts in governance in the Western capitalist countries occurred because of growth in mass private property (Shearing & Stenning, 1981), consumerism (Loader, 1999), or a governance deficit (Shearing & Wood, 2003), one of the more significant reasons for such transformation is due to unintended consequences of weak states, failed security, and the rapid growth of capitalism that followed the revolution of 1989–1991 and the collapse of the socialist-centred states (Born et al., 2007). Many countries in the region experienced massive retrenchment and reduction in the employment of the state police apparatus, resulting in the demand of secondary social control. This was the case not just for countries in the Balkan Peninsula but was also evident in countries in post-socialist countries in East Central and Central Europe as well as the post-Soviet republics in Central Asia.

Though we are limited in the availability of the most accurate and comparable data on PSG employment, we find significant disparity in the employment ratios with police officers across these nations. This discussion is important in light of the growth and maturation of the PSG industry in developed and more aggressive emerging markets such as Poland, Romania, and Hungary. The presence of a higher ratio of PSGs to public police was attributed to changes in property relations with increases in mass private properties (Shearing & Stenning, 1981) and increased fear of crime and victimization due to growth in night-time leisure activities (Hobbs et al., 2000). Others have argued that these developments can be attributed to the changing nature of the public police's primary role in crime prevention activities in neoliberal democracies (Garland, 1996); deficit governance (Shearing & Wood, 2003); and the development of cultures of consumerism, managerialism, and consumption (Loader, 1999). The commodification of security (Zedner, 2000) has resulted in the pluralisation of policing (Bayley & Shearing, 1996; Loader, 2000), emergence of secondary social control occupations (Newburn, 2001), and multiple governance structures (Wood & Dupont, 2006). Thus, examining the ratio of police officers versus PSGs in the post-socialist countries may offer some insight to the nature of economic development and/or democratization and expansion of the market economies. Yet data from other research (van Steden & Sarre, 2010a, 2010b) suggest that such comparisons may not hold true even in some developed market economies such as Austria or Portugal. However, this issue requires further exploration.

These developments also raise questions relating to the stringency of PSC regulations in these countries. In some of these new republics in the Balkans, as well as in other subregions that include countries like Bulgaria and Russia, among others, operative PSCs and their employees for the most part are early retired or retired police/military personnel whose training and experience offers greater legitimacy and confidence in their services relative to poorly trained PSGs in the open market. In Moldova, the Ministry of Interior has created its own PSC called the State Security Service (SSS), with its employees being former police officers. This unit is self-sufficient, earning over US$11.5 million in 2009, and their guards have more perks than those working as regular police officers (Lazur, n.d.). Further, the SSS in Moldova has the largest number of employees compared to the largest PSC, which has no more than 300 guards, and the Licensing Chamber withdrew permits of 19 PSCs in the last 6 years (Lazur, n.d.). The state is a competitor with PSCs but also has the oversight function, bringing into question conflict of interest.

Another theme we draw from this study is that there is a wide discrepancy in the employment of PSGs relative to public police officers in these countries. There are no clear trends that delineate variations in PSGs versus police officers in different countries. That is, can national characteristics based on political and economic indices help us distinguish which countries would have more police officers relative to PSGs? Data from Western Europe suggest that countries such as Austria, Belgium, the Netherlands, and Sweden that rank high on political and economic indices have a higher ratio of police officers compared to security guards relative to countries such as the United

Kingdom and Ireland, which have the opposite (van Steden & Sarre, 2007). Data from this study also show a wide range in the employment ratios of police officers and PSGs in many of the Eastern European subregions. This is an important issue for future research since these variations may offer insights for understanding the nature of governance, governance deficit, and shifts in policing.

The last theme we note from this review is that there is a significant variation in the regulatory mechanisms relating to PSG regulations regarding recruitment, legal powers, and minimum standards of recruitment and training. More important, the minimum standards that govern security guard employment appear to be rather relative to the responsibility that is associated with their job descriptions. However, these findings are not remarkably different than those found in many nations in other parts of the world. A review of the CoESS report of 2013 shows that there is a fair amount of variation even among the more developed Western European nations (Button & Stiernstedt, 2016). Similar variations are observed in this research as well. For instance, there is a significant variation regarding special powers among Austria, Belgium, Germany, Norway, Sweden, and Switzerland among Western European nations that have limited search and seizure (Button & Stiernstedt, 2016) similar to what we had seen in the countries covered in this research. Future research on the cross-national comparative analyses of PSCs statutory regulations may help offer insights into factors that identify conditions that predict the nature of regulatory stringency in these countries.

Conclusion

We believe that PSGs perform an important task for the state. Though private entities sponsor their employment for protection from crime and hazards, PSGs – if not identical to public police, which is an agency of the sovereign state – play an important supplemental role to the public police. This is particularly true in states where security guards far outnumber public police officers and in states such as those in the Balkan region that are in political, economic, and social transition. Not all interactions between PSGs and citizens can be assumed to be cordial and helpful. By their very nature, security guards are employed to exercise social regulation over citizens. The importance of training and the consequent civil and criminal liability in actions that lead to injury or civil rights violations for both police officers (Ross, 2000) and PSGs (Moore, 1988) has been well established in developed economies. This highlights the cultural context relating to democracy, accountability, and legitimacy measured by citizen confidence and trust in public and private regulatory agencies in mature democracies. Contrary to these measures, as we know from developed economies, existing research on citizen confidence in governance of social order in these emerging and transitory states is limited, barring for a few EU post-socialist nations such as Czech Republic, Estonia, Poland, and Slovenia (Kääriäinen, 2007). Much less is known about the citizen responses to non-state policing activities. Given that the regulatory framework in most countries mandates minimum or no qualifications or training requirements in legal matters, civil rights, or conflict resolution, among others, these are significant issues that warrant further exploration.

References

Abrahamsen, R., & Williams, M. C. (2005). *The globalization of private security: Country report: Nigeria.* Aberystwyth: University of Wales.

Azizov, D. (2014, January 28). Uzbekistan bans private security agencies. *Trend News Agency.* Retrieved from https://en.trend.az

Bayley, D. H., & Shearing, C. D. (1996). The future of policing. *Law and Society Review, 30,* 585–606. doi:10.2307/3054129

Berend, T. I. (2009). *From the Soviet bloc to the European Union: The economic and social transformation of Central and Eastern Europe since 1973.* Cambridge: Cambridge University Press.

Born, H., Caparini, M., Cole, E., & Scherrer, V. (2007). *Regulating private security in Europe: Status and prospects.* Geneva: Centre for the Democratic Control of Armed Forces (DCAF).

Button, M. (2007). Assessing the regulation of private security across Europe. *European Journal of Criminology, 4* (1), 109–128. doi:10.1177/1477370807071733

Button, M. (2012). *Private policing.* New York: Routledge.

Button, M., & George, B. (2001). Government regulation in the United Kingdom private security industry: The myth of non-regulation. *Security Journal, 14*(1), 55–66. doi:10.1057/palgrave.sj.8340073

Button, M., & Stiernstedt, P. (2016). Comparing private security regulation in the European Union. *Policing and Society,* 1–17. doi:10.1080/10439463.2016.1161624

CoESS. (2013). Private security services in Europe CoESS facts and Figures 2013. Retrieved July 17, 2016, from http://webcache.googleusercontent.com/search?q=cache:Yn-i98aIC00J:www.coess.org/newsroom.php%3Fpage%3Dfacts-and-figures+&cd=3&hl=en&ct=clnk&gl=us&client=safari

de Waard, J. (1999). The private security industry in international perspective. *European Journal on Criminal Policy and Research, 7*(2), 143–174. doi:10.1023/A:1008701310152

Dojčinović, S. (n.d.). Serbia: Tracing a fugitive's business deals. Retrieved July 3, 2016, from https://www.reportingproject.net/security/index.php/serbia/10-serbia-tracing-a-fugitives-business-deals

Dyrmishi, A., & Madhi, G. (2015). Albania. In F. Klopher & N. van Amstel (Eds.), *Force for good? Mapping the private security landscape in Southeast Europe* (pp. 7–29). Belgrade: Geneva Centre for the Democratic Control of Armed Forces.

Dzhekova, R., & Rusev, A. (2015). Bulgaria. In F. Klopher & N. van Amstel (Eds.), *Force for good? Mapping the private security landscape in Southeast Europe* (pp. 31–60). Belgrade: Geneva Centre for the Democratic Control of Armed Forces.

Emini, D., & Vrajolli, M. (2015). Kosovo. In F. Klopher & N. van Amstel (Eds.), *Force for good? Mapping the private security landscape in Southeast Europe* (pp. 61–81). Belgrade: Geneva Centre for the Democratic Control of Armed Forces.

Evans, R. (2011, July 7). World has more private guards than police. *Reuters.* Retrieved from http://in.reuters.com

Frye, T. (2002). Private protection in Russia and Poland. *American Journal of Political Science, 46,* 572–584. doi:10.2307/3088400

Garland, D. (1996). The limits of the sovereign state: Strategies of crime control in contemporary society. *British Journal of Criminology, 36,* 445–471. doi:10.1093/oxfordjournals.bjc.a014105

Generalov, V., & Gorlov, S. (Генералов, В. А., & Горулёв, С. Е.) (2001). *Сравнительный анализ правового регулирования частной охранной деятельности во Французской Республике, Российской Федерации и Республике Беларусь* [Comparative analysis of the legal provisions regarding private security activity in the Republic of France, Russian Federaton, and Republic of Belarus] (pp. 51–53). Retrieved July 17, 2016, from http://elib.bsu.by/bitstream/123456789/29363/1/2001_3_JILIR_generalov_goruliov_r.pdf

Gorta, A. (2009). Illegal drug use by police officers: Using research and investigations to inform prevention strategies. *International Journal of Police Science & Management, 11*(1), 85–96. doi:10.1350/ijps.2009.11.1.112

Head, SEESAC, & Brigada, I. (2005, August). *SALW and private security companies in South Eastern Europe: A cause or effect of insecurity?* (2nd ed.). Belgrade, Serbia and Montenegro: SEESAC. ISBN: 86-7728-007-3.

Hiscock, D. (2006). The commercialisation of post-Soviet private security. In A. Bryden & M. Caparini (Eds.), *Private actors and security governance* (pp. 129–140). Zurich: Lit Verlag GmbH & Co. KG Wien.

Hobbs, D., Lister, S., Hadfield, P., Winlow, S., & Hall, S. (2000). Receiving shadows: Governance and criminality in the night-time economy. *The British Journal of Sociology*, *51*(4), 701–717. doi:10.1080/00071310020015334

Johannes, N. (2009). Report on Armenia's private security sector: An outline of the industry's activities, review of current oversight mechanisms and analysis of international regulation good practices. Retrieved from http://www.osce.org/yerevan/75110?download=true

Jones, T., & Newburn, T. (1998). *Private security and public policing.* Oxford: Clarendon.

Juska, A. (2009). Privatisation of state security and policing in Lithuania. *Policing & Society*, *19*(3), 226–246. doi:10.1080/10439460902863329

Kääriäinen, J. T. (2007). Trust in the police in 16 European countries: A multilevel analysis. *European Journal of Criminology*, *4*(4), 409–435. doi:10.1177/1477370807080720

The Law of Georgia. (2015). No 536-IIc. On private security activity. Adopted on November 21, 2008 (amended on March 20, 2015). Retrieved from https://matsne.gov.ge/ru/document/download/19414/1/ru/pdf

The Law of Ukraine No. 4616-VI. (2012). On security activity. Adopted on March 22, 2012 (last amended on November 26, 2015). Retrieved from http://search.ligazakon.ua/l_doc2.nsf/link1/T124616.html

Lazur, D. (n.d.). Moldova's past, present merge in private security sector. Retrieved July 17, 2016, from https://www.reportingproject.net/security/index.php/stories/1-stories/2-moldovas-past-present-merge-in-private-security-sector

Loader, I. (1999). Consumer culture and the commodification of policing and security. *Sociology*, *33*(2), 373–392. doi:10.1177/S003803859900022X

Loader, I. (2000). Plural policing and democratic governance. *Social & Legal Studies*, *9*(3), 323–345. doi:10.1177/096466390000900301

Marat, E. (2012). Regulating private security companies in the Central Asian states. Central Asia Policy Brief. No. 1. The Elliott School of International Affairs, George Washington University. Retrieved from http://centralasiaprogram.org/wp-content/uploads/2015/04/Policy_Brief_1_May_2012.pdf

Ministry of Education. (2010). Decree of the Ministry of Education of the Russian Federation, No. 430. On the requirements to the minimal content of the professional training program for the private security guards. Adopted on April 26, 2010. Retrieved from http://www.umvd56oren.ru/uslugi/lrr/administrativnye_reglamenty_predostavleniya_uslug/prikaz_minobrnauki_rf_ot_26042010_n_430/

Moore, R. H., Jr. (1988). Civil liability for negligent and inadequate training: A private security problem. *Journal of Contemporary Criminal Justice*, *4*(2), 106–118. doi:10.1177/104398628800400205

Nalla, M. K., & Crichlow, V. J. (2017). Have the standards for private security guards become more stringent in the post 9/11 era? An assessment of security guard regulations in the US from 1982 to 2010. *Security Journal*, *30*(2), 523–537. doi:10.1057/sj.2014.21

Nalla, M. K., Gurinskaya, A., & Dzmitryieva, A. (2015, May, 27-28). Exploring the nature of the private security guard industry in Russia: How does it compare with other Eastern European countries? In V. Y. Smorgunova, Y. I. Gilinskiy, & N. A. Isaev (Eds.), *Proceedings of the XXVIII international Baltic criminological conference on Преступность и социальный контроль в обществе постмодерна* [Crime and social control in the society of postmodern] (Vol. 2, pp. 42–53). St. Petersburg: Publishing house "Alef-Press".

Newburn, T. (2001). The commodification of policing: Security networks in the late modern city. *Urban Studies*, *38*(5–6), 829–848. doi:10.1080/00420980123025

Ortiz, C. (2010). The new public management of security: The contracting and managerial state and the private military industry. *Public Money & Management*, *30*(1), 35–41. doi:10.1080/09540960903492356

Petrović, P., & Milošević, M. (2015). Serbia. In F. Klopher & N. van Amstel (Eds.), *Force for Good? Mapping the private security landscape in Southeast Europe* (pp. 83–106). Belgrade: Geneva Centre for the Democratic Control of Armed Forces.

Prenzler, T., & Sarre, R. (1999). A survey of security legislation and regulatory strategies in Australia. *Security Journal*, *12*(3), 7–17. doi:10.1057/palgrave.sj.8340026

Rigakos, G. (2002). *The new parapolice: Risk markets and commodified social control.* Toronto: University of Toronto Press.

Ross, D. L. (2000). Emerging trends in police failure to train liability. *Policing: An International Journal of Police Strategies & Management*, *23*(2), 169–193. doi:10.1108/13639510010333796

Shearing, C., & Wood, J. (2003). Nodal governance, democracy, and the new "denizens". *Journal of Law and Society*, *30*(3), 400–419. doi:10.1111/1467-6478.00263

Shearing, C. D., & Stenning, P. C. (1981). Modern private security: Its growth and implications. In M. Tonry & N. Morris (Eds.), *Crime and justice: An annual review of research* (Vol. 3). Chicago: University of Chicago Press.

Small Arms Survey. (2011). Global private security/police officer personnel levels by country/per capita 2011. Retrieved July 17, 2016, from http://www.publicintelliegence.net/global-private-securitypolice-officer-personnel-levels-countryper-capita-2011

Sotlar, A. (2009). Post-conflict private policing: Experiences from several former Yugoslav countries. *Policing: An International Journal of Police Strategies & Management*, *32*(3), 489–507. doi:10.1108/13639510910981626

Stenning, P. C. (2000). Powers and accountability of private police. *European Journal on Criminal Policy and Research*, *8*(3), 325–352. doi:10.1023/A:1008729129953

Sultanov, A. (2016, September 30). Kyrgyz security firms to contribute to regional security. *Caravanserai*. Retrieved from http://central.asia-news.com

Taylor, B. D. (2014). Police reform in Russia: The policy process in a hybrid regime. *Post-Soviet Affairs*, *30*(2–3), 226–255. doi:10.1080/1060586X.2013.860752

Tomovic, D. (2015). Boom in private security causes concern in Montenegro. Retrieved July 17, 2016, from http://www.balkaninsight.com/en/article/growing-private-police-raise-concern-in-montenegro

UNODC. (2005–2006). Azerbaijan police. Retrieved from http://www.unodc.org/documents/data-and-analysis/Azerbaijan.pdf

UNODC. (2015a). Total police personnel at the national level. Retrieved July, 2016, from https://мвд.рф/Deljatelnost/civil/safety_discord

UNODC (2015b) Data source for the number of police personnel. Retrieved July 1, 2016, from http://www.unodc.org/unodc/en/data-and-analysis/statistics/data.html

van Steden, R., & Sarre, R. (2007). The growth of privatized policing: Some cross national data and comparisons. *International Journal of Comparative and Applied Criminal Justice*, *31*(1), 51–71. doi:10.1080/01924036.2007.9678760

van Steden, R., & Sarre, R. (2010a). Private policing in the former Yugoslavia: A menace to society?. *Journal of Criminal Justice and Security*, *12*(4), 424–439.

van Steden, R., & Sarre, R. (2011). The growth of private policing: Some cross-national data and comparisons. *International Journal of Comparative and Applied Criminal Justice*, *31*(1), 51–71. doi:10.1080/01924036.2007.9678760

van Steden, R. V., & Sarre, R. (2010b). The tragic quality of contract guards: A discussion of the reach and theory of private security in the world today. *The Journal of Criminal Justice Research*, *1*(1), 1–19.

Volkov, V. (1999). Violent entrepreneurship in post-communist Russia. *Europe-Asia Studies*, *51*(5), 741–754. doi:10.1080/09668139998697

Volkov, V. (2016). *Violent entrepreneurs: The use of force in the making of Russian capitalism*. Ithaca, NY: Cornell University Press.

Wood, J., & Dupont, B. (Eds.). (2006). *Democracy, society, and the governance of security*. Cambridge: Cambridge University Press.

Zedner, L. (2000). The pursuit of security. In T. Hope & R. Sparks (Eds.), *Crime, risk and insecurity* (pp. 200–214). London: Routledge.

Private security services regulations in the United States today

Robert McCrie

ABSTRACT

Security services regulations in the United States began formally in the second half of the twentieth century. Many states – never the federal government – first set and then increased, and sometimes decreased, standards over the years. With the shock from the events of 11 September 2001 (9/11) and the subsequent war on terrorism, the pace of regulatory growth increased. Even so, regulations for security personnel – especially security guards – remain at an indefensibly low level with 12 states having no requirements at all for unarmed security personnel and 14 having none for armed. Yet along the way, regulatory pre-employment screening requirements have incrementally improved, training demands, less so. Expecting a security officer with zero-to-a-few hours preassignment training to be a competent first responder, a skilled communicator with the public, a knowledgeable person about applicable law, an informed user of security technology, and a worker educated on the mission and operations of the workplace is not a convincing point of view. The security industry espouses higher standards, including through regulation, but then does not act upon its aspirations. For other security services – alarm installation and monitory personnel, investigators/private detectives, and locksmiths – regulations vary widely according to state. They don't exist at all for security consultants. This article comments on and reviews regulations for all these security services.

Introduction

Security services in the United States have undergone discernible regulatory change in the past two generations, increasingly so since the tragic events of 11 September 2001 (9/11) and the subsequent war on terror. Even the definition of what private *security* means has changed. Up until the 1980s and 1990s, a widely used definition for security was *private people protecting private property*. This was a defensible and logical definition for the time. Private security resources were devoted to safeguarding proprietary assets in many ways and the workplace was exclusively paying for them. Managers in those years thought in fiduciary and material terms, like protection of cash and assets with a liquefiable value. Security program planners and managers didn't care much about an enterprise or institution across the street or down the block. Why should they? That perception now has changed.

A newer working definition for security is *protection of assets from loss*. What are those assets? Most important of all, in a contemporary perspective, are not only people and their well-being – employees, of course, but also customers and clients, visitors, contractors, and anybody else who ambles onto a private protected area. Other assets of significance are like the historical physical ones – merchandise, raw materials, cash, and cash equivalents. Moving into this sphere of protection are computer-related assets – proprietary communications, records, and databases – all of which remain vulnerable to loss, theft, and other types of criminal misuse at any nanosecond the system is accessible. Data security is clearly a critical duty not only of security personnel but also of everybody else who accesses the network of a workplace and has interests of the workplace at heart. Well-established standards and certifications and even international resolutions exist for cyber security policies, programs, and workers (e.g., Chang & Grabsky, 2014; CISSP®, 2017) but no regulations, at present.

The new definition of security is broad enough to recognise other important qualities of contemporary protection operations. For example, interruption of a supply chain puts an enterprise at risk of missing production targets. Protecting it outright or arranging collateral supply sources generally is a security planning function requiring competent service providers to achieve. Further, any failure to assess, mitigate, respond to, and recover from an untoward event could be deemed a deficiency in a security program. Such an encumbrance on normal operations has economic consequences leading to diminished reputation and loss of programmatic opportunity. Additionally, executive and staff personal protection has grown in significance. In all of these circumstances, the theoretical basis of situational crime prevention (SCP) serves as a way of evaluating, implementing, and justifying specific strategies for loss mitigation. SCP argues that vulnerability eventually is exploited; therefore, risk mitigation is an imperative for loss conscious managers (Clarke, 1997; Clarke & Newman, 2005). Attentive security services are required to make these programs a success.

The events of 9/11 and the subsequent domestic war of terrorism have forced a new appraisal of the role private security services plays in civil society. Namely, they have, in many respects, created a quasi-private sector duty to act for the public good, in addition to their assumed proprietary responsibilities. This trend has actually been years in the making, particularly in the case of physical guarding which is often considered as the visible face of private security. A sociologist directed attention to evolving public functions of proprietary protection, using the term *private police*, years ago during a period of rapid security industry growth (Becker, 1974). More recently, two law school professors, Sklansky (1999, 2006) and Joh (2005), liberally again use the term *private police* in referring to such services. Most security business operators and proprietary directors likely would vigorously reject such terminology for security officers, fearing the unwillingly imposed assumption of civil liability from potential negligence if their personnel are considered *private police*. Still, the forced evolving societal role of private security services, though not quite yet a duty, cannot be ignored and in fact might be celebrated as a manifestation of civic responsibility workplaces is capable of, if not willing, to assume. Inasmuch as far more persons are employed in private security than in public law enforcement (over 1 million contract security guards alone vs. about 850,000 sworn law enforcement personnel), the expanded expectations of the proprietary sector is a reasonably understandable development, whether anybody likes it or not, as a reality of evolving public policy.

Such a developing role, for both private and public security businesses and personnel, inevitably must have some connection with clear goals, standards, and regulations of those who own and direct such enterprises and work within them. These terms – goals, standards, and regulations – have different meanings and significance. *Goals* are aims for public policy or desires. They may be well intentioned and possess some urgency but without force of law to achieve them. *Standards* are models or combinations of elements for protocols or performance accepted as being correct. They can be created as an outcome of previously established goals. Standards are significant legally in the sense of defining "standard of care" in tort litigation. But standards usually lack a legislative mandate and a means of enforcing them; tort litigation achieves that goal. *Regulations*, by differentiation, are issued by various government departments and have the intent of law because state legislatures initially have to put them into place. Typically, legislatures will pass a law establishing an intent in a piece of legislation. A state-operated agency with their own staff will develop procedures to achieve the presumed legislative intent and oversee the application of the law (Prenzler & Sarre, 2014).

Regulatory activities, including those that are security related, expanded robustly in the second half of the twentieth century. Surely, regulations didn't come easy to the American economic scene. Regulation meant meeting minimum agreed-to standards that could marginally add to the cost of doing business. Further, opponents to such measures argued that regulations restrained trade, added to bureaucracy, and placed unjustified burdens on business operators. This argument in itself is subject to debate: regulations, it could be argued, can make a type of service more reliable for the general public, by providing better selected, trained, supervised, and managed enterprises and employees. The commercial enterprises providing these services would be operated by vetted managers and principals. The businesses themselves would possess a minimum level of liability insurance coverage. Costs would be lowered over time through greater reliability of the services with fewer untoward events and lower personnel turnover. State regulation meant that government (in some cases independent, adequately supported trade and professional organisations) must create a bureaucracy to receive applications and vet them. The regulations may change over time, reflecting evolving mores and circumstances. Regulatory bureaucracies, further, must provide mechanisms for assuring that regulation compliance is achieved. When registrants fail to meet standards, a means to sanction or even revoke registration is usually provided. That means that staff investigators are normally provided to check on compliance and evaluate complaints.

Documenting and understanding private security services and their regulations

The need for security has existed since time immemorial. But as an organised, sustained industry, private security corporate activity began in the third quarter of the nineteenth century within the United States (McCrie, 2006). Many years were to pass before security services were to face state regulations according to researchers.

The first critical analysis of private security services came from the RAND Corporation (Kakalik & Wildhorn, 1972). The researchers noted at the time that few states regulated any aspect of the security industry. Of those that did, few had adequate staffing. According to RAND, only one-half of the private security regulatory agencies surveyed at the time possessed sufficient office personnel to adequately perform their duties. Some states had only one to five persons working in a division that might be responsible for licensing a dozen to a score or more of business types and vocations involving thousands of people. Further, few adequately supported field investigators of licensing compliance were on staff. Therefore, through the third quarter of twentieth century, licensing provided some government revenues and expressed a sense of what requirements service organisations were expected to meet, but the regulatory measures themselves had little teeth in them. Yet through its publication, the RAND Report had documented the importance of private security activities and beckoned a more discursive follow-up.

Subsequently, a major survey of private security was commissioned by the Law Enforcement Assistance Administration (LEAA), created in an era of trying to understand and combat increasing criminality and urban disorder. This research initiative was funded as part of President Lyndon B. Johnson's broad Great Society domestic program. Along with Medicare and Medicaid and Volunteers in Service to America, LEAA was established to support research on law enforcement processes and procedures and to provide some direct federal financial support for local and state law enforcement. Private security services had never been considered part of the public sector. However, the industry, in its various components, had become substantial and its public impact akin to public service seemed clear enough to justify formal, disinterested query. To facilitate this research, LEAA established the National Advisory Committee on Criminal Justice Standards and Goals. This committee approved a variety of reports on criminal justice practices and challenges and protective issues including the Report of the Task Force on Private Security (RTFPS), published in 1976.

While the RAND Report depended primarily upon the skills of 2 social science researchers, the RTFPS required a research staff of 11 persons, including the well-regarded executive director, Clifford W. Van Meter, and an editorial staff of at least 19 persons. Further, the TFPS was guided by 13 advisory members, including representatives from private organisations using security services, the security industry itself, government representatives, and a judge and an academic. Further, the document lists 14 consultants and over 75 contributors to the final report. This approach aided the RTFPS to achieve a depth of understanding of the industry and its role in society never before available to legislatures or the general public. Also, the federal imprimatur of the document gave it a *gravitas* with its broad perspective never experienced previously (or since!) concerning the security industry. The Task Force provided factual findings and metrics on the operations of private security services and, after considering them, provided goals for different aspects of protective services. These also included standards to be considered and hopefully adopted by state governments for security businesses, the users of such services, and individual security workers. In addition to standards, state regulations were also proposed, though some were already in existence. The RTFPS included an extensive model state statute. The statute required the licensing of all contract security companies, encompassing in its requirements security guards, armored car guards, armed courier guards, and alarm response runners (RTFPS, 15–16).

One of the concerns of the RTFPS was that regulation should provide a light touch on subsequent requirements for security services. The document sought not to press for onerous demands on the field but would propose only that "The standards are considered necessary for the protection of the public." But one standard was unambiguous that each state should regulate the private security industry through legislation to protect the interests of the public without excessively burdening an industry. The RAND Report had earlier expiated on the same issue. A government office would set requirements, issue licenses and later renewals, and register or license private security businesses and the personnel they employed. A specific board to regulate security services alone was advocated. The standards would guide the language and outcomes of the new regulations. These regulatory agencies would report to a state government office and produce an annual report of their performance. The regulations would also provide for means of suspending or revoking licenses and registrations that failed to meet the enunciated requirements. In 1976, 34 states licensed some aspect of the industry, but only 11 had specific private security regulatory boards. The remaining states enforced regulations, if at all, through state police departments, the state attorney general's office, the secretary of state's office, or some other accommodation. RTFPS called for the officers, directors, and partners of small privately held companies to undergo an evaluation by the private security regulatory board as a condition to receive a license. The purpose for vetting such owners-operators was in part to "determine if organized crime has any interests in the business, or if threatening conflicts of interest or other improprieties exist" (RTFPS, 301).

RTFPS reported that 31 states processed 7421 security license applications in that year. The total number of licensed employees in 25 states for which data were available reached 278,165. These included mostly licensed private detectives and investigators and guard, watchmen, and patrol services employees mixed together. How many security workers were employed as employees compared with contract security guard services was not known, though the report mentioned that over 200,000 security personnel were identified in a reporting unit of the Standard Industrial Category, established by the US Bureau of the Census, US Department of Commerce. These numbers would rise dramatically in the years to come. Similarly in the subsequent years, regulatory agencies gained increased staffing, duties, and operational proficiency.

Following the RTFPS, the National Institute of Justice, US Department of Justice, provided grants to Hallcrest Systems, an independent consultancy, to conduct literature searches, to hold focus group interviews with private security and law enforcement practitioners, and to analyse security industry trends. Two studies were authorised. Hallcrest Report I was intended to ascertain the development of security services since the RTFPS (Cunningham & Taylor, 1985). In part, the study sought to describe how private security contributed to crime control and order maintenance and how such services could be improved. Over 400 law enforcement and contractual security workers were interviewed. The report found that police tended to have a negative stereotype towards private security guards due to their excessive use of force and weapons. Further, police reported that up to 12% of their entire service time was allocated to responding to false burglar alarms. Hallcrest I called for upgrading private security, increasing police knowledge of what the private sector was doing, encouraging the sharing of any private security resources with the public sector, and advocated that the private sector should be more fully engaged in validating burglar alarms themselves, rather than drawing upon public services to respond to an alarm condition.

A second research endeavour, Hallcrest II, further updated the material. The industry was continuing to grow rapidly offering diverse services – like guarding, alarm services, investigations, and armored car services – but generally not linked by common ownership of different types (Cunningham, Strauchs, & Van Meter, 1990). However, this iteration also included other issues: the extent of economic crimes impacting the nation, the growth of global terrorist incidents since 1968, and the rising fear of crime that had become an American urban fact of life. Hallcrest II also discussed a matter that had previously escaped the attention of policymakers and the public: how private security provides a social and economic benefit to communities and cities as a whole. Cited was a pioneering study by researchers at Penn State on how private security contributed to the livability of Starrett City, a large residential complex located within then one of the most violent crime beleaguered police precincts, the 75th, in Brooklyn, a borough of the City of New York. Walking across one side of an avenue in the 75th precinct to the side of Starrett City was a difference statistically between substantial risk and safety. Starrett City residents informed researchers that without private security there, the complex would not be safe (89.1%), would be a bad place in which to live (83.5%), and residents responding claimed they would have to change their way of life if they couldn't move out, should private security be eliminated (52.5%). The researchers further calculated that Starrett City's private security saved taxpayers substantial costs for lessening the need for police services (Donovan & Walsh, 1986).

Pressure from the disinterested federally funded research reports just discussed, nonetheless, created an environment that supported further evolution of state regulations. Then, 9/11 and subsequent events caused law enforcement, legislators, and the public at large to regard private security with a sense that it, too, was significant for public protection. Still, no further comprehensive, research-based analysis of the industry was funded or published, though a US Department of Justice funded report summarised the status quo (Strom et al., 2010).

No federal standards for security services have ever been passed or are currently seriously being considered, though bills to support public-private cooperation in security matter have been raised in Congress. Conceivably, in a national emergency, certain private security forces could be federalised for the duration of the emergency. These likely would include services protecting the critical national infrastructure, as defined by the USA PATRIOT ACT of 2001. Yet even with 9/11 and subsequent demands and expectations placed on private security, regulation of security services remains a state's rights issue and not conferred to the federal government according to the 10th Amendment of the US Constitution. [The federal government is a major user of private security services and could set its own high standards for such services but has not led in any discernible way in doing so (e.g., Roberts, 2012).] Nemeth (2012) writes: "The impetus for federal legislation is real and forceful. So much of what the industry does has grave consequences" (30). Yet, that impetus has been slow to activate.

Poulin and Nemeth (2005) noted that state and federal governments are not the only mechanism by which security services might be regulated. Trade and professional organizations, like the

American Medical Association for physicians or the American Bar Association for lawyers, could have a role to play:

> An independent organization such as [ASIS International] or The International Foundation for Protection Officers (IFPO) would be appropriate candidates for accreditation oversight. Although talk of professionalism is rampant, the industry will have to invest in its people and infrastructure. Standards of all sorts must rise. (311)

State regulations of the security industry are constantly in flux, including facing serious challenges for their continued existence that could include selective state elimination or weakening of requirements. Sometimes, state regulatory agencies make significant operational changes that are not well communicated to the various parties affected by or interested in them. Sentiment always exists somewhere to seize the opportune moment and eliminate or substantially weaken hard achieved regulations through legislative *leger-de-main*.

Regulations next are discussed for security companies generally, then unarmed and armed security guards, alarm security personnel, investigators/private detectives, security consultants, and locksmiths. This article concentrates on requirements involving domestically focused security companies, independent practitioners, and services they provide. It does not consider companies or workers providing services and materials for the international war on terror, an entirely different sense of the word *security*. These enterprises almost exclusively serve the federal government and are a separate topic (Krahmann, 2002; Richemond-Barak, 2014; Spearin, 2014). We shall concentrate on the work of private security services and their workers serving domestic needs.

Watch, guard, and patrol services

The largest segment of the security industry in the United States, as measured by employment, public consciousness, and economic importance, constitutes unarmed security watch, guard, and patrol personnel. The economic importance of security guards in the United States exceeds $19 billion in a recent year (Freedonia Group 2015). These workers are the men and women who are present at access points, conduct physical tours of locations, interact with the public, and respond to incidents or events. During emergencies, they may be described as the true first responders. As the demands of the workplace evolved, the expectations of how these security workers should respond similarly have changed.

Over 8000 establishments provide contract private security guard services. Over 1800 of these employ 100 or more security officers, 49 of them, more than 1500 each. Over 1 million contract security guards are employed, unarmed, and armed (Valiant Solutions 2017). In addition, hundreds of thousands more are employed by organisations in a proprietary status. Thus, the private security guard sector alone far exceeds employment of sworn federal, state, and local officers. A recommendation for minimum standards for security officers and companies has been proposed by a committee of ASIS International (Table 1).

Tort law was increasing prior to 9/11, shaping the way by which security services companies operated, including for guarding. One aspect was mandating that security personnel be vetted for any relevant criminal justice history. Other factors, too, were considered significant. By 1982, statutory requirements evolved requiring such factors as a minimum age to be an unarmed guard, proof of citizenship or permanent residency status, a minimum level of education, a background check of criminal records and fitness to work, and a formal training program. That year, 14 states required a fingerprint check and full-face photo and 13 required a background check. By 1998, every measurement showed expansion of minimum requirements by law in those states that chose to regulate security services (Hemmens, Maahs, Scarborough, & Collins, 2001).

By 2010, again minimum requirements had expanded in all states that in any way regulated security guard companies and their employees (Nalla & Crichlow, 2014). By early 2017, a majority

Table 1. Recommended state regulation of private security.

Topic	Recommendation
Regulatory body	Under direction of a state agency for both proprietary and contract security entities
Fees	Commensurate with the need to support processing and enforcement. Administrative fines for violators are supported
Qualifying licensee	Those licensee-in-charge/qualifying agent for both proprietary and contract entities should possess adequate education and experience and pass a written exam
Insurance	Requirements for liability insurance (e.g., minimum of $1 million per occurrence)
Individual registration	Private security officers should be registered/licensed for all private security officers
Background investigation	All candidates must successfully pass a background investigation prior to registration/licensure as a security officer
Training/Unarmed guards	Required to include: pre-assignment training in accordance with all legal requirements; on-the-job training commensurate with position requirements (e.g., 8–16 h) and annual training sufficient to maintain job proficiency (e.g., 8 h). A written and/or performance examination should be passed
Training/Armed guards	The above requirements for unarmed guards plus training in a range and classroom "taught and administered by a state certified firearms instructor or approved current law enforcement or military firearms instructor"

The Private Security Officer Selection and Training Guideline was proposed by the ASIS International Guideline Committee (ASIS GDL PSO-2010). In some ways, it is advanced, for example, calling for a pre-employment drug test and a criminal history check and employment verification for at least the previous seven years. However, an early proposal for 40 h pre-employment training was rejected, resulting in "a requirement for private security officer training" but leaving pre-assignment not specified.

of states required training for unarmed and armed security personnel, though the extent of such training varied substantially. The sweep of changes in statutory requirements for security guard services alone is impressive, less impressively so when the details are closely examined (Table 2).

Regulatory development of security guard services

The familiar watch, guard, and patrol personnel have existed as contractual services in the United States since the third quarter of the nineteenth century. Alan Pinkerton founded his enterprise soon after 1850 (Horan, 1967; Morn, 1982). The Pinkerton enterprise began as an investigative organisation that evolved into becoming for many generations the nation's largest contractual guard services business. The Pinkerton model reflected hierarchy, centralisation, chain of command, but on-site resourcefulness was to inspire the creation of immeasurable guarding enterprises. For most of the twentieth century, organisations hired their own security personnel as

Table 2. Statutory requirements of security guard regulations (N = 51).

	1982		1998[a]		2010[b]		2017[c]	
	N	%	N	%	N	%	N	%
Minimum age requirement for unarmed guards	10	19	21	41	43	84	41	80
Proof of citizenship or permanent residency	9	17	14	27	35	67	47	92
Fingerprint check and full-face photo	14	27	23	47	39	76	38	74
Formal written application used	–	–	–	34	67	–	–	–
An application fee charged	–	–	–	35	69	39	76	–
Minimum level of education required	2	4	3	6	15	29	–	–
Background check required	13	25	20	39	43	84	49	96
Denial for past misdemeanour related to security	–	–	–	–	4	8	–	–
Unarmed training required	2	4	8	16	7	13	32	64
Armed training required	–	–	3	6	16	31	41	80

Growth in minimum required standards for the 50 states plus the District of Colombia (N = 51) shows a trend in increased requirements over a 35-year period.
Sources: [a]Hemmens et al. (2001).
[b]Nalla and Crichlow (2014).
[c]Data derived from analysis of state regulation requirements compiled for the National Association of Security Companies (NASCO) as of 1 March 2017.

direct employees. As the century progressed, businesses steadily decreased using proprietary workers in security positions, turning to the contract sector.

The industry during most of its history was characterised by ease-of-entry for new operators. A retired sheriff or independent business operator was able to open an enterprise with a security guard operation, facing few impediments. A paucity of regulations was one of these characteristics. International developments were to change this. The Cold War (1945–1989) was a term coined to describe the hostilities between the United States and the Soviet Union. Each believed the other was planning world conquest and was amassing nuclear might to achieve national ends. This created a contract industry to serve defence and intelligence needs that required protection with a high order of reliability (McCrie, 2005). Physical security was supported with guards, often armed, who were a routine part of these organisations. Yet, the growth of proprietary and contract security did not result in the rapid evolvement of formal, state-mandated minimum standards for the guards themselves and for the owners and operators of these contractual facilities.

Vetting security business owners and personnel

A critical, even fundamental, aspect of raising security personnel standards is to conduct a background check for past criminal convictions of security business owners and personnel. The process of state licensing always includes access to state criminal justice records. Further, any state legislature that wishes to also may and should include a check of federal criminal justice records maintained by the Federal Bureau of Investigation (FBI). States that license are interested in the fitness of security business proprietors, partial owners, directors, and senior operating personnel. Experience, education, and personal reputation are assessed when most of such individuals apply for a security services business licenses. Office support employees usually are not required to undergo such screening but sometimes do.

The predisposition among human resources managers in non-security-related workplaces today is to not automatically screen-out individuals with a criminal record but not relevant to workplace circumstances. For security positions, however, where trust is essential, the screening-out of applicants with a felony conviction or those with a relevant misdemeanour conviction remains a constant commitment and is, or should be, at a higher level. Vetting for such security positions has evolved with the capacity to search criminal databases. Over the sweep of recent years, particularly since 9/11, issues like employee vetting have advanced. Laws permit states to access criminal records from the FBI. Similarly, state criminal records are available in addition to, or as an alternative to, FBI records check.

Over a 35-year period, statutory requirements for unarmed security personnel grew by several measurements. A required background check was particularly notable, rising from 13 states in 1982 to 49 in 2017. The quality of this check also improved along the way. Initially, state criminal justice service bureaus might only check their own databases for a criminal records history. However, a prospective security guard might be convicted of a misdemeanour or felony in one state, where a record would be discoverable, and then move to another where he or she could seek employment. In such a case, the offense might not be discovered, lacking a diligent background check. The solution was to conduct also a federal criminal records check of the database of the Criminal Justice Information Service (CJIS) maintained by the FBI.

Any state with a legislative mandate could require unarmed or armed security personnel applicants – or for that matter any licensed worker – to undergo a CJIS check. The prospective security worker would be fingerprinted by a local criminal justice agency or an authorised independent service bureau which would transmit the physical or electronic set of prints to a state agency for a state records check. Following this, they would be sent to the CJIS. States may allow security officers to work provisionally until the screening process was completed. If the applicant was found to be convicted of a felony or a relevant misdemeanour, he or she would be terminated immediately, though possibly with the opportunity for appeal. Otherwise, the formal license would be granted.

Licensing always requires minimum standards and the marketplace may demand standards considerably higher than the stated minimum. Therefore, both proprietary and contract security services may require vetting and training that go far beyond the minimums. Some security positions require and provide considerably more training than state minimums. Further, some organisations incentivise workers to develop further security knowledge on their own during employment. Finally, individual cities and cities in states where no requirements are in place may enact and enforce their own regulations for any category of security services worker.

Training of security guards

The TFPS had a clear notion that security guard training should be emphasised. Effective training programs can decrease the time it takes to perform a task, increase effectiveness and efficiency for maximum productivity and positive "bottom-line" impact, improve the quality of products and services, reduce accidents and lower insurance premiums, implement new systems or procedures, and even reduce employee illness and stress through health-oriented work approaches (Lee, 2009, p. 198).

The proposed minimum standard in 1975 called for an 8-h preassignment training course. This would be equally divided into four areas: orientation to the vocation; legal powers and limitations; handling emergencies including during fires, explosions, floods, and riots; and general duties. While the report does not suggest who pays for this training, by default prospective private security guard applicants usually would pay for themselves. In states where such requirements existed, the training would be provided by independent schools or academies whose curriculum would be reviewed and approved by a state agency. From personal observations, some of these schools in New York City for most of the years were absolute shams.

The TFPS added that the employee should be allowed to begin work with the expectation of further training. The standard advises "a realistic minimum of 32 hours of basic training ... recommended in addition to preassignment training. This training should be completed over a 3-month time period and may include a maximum of 16 hours on-the-job training" (103). The report notes that while the 32-h preassignment training proposal may be considered "inadequate" by some, it should be regarded as "a progressive step," pointedly adding: "Admittedly, it is far short of the 400 hours recommended in 1973 for sworn police officers by the National Advisory Commission on Criminal Justice Standards and Goals."

Following 9/11, the US Department of Homeland Security recognised ASIS International for its interest in private security officer selection and training goals and standards and welcomed a statement concerning the organisation's professional opinion on training requirements revisiting its first document published in 2004. The ASIS Standards and Guidelines Commission established a Private Security Officer Guideline Committee of nine persons. Neither termed a goal nor a standard, the guideline provided "recommended minimum qualifications in order to improve the performance of private security officers and the quality of security services" (Private Security Officer, 2010). The guidelines called for state regulation of private security over a variety of topics. In its development, the regulated minimum pre-employment training for security officer candidates was proposed as 40 h, the training standard advocated by the International Federation for Protection Officers (IFPO). The IFPO director, serving as the initial chair of the ASIS committee, expressed the view that her organisation would like to see a national standard of 60–80 h of guard training (Bergel, 2015). However, she resigned the committee when members obstructed recommendation for lengthier training requirements. The committee eventually endorsed only the 8 h pre-assignment training currently recognised. Independently, the IFPO had created a self-paced, facultative training programme for security personnel leading to a Certified Protection Officer designation.

Unarmed security guard services

State criminal justice records checks are the fastest and cheapest for states to conduct on prospective security personnel. But as we observed, an applicant may be convicted of a relevant offense across a state line and never be discovered, assuming that a diligent of the applicant's background was not conducted. Such an inquiry is required by 37 states plus the District of Columbia (Table 3). That leaves 13 states without such a criminal record screen, though, as mentioned, cities could set their own regulations that could require a state background check. In a contrast to just a few years earlier, all these state criminal records checking states now also include an FBI records check, except for Kentucky.

Similarly, training has increased, both pre-assignment and post-employment. The table indicates that 28 states provide basic training, normally in-class and led by an instructor whose curriculum has been approved by a state agency. The length of such training extends from 4 h (two states, South Carolina and Tennessee) up to 40 h (three states, Florida, Oklahoma, and Vermont). Total training ranges from 0 to 48 h (Two states, Alaska and Oklahoma).

Table 3. Unarmed security officers and their requirements.

State licensed	Fed. check criminal database	State check criminal database	Basic training	In service training	Total
Alabama	Y	Y	8	0	8
Alaska	Y	Y	8	40	48
Arizona	Y	Y	8	0	8
California	Y	Y	8	0	8
Colorado	N	Y	8	0	8
Connecticut	Y	Y	8	0	8
Delaware	Y	Y	16	0	16
District of Columbia	Y	Y	24	16	40
Florida	Y	Y	40	0	40
Georgia	Y	Y	24	0	24
Idaho	Y	Y	0	0	0
Illinois	Y	Y	20	0	20
Kentucky	N	Y	8	0	8
Louisiana	Y	Y	8	0	8
Maryland	Y	Y	0	0	0
Minnesota	Y	Y	12	6	18
Missouri	Y	Y	0	0	0
Montana	Y	Y	0	0	0
Nevada	Y	Y	0	0	0
New Hampshire Y	Y	0	0	0	Y
New Jersey	Y	Y	24	0	24
New Mexico	Y	Y	20	4	24
New York	Y	Y	8	16	24
N. Carolina	Y	Y	16	0	16
Ohio	Y	Y	0	0	0
Oklahoma	Y	Y	40	8	48
Oregon	Y	Y	14	0	14
Pennsylvania	Y	Y	26	14	40
Rhode Island	Y	Y	0	0	0
S. Carolina	Y	Y	4	0	4
Tennessee	Y	Y	4	0	4
Texas	Y	Y	0	0	0
Utah	Y	Y	24	0	24
Vermont	Y	Y	40	0	40
Virginia	Y	Y	18	0	18
Washington	Y	Y	8	4	12
W. Virginia	Y	Y	30	0	30
Wisconsin	Y	Y	0	0	0

States with no data: Arkansas, Hawaii, Indiana, Iowa, Kansas, Maine, Massachusetts, Michigan, Mississippi, Nebraska, North Dakota, South Dakota, Wyoming.
Source: Nalla and Crichlow (2014); National Association of Security Companies (NASCO) database, 2017.

Armed security guard services

The RAND study of 1969 found that 50% of both contract and proprietary guards carried a firearm at least 25% of the time. However, the use of firearms declined, driven by concerns of liability to the employer or contract guard company from possible negligent use of a weapon. By 1981, Hallcrest surveys found that less than 10% of personnel were armed, "a dramatic decrease in the carrying of firearms by security guards" (Hallcrest I, 143). By the twenty-first century, the Hallcrest staff project opined that "not more than 5% of private security operational personnel will be armed" (144).

The TFPS proposed that a 24-h firearm training programme prior to assignment served as a minimum requirement. The ASIS International Private Security Officer Guideline left open any minimum proposed requirement leaving the extent of training up to the state. Our research showed 10 states required a discharge report. This indicates a discharge under criminal law in which a first offender, usually, was found guilty of a crime but for which the person does not receive a criminal record of conviction. Then, 36 states plus the District of Columbia conducted state and federal criminal records checks prior to licensing. In 26 of these states, basic training is required ranging from 4 to 48 h. Additionally, 28 states require firearms training on the range, extending from 4 to 47 h. Ten states that conduct criminal records checks do not require basic training and eight such states do not require firearms training (Table 4).

Alarm systems businesses and personnel

Mechanical alarms began providing protection to residences and organisations in the third quarter of the nineteenth century. By the fourth quarter, alarm systems became electrified. From the earliest years, alarms provided a limited repertoire: receiving, acknowledging, and responding if necessary to any deviation in openings and closings and any distress signals. Generally, the providers of monitoring and installation services would not dispatch their own employees to evaluate an alarm condition but rather would contact police or a private security contractor for timely response. Alarm monitoring and installation – sometimes involving systems integration – is now the second largest portion of the private security services market in the United States. Alarm monitoring alone was responsible for $17.1 billion in revenues in 2014; systems integration and management produced another $2.8 billion of turnover in thousands of enterprises (Freedonia, 2015).

Security alarm companies and their personnel have intimate knowledge of the systems they sell, install, and sometimes manage or monitor in commercial and residential properties. It is reasonable as a matter of public policy to be assured that persons engaged in these endeavours do not possess criminal records that could put the security of the customer base at risk. Twenty-nine states have license requirement for security and fire alarm businesses or personnel (Table 5). Six states have licenses for security alarm contractors and installers exclusively. Additionally, 17 states require licenses for some combination of fire protection system businesses, apprentices, installers, contractors, and inspectors.

Investigators and private detectives

Investigators – private detectives or fact-finders – seek answers to questions important for organisations or individual clients. They are adept at finding information on how, when, where, who, and why certain incidents occurred or individuals acted. According to the Bureau of Labor Statistics (2015), employment is over 30,000. The largest percentage is employed in investigation and security services, followed by management, scientific, and technical consulting services; local government; computer systems design and related services; and state government. On a national basis, law firms and financial institutions retain on staff hundreds of investigators.

Table 4. Armed security officers and their requirements.

State licensed	Discharge report	Fed. and state criminal records	Basic training	Firearms training	Total training
Alabama	N	Y	8	4	12
Alaska	N	Y	48	8	56
Arizona	N	Y	8	16	24
California	Y	Y	40	14	54
Connecticut	N	Y	8	8	16
Delaware	N	Y	16	40	56
District of Columbia		Y	NR	NR	
Florida	Y	Y	40	28	68
Georgia	Y	Y	24	15	39
Hawaii	N	Y	8	0	8
Illinois	Y	Y	20	40	60
Indiana	N	Y	0	0	0
Iowa	N	Y	0	0	0
Louisiana	Y	Y	16	0	16
Maryland	N	Y	0	16	16
Mississippi	N	Y	0	0	0
Montana	N	Y	0	0	0
Nevada	N	Y	0	13	13
New Hampshire	N	Y	0	4	4
New Jersey	N	Y	24	0	24
New Mexico	N	Y	8	40	48
New York	N	Y	24	47	71
N. Carolina	Y	Y	16	20	36
N. Dakota	N	Y	12	44	56
Ohio	N	Y	0	20	20
Oklahoma	Y	Y	40	32	72
Oregon	N	Y	12	24	36
Pennsylvania	N	Y	26	14	40
Rhode Island	N	Y	0	0	0
S. Carolina	N	Y	4	4	8
Tennessee	N	Y	4	12	16
Texas	Y	Y	30	10	40
Utah	N	Y	24	12	36
Vermont	N	Y	40	16	56
Virginia	Y	Y	18	32	50
Washington	N	Y	16	8	24
Wisconsin	Y	Y	0	36	36

State with no data: Arkansas, Colorado, Idaho, Kansas, Kentucky, Maine, Massachusetts, Michigan, Minnesota, Missouri, Nebraska, South Dakota, West Virginia, Wyoming.
NR: Not regulated currently.
Source: Williams (2014); NASCO database. 2017.

Investigators and private detectives are licensed in 47 states plus the District of Columbia (Table 6). Training or experience for those states specifying a minimum extend from 500 h to 6 years. Within the more populous states, such licensing is not granted casually. Typically, a retired law enforcement officer can obtain a state license as a private investigator with processing delay but without significant impediments following a background check. By contrast, those without such a law enforcement background are required to work under the supervision of a licensed investigator for a period of time. For example, in New York State, an investigator-to-be needs to have worked in such an acolyte role for at least 3 years. Then, the individual needs to provide investigative case files, indicating fact-finding that began, continued over surveillance or a research period, and ended when the investigator provided a report summarising facts found. Only then will the license be granted, usually many months later.

An untold number of persons work under the supervision of a licensed investigator. The training and education for such individuals may be strictly on the job, with college courses or through brief programs. Sennewald and Tsukayama (2015) note:

Table 5. State license requirements for security alarm and fire systems.

States	License types	Licensing agencies
Alabama	Security alarm installer	Electronic Security Board of Licensure
Arkansas	Alarm system technician, agent manager, monitor	State Police Regulatory Service Div. Private Investigator & Alarm Installation Monitoring
California	Alarm company agent	Dept. of Consumer Affairs, Bureau of Security & Investigator Service
Connecticut	Fire protection journeyperson/contractor	Dept. of Consumer Protection
Florida	Certified alarm system contractor I and II; registered residential alarm system contractor	Dept. of Business and Professional Regulations
Georgia	Low voltage-alarm, unrestricted	Construction Industry License Board
Illinois	Fire equipment employee and distributor	State Fire Marshall
Iowa	Security and fire alarm installers; fire protection contractors and installers	State Fire Marshall. Div. Dept. of Public Safety
Kentucky	Fire alarm system inspector	Dept. of Housing Building & Construction
Louisiana	Sprinkler system installer	Office of the State Marshall
Massachusetts	Fire alarm system installer and technician	Board of the State Examiner of Electricians, Div. of Professional Licensure
Michigan	Fire Alarm specialty apprentice technician; fire alarm contractor; fire alarm specialty technician; security alarm contractor	Dept. of Licensing and Regulatory Affairs, Bureau of Construction Codes Electrical Division
Minnesota	Fire protection sprinkler systems contractor license	Dept. of Public Safety State Fire Marshall
Montana	Fire prevention system installers security alarm installers	Fire Prevention Licensing Program, Board of Private Security Patrol Officers & Investigators
Nebraska	Fire alarm inspector; fire sprinklers contractor	State Fire Marshall
Nevada	Fire protection equipment installers and repairs	State Fire Marshall
New Jersey	Burglar alarm mechanic; fire alarm technician	Dept. of Law and Public Safety, Div. of Consumer Affairs, Burglar Alarm, Fire Alarm & Locksmith Advisory Committee
New York	Security and fire alarm installers	Dept. of State, Div. of Licensing Services
North Carolina	Alarm installer and alarm system business licensee	Dept. of Public Safety Alarm System Licensing Board
Oklahoma	Fire sprinkler technician; CCTV technician; fire sprinkler technician trainee; burglar alarm, commercial fire alarm company manager technician	Dept. of Labor Alarm & Locksmith Div.
Pennsylvania	Fire inspector	Dept. of Labor and Industry; Certification, Accreditation and Licensing Div.
Rhode Island	Fire alarm installer; burglar and hold-up alarm agent	Dept. of Labor and Training Professional Regulations
South Carolina	Fire alarm; burglar alarm	Board of Contractors
Tennessee	Alarm system contractor	Board for Licensing Alarm System Contractors, Div. of Regulatory Board, Dept. of Commerce and Insurance
Texas	Fire protection system contractor; fire protection personnel, firefighter	Fire Marshall Office, Commission on Fire Protection
Utah	Alarm system installer	Dept. of Commerce, Div. of Occupational & Professional Licensing
Vermont	Fire alarm inspector	Fire Safety Div., Dept. of Public Safety
Virginia	Inspector, fire protection systems	Dept. of Housing and Community Development, Training and Certification Office

Source: State licensing regulatory agencies.

Professional specialty societies have formed that offer certifications subject to education, experience, and examination requirements as rigorous as those applied to certified public accountants and other professions. The Certified Protection Professional (CPP) and Professional Certified Investigator (PCI) designations earned through ASIS International, the Certified Fraud Examiner (CFE) designation awarded by the Association of Certified Fraud Examiners, and the Certified Security Consultant (CSC) awarded by the International Association of Professional Security Consultants are four of the gold standards by which modern practitioners in security and investigation are measured and known.... There is still a large number of unprofessional, unsophisticated, and unskilled "investigators" in the security industry. (13)

Table 6. Investigator/Private detective required license and vetting.

States	Criminal history check	License required	Experience/Training
Alabama	Y	Y	
Alaska	Y	Y	2 years
Arizona	Y	Y	3 years
Arkansas	Y	Y	2 years
California	Y	Y	2000 h per year
Colorado	Y	Y	4000 h
Connecticut	Y	Y	5 years
Delaware	Y	Y	5 years
D.C. Washington	Y	Y	NR
Florida	Y	Y	2 years
Georgia	Y	Y	2 years
Hawaii	Y	Y	4 years
Idaho	Y	N	500 h
Illinois	Y	Y	3 years
Indiana	Y	Y	4000 h
Iowa	Y	Y	2 years
Kansas	Y	Y	1 year
Kentucky	Y	Y	240 h per year
Louisiana	Y	Y	3 years
Maine	Y	Y	3 years
Maryland	Y	Y	5 years
Massachusetts	Y	Y	3 years
Michigan	Y	Y	3 years
Minnesota	Y	Y	6000 h
Missouri	Y	Y	2 years
Montana	Y	Y	5400 h–3 years
Nebraska	Y	Y	3000 h
Nevada	Y	Y	1000 h
New Hampshire	Y	Y	4 years
New Jersey	Y	Y	5 years
New Mexico	Y	Y	6000 h–5 years
New York	Y	Y	3 years
North Carolina	Y	Y	3 years
North Dakota	Y	Y	2000 h
Ohio	Y	Y	4000 h–2 years
Oklahoma	Y	Y	1 year
Oregon	Y	Y	1500 h
Pennsylvania	Y	N	
Lehigh County	Y	Y	3 years
Rhode Island	Y	Y	5 years
South Carolina	Y	Y	3 years
Tennessee	Y	Y	2000 h
Texas	Y	Y	3 years
Utah	Y	Y	2000 h
Vermont	Y	Y	2 years
Virginia	Y	Y	5 years
Washington	Y	Y	3 years
West Virginia	Y	Y	2 years
Wisconsin	Y	Y	1000 h

NR: Not regulated currently.
States that neither require a license or criminal records check: Delaware, Mississippi, South Dakota, Wyoming.
Source: State licensing regulatory agencies.

Security consultants

A trend in management strategy in recent decades has reduced the desire for in-house specialists and increased the need for outside consultants to analyse or opine on particular issues. Additionally, new risks to organisations have risen that require assessment by someone with skills who otherwise is not likely to be employed in the workplace where such expertise is needed. That is certainly the case for security where thousands of ex-practitioners, independent experts, and academics offer their services as independent consultants. No state or federal licensing exists for this category of worker. The International Association of Professional Security Consultants offers a Certified Security Consultant designation for those who possess "a combination of experience and education, as well as independence (professional objectivity) and adherence to a Professional Code of Ethics." The examination and requirements "are designed to screen out product-affiliated salesmen who call themselves security consultants" (2017).

People who promote themselves as security consultants usually – but not necessarily – possess considerable relevant experience and have been recognised in their field for their successful endeavours. They are likely to hold pertinent, up-to-date certifications in the field and may have published research-based articles that establish their mastery of their subject expertise. Security consultants who conduct forensic studies and testify to their conclusions in federal court must meet legal requirements of rules of evidence, including reliability and relevancy (Keller, 2004; McCrie, 2004).

Locksmiths

The locksmith is the forgotten service provider in most discussions about protection. Yet, locks are the oldest specifically created security device. A model of a four thousand year old Egyptian pin tumbler lock is on display in the Lock Museum of America in Terryville, Connecticut. In contemporary situations, locksmiths also may be concerned with other types of physical assets protection: chests, safes, and vaults. Increasingly, lock applications have electronics components – demanding a different type of skill but always requiring a high level of trust.

Currently, the Bureau of Labor Statistics reports employment of 17,800 locksmiths and safe repairers (2015). Most of them (72%) are employed throughout the United States in independent businesses and in investigations, the remainder work in educational institutions, general medical and surgical hospitals, and for local government. Locksmiths know the strengths and weaknesses of locks and locking systems – mechanical and often electrical – in locations where they have provided services and even where they have not. They are privy to secret places where valuable assets are stored.

Thirteen states license locksmith businesses and locksmiths: Alabama, California, Connecticut, Illinois, Louisiana, Maryland, New Jersey, North Carolina, Oklahoma, Oregon, Tennessee, Texas, and Virginia. In addition, Florida's Miami Dade County and New York City's five boroughs plus New York State's Nassau County have regulations. Four of them – Alabama, Illinois, Tennessee, and Virginia – require certified locksmith training. Within those states that require licensing, individual cities may establish additional local law. For example, the Los Angeles Code requires a permit from the Board of Police Commissioners, requiring five character references to determine the trustworthiness of the applicant. Additionally, fingerprints of the applicant are furnished at the time of application for a criminal records check (Phillips, 2016). The Associated Locksmiths of America provides a certification programme for locksmiths which is pertinent nationally but which does not rise to the level of a regulation.

Conclusion: Evaluating the current realities of state regulations

This paper was written by reading and assessing the (not extensive) literature on the topic of security services regulations. Additionally, databases for each state were consulted numerous times to ascertain regulations for our tables. Where available, we accessed databases maintained by professional and trade organisations. Further, in some cases, we spoke with licensing officials to make sure that we understood what their websites were intended to convey. Finally, along the way of completing this paper, we also discussed with personnel in the security industry their perceptions and experience with the realities of contemporary licensing.

State licenses for security services are not especially complex but have infinite variety. Our tables fail to identify the minutia on the contemporary licensing scene. For business owners and operators: the extent of background checks where required and the means by which they occurred. For security guards: the offenses that could screen them out for consideration in one state but not affect their employability in another. For investigators/private detectives: the extent to which regulator accept credentials from one applicant but reject another who possesses approximately the same experience. In all cases, fees for applications and renewals, processing time for applications, and the quality and quantity of pre-employment and post-employment training vary significantly. We did not seek to consider regulations found in many urbanised states on independent and proprietary training schools and programs. Also, cities or counties may establish their own regulations for any aspect of the security industry, though no publicly available database for such measures has been found.

To assess state regulations for security services is to describe a moving target. A current subjective judgment of personnel licensing status indicates the reality (Table 7). People with an image that progress is linear, albeit at variable rates of change over time, could be fooled by these regulations. Perhaps, the editors of this volume thought that contributions would describe a trend to more specific, demanding, and well-managed state regulations, to an extent that has occurred. But we also encountered, occasionally, situations in which licensing agencies quietly backtracked on the measures they were expected to regulate without the industry being aware of these adjustments. Further, from the security services industry itself, we found unmistakable ambiguity: the persistent public support for higher industry standards, perhaps through tighter state-by-state regulation, while at the same time through lobbying efforts opposition to increased regulations to prevent their actual development. To focus just on security guards, can society expect reasoned, appropriate response to circumstances in which even 8 h pre-employment screening is deemed to be an economic burden and in which 12 states have no requirements whatsoever for such training? Or for armed security personnel in which 24 states require no classroom basic training, or in which 22 states require no range experience?

What is missing in this paper are lists of malfeasance and nonfeasance of security service personnel when uneven selection, training, and support requirements have resulted in felonies and misdemeanours by security workers who should have been screened out. Ample examples exist but are beyond the scope of this paper. State regulations go only so far in raising industry standards. It must be the tort bar that will advance such measures or a torrent of horrible occurrences that are too pervasive for the media, state legislatures, and congress to ignore.

Table 7. Summary of security personnel licensing status.

Vocation	Assessment high points
Unarmed security guards	Pre-employment screening through state and federal databases now widespread; training standards substantially insufficient; regulation by states uneven; no federal minimum statutes envisioned
Armed security guards	Fair to good classroom and range training standards in some states; non-existent or cursory in others; state regulations vary widely in reliability
Alarm systems personnel	Not licensed in most states
Investigators/Private detectives	The most reliable licensing, in states where regulations exist
Security consultants	No legislatively set standards; however, adequate experience and the ability to use scientific methods to arrive at conclusions for forensic consultations are the norm
Locksmiths	Licensing and criminal record check required in some states. Certifications of competence are the norm

References

Becker, T. M. (1974). The place of private police in society: An area of research for the social sciences. *Social Problems, 21,* 438. doi:10.2307/799910

Becoming a Certified Security Consultant. 2017. Retrieved from: https://iapsc.org/about-us/certification.

Bergel, J. (2015, Nov 10). *In many states, security guards get scant training, oversight.* HuffPost.

Chang, L. Y. C., & Grabsky, P. (2014). Cybercrime and establishing a secure cyberworld. In M. Gill (Ed.), *Handbook of security.,* London & New York: Palgrave Macmillan.

CISSP* ¯ Certified information systems security professional.2017 Retrieved from: https:www.isc2.org/template-three-column-certificate-pages.aspex

Clarke, R., & Newman, G. (2005). *Designing out crime from products and systems.* Monsey, NY: Criminal Justice Press.

Clarke, R. V. (Ed.). (1997). *Situational crime prevention: Successful case studies* (pp. 2nd). Guilderland, NY: Harrow and Heston.

Cunningham, W., & Taylor, T. (1985). *The Hallcrest report: Private security and police in America.* Boston, MA: Butterworth-Heinemann.

Cunningham, W. C., Strauchs, J. J., & Van Meter, C. W. 1990. *The Hallcrest report II: Private security trends 1970-2000.* Stoneham, MA: Butterworth-Heinemann.

Donovan, E., & Walsh, W. (1986). *An evaluation of Starrett City security services.* University Park, PA: Pennsylvania State University.

Freedonia Group. (2015, June 20). *Private security service revenues.* Cleveland, OH: Freedonia Group, Inc.

Hemmens, C., Maahs, J., Scarborough, K. E., & Collins, P. A. (2001). Watching the watchman: State regulations of private security 1982-1998. *Security Journal, 14*(4), 17–28. doi:10.1057/palgrave.sj.8340095

Horan, J. D. (1967). *The Pinkertons: The detective dynasty that made history* (pp. 50). New York: Bonanza Books.

Joh, E. E. (2005). Conceptualizing the private police. *Utah Law Review, 573,* 578–579.

Kakalik, J. S., & Wildhorn, S. 1972. Private police in the United States: Findings and recommendations, Government Printing Office, Washington, DC, vol. 5, 30. (The Rand Report)

Keller, K. S. (2004). Securing security expert testimony: Overcoming the *Daubert* challenge to reach the witness stand. *Security Journal, 17*(3), 21–29. doi:10.1057/palgrave.sj.8340174

Krahmann, E. 2002. Private firms and the new security governance. Retrieved from http://www.isanet.org/noarchive/krahmann.html

Lee, L. (2009). *Homeland security and private sector business: Corporations' role in critical infrastructure protection.* Boca Raton, FL: CRC Press.

McCrie, R. (2005). ASIS International. In L. E. Sullivan (Ed.), *Encyclopedia of law enforcement, vol. 2* (pp. 547–549). Thousand Oaks, CA: Sage Publications.

McCrie, R. (2006). A history of security. In M. Gill (Ed.), *Handbook of security.* London & New York: Palgrave Macmillan.

McCrie, R. D. (2004). The history of expertise in security management practice and litigation. *Security Journal, 17* (3), 11–19. doi:10.1057/palgrave.sj.8340173

Morn, F. (1982). *The eye that never sleeps.* Bloomington, IN: Indiana University Press, p. 98.

Nalla, M. K., & Crichlow, V. J. (2014). Have the standards for private security guards become more stringent in the Post 9/11 Era? An assessment of security guard regulations in the US from 1982 to 2010. *Security Journal, 27,* 1–15.

National Advisory Committee on Criminal Justice Standards and Goals. 1976. Private security: Report of the task force on private security. Government Printing Office, Washington, DC.

Nemeth, C. P. (2012). *Private security and the law* (4th ed.). Waltham, MA: Butterworth-Heinemann.

Phillips, B. (2016). *The complete book of locks and locksmithing* (7th ed.). New York: McGraw-Hill.

Poulin, K. C., & Nemeth, C. P. (2005). *Private security and public safety: A community-based approach.* Upper Saddle River, NJ: Pearson Prentice Hall.

Prenzler, T., & Sarre, R. (2014). Regulation. In M. Gill (Ed.), *The handbook of security* (2nd ed.). London & New York: Palgrave Macmillan.

Private Security Officer Selection and Training. (2010). *ASIS GDL PSO-2010.* Alexandria, VA: ASIS International.

Private Security Service Demand in the United States. (2015). Cleveland, OH: Freedonia Group.

Richemond-Barak, D. (2014). Can self-regulation work? Lessons from the private security and military industry. *Michigan Journal of International Law, 35*, 773.

Roberts, C. (2012). The U.S. Federal Protective Service: A troubled agency–The need for improved contract guard training and oversight. *Journal of Applied Security Research, 7*(4), 478–488. doi:10.1080/19361610.2012.710539

Sennewald, C. A., & Tsukayama, J. K. (2015). *The process of investigation: Concepts and strategies for investigators in the private sector* (4th ed., pp. 13). Waltham, MA: Butterworth-Heinemann.

Sklansky, D. A. (1999). The private police. *UCLA Law Review, 46*, 1165–1287.

Sklansky, D. A. (2006). Private police and democracy. *American Criminal Law Review, 43*, 89–105.

Valiant Solutions . (2017, June 7). *Personal communications.* Woodbury, NY: Valiant Solutions, Inc.

Spearin, C. (2014). Special operations forces & private security companies. *Parameters, 44*(2), 61.

Strom, K., Berzofsky, M., Shook-Sa, B., Barrick, K., Daye, C., Hortstmann, N., & Kinsey, S. (2010). *The private security industry: A review of the definitions, available data sources, and paths moving forward.* Washington, DC: US Department of Justice.

USA PATRIOT ACT 2001. http://www.gpo.gov/fdsys/pkg/PLAW-107publ56/pdf/plaw-107publ56.pdf

Williams, A. (2014). Guards with guns [online]. [2016, July 27]. Available: htpps://apps.cironline.org/hired-guns

Index

www.ingramcontent.com/pod-product-compliance
Ingram Content Group UK Ltd.
Pitfield, Milton Keynes, MK11 3LW, UK
UKHW010020280225
455677UK00023B/706